Human Rights:
From Rhetoric to Reality

Human Rights:
From Rhetoric to Reality

Edited by

Tom Campbell, David Goldberg,
Sheila McLean and Tom Mullen

Basil Blackwell

British Library Cataloguing in Publication Data

Human rights: from rhetoric to reality.
  1. Civil rights
  I. Campbell, Tom
  323.4   JC571

  ISBN 0–631–14361–0
  ISBN 0–631–14362–9 Pbk

Library of Congress Cataloging in Publication Data
Main entry under title:

Human rights.
  Includes index.
  1. Civil rights. I. Campbell, Tom.
K3240.4.H836   1986   323.4   85–15826
ISBN 0–631–14361–0
ISBN 0–631–14362–9 (pbk.)

Typeset by Cambrian Typesetters, Frimley, Surrey
Printed in Great Britain by TJ Press Ltd, Padstow

Contents

Preface

This book tackles, in concrete contexts, problems which arise in translating the idea of universal human rights into specific practical requirements. It explores ways in which the simple and uncompromising moral imperatives which are expressed in the rhetoric of human rights may be applied to actual social circumstances in a manner which can be accurately monitored and adjudicated in courts of law.

Whilst the contributors have their own particular views on the analysis and significance of human rights discourse, the extended discussions to which the preparation of this book gave rise have given substance to the view that, whatever institutional arrangements are adopted to protect and further human rights, these cannot operate satisfactorily without some agreement as to the essential purposes of each right. From these flow both the fundamental duties of government and the definitive limits to its authority. In working together on the shared idea that, to be effective, human rights must be given legal formulation in a manner which gives effect to the concerns underlying the use of the rhetoric of human rights, we have sought to make a collective contribution to the study of human rights.

The editors wish to thank Fiona McKinlay, Liz Doherty and Marjory Wilson for their assistance in the preparation of this manuscript.

1

Introduction:
Realizing Human Rights

Tom Campbell

The rhetoric of human rights draws on the moral resources of our belief in the significance of an underlying common humanity, and points us in the direction of a type of society which ensures that the basic human needs and reasonable aspirations of all its members are effectively realized in, and protected by, law. Human rights discourse can, therefore, serve both as a potent source for radical critiques of actual social arrangements and also as a powerful basis for working out and presenting alternative institutional practices.

The language of human rights carries great rhetorical force of uncertain practical significance. This is both its persuasive strength and its legislative weakness. At the level of rhetoric, human rights have an image which is both morally compelling and attractively uncompromising. But, when it comes to making legislative provision for the favoured objectives, then the idea of universal, inalienable and indefeasible rights offers depressingly little guidance. The stance that all human beings have certain rights by virtue of their humanity, rights which are not to be set aside for any purpose whatsoever, is a hypnotically arresting ideology. But no more than any other ideology does it determine the particular legislative and judicial decisions which directly affect the well-being of those whose interests are in question. Yet, ultimately, the success of critiques and proposals presented in the name of human rights requires that highly general statements of rights be transformed into more particular formulations, using the specific terms in which the fate of human beings is decided.

To classify human rights discourse as a form of rhetoric is not disparaging in itself. Rhetoric may be regarded as the art of expressing, in linguistic form, thoughts and feelings in ways which most efficaciously communicate them to others. Its object is persuasion, and its method is argumentation rather than deliberate manipulation. It seeks to convince, but not to deceive. Often, however, rhetoric is regarded as the use of language to arouse attitudes in a partisan way, without actually saying anything of substance. Hence its association with simplistic and unsubstantiated slogans. This latter, pejorative, definition is, however, best restricted to what is often referred to as 'mere rhetoric': a dismissive phrase which is appropriately deployed when grand-sounding phrases are substituted for more informative assertions in situations which call for information. This leaves open the possibility that rhetoric has a proper and valuable place in the communication of the feelings, attitudes and orientations which characterize any intellectual, moral and emotional outlook.

Thus, in the political sphere, rhetoric has a function in the presentation of broad approaches to political issues. Catch-phrases, provocative slogans and dramatic images have a role to play in communicating, commending or condemning the gist of any political programme.[1] This deployment of political language, which is essential to the success of any ideology (in the sense of a set of general practice-orientated social beliefs and values), may be criticized as 'mere rhetoric' when it is presented in place of specific policy recommendations. When actual political decisions are required, rhetoric, that is the general statement of an outlook in a persuasive form, requires supplementation by more specific and informative formulations of policy objectives.

In this non-pejorative sense of rhetoric, human rights discourse may be regarded as a proper type of rhetorical expression, which is exemplified in the Universal Declaration of Human Rights (1948)[2] as well as in the common currency of political debate and in the preambles to numerous policy documents or legislative enactments. No doubt such human rights rhetoric requires to be transformed into the practical terms of everyday circumstances, but this does not make it redundant. Indeed, several of the contributors to this book argue for the significance of human rights rhetoric in setting the agenda for political debate, indicating the importance of certain types of person-centred reasons for government action or inaction, and heightening popular consciousness with respect to the imperative force of basic human needs and aspirations.

Nevertheless, working out the specific implications of highly general statements of human rights is a necessary move, if the rhetoric of human rights is to have major impact on the resolution of social problems. The meaning and scope of each right has to be clarified, the content and location of any correlative duties to which it gives rise must be spelled out, and the permissible range of exceptions and limitations specified. Whether this work is done by the framers of constitutions, the ordinary law-making procedures or the activities of courts themselves, it may be regarded as realizing, or positivizing, human rights through law. The most obvious form in which this is done is through specific constitutional provisions which incorporate a statement, or Bill, of rights which are given the status of fundamental law. These rights are then regarded as superior to ordinary legislation, and are used to render invalid any legislative action, administrative or other governmental decisions which are held to run counter to the listed rights. Institutionally this invalidation is normally achieved through the medium of special courts whose task it is to rule on the constitutionality of ordinary legislation, and to determine whether the fundamental rights of the citizen have been infringed in particular cases.

This model, which is typified by the US Constitution, is found with variations in Canada and the civil-law jurisdictions of continental Europe.[3] In effect, this mechanism gives major power in positivizing human rights to courts, since the type of decision to be made in applying highly general statements of rights to specific circumstances is tantamount to creating the detailed rules which are decisive in the particular circumstances of each case. This mechanism has the advantage that there is an institutional avenue for challenging violations of human rights by governments, but it is open to the charge that it is undemocratic. Perhaps for reasons of democracy and accountability, the protection of human rights may be left to elected legislative bodies, as is largely the case in the UK, for instance, where courts are in effect limited to the determination of whether the executive organs of government have acted within the law.[4] However, this apparently more democratic process leaves human rights vulnerable to the decisions of bodies which have much more on their collective minds than the protection of human rights, and are subject to the sort of majoritarian populist pressure and reasons of state which so often lead to human rights violations. It is therefore argued that the special function of human rights in placing limits on legitimate state actions cannot be left safely in the hands of state legislatures or the ordinary processes of law.

This constitutional debate is essentially about the best mechanism for realizing human rights through law. Are human rights to be positivized through elected legislative assemblies or through Bills of Rights and constitutional courts? It is a debate which is touched on in this book and to which much of the analysis of what is involved in realizing human rights is highly relevant. In this context, the frequent references throughout the book to the European Convention on Human Rights indicates the extent to which, through the European Commission and Court of Human Rights, the positivizing of human rights is having an effect in the UK.

International law in general features in the book as a prime expression of the significant rhetoric of human rights, although there is little evidence of it having much direct impact on the human rights practice of states. This reflects the general weakness, in terms of enforcement, of a system of law which leaves declarations and covenants to be applied at the discretion of the states whose behaviour they are designed to regulate.

Whatever the realities of international politics, and whichever way the constitutional debate about the implementation of human rights is resolved, there are certain prior questions which arise over the nature and content of the rights which it is sought to enforce. If human rights are to be more than mere rhetoric, it is clear that some strategy must be devised for overcoming certain general problems which arise in the process of realizing human rights through law. It is with these problems that this book is largely concerned.

For instance, it is often the case that such 'legislative' processes, whatever constitutional channels they take, appear to involve the diminution of the rights in question to the point at which they cease to match up to the moral objectives which motivate those who are moved to speak of human rights when confronted with particular evils. In practice, it may be argued, legislation compromises human rights. Certainly, narrowing the scope of human rights as they are stated in the general terms of, for instance, a Bill of Rights, is inevitable if it is to be made clear what it is to be protected by the enforcement of such rights.[5] Only then is it possible to formulate attainable human rights objectives and mount effective challenges against authorities which violate or neglect human rights. Realizing human rights is a matter of translating idealized objectives into justiciable rules which require a precision and clarity untypical of ideological discourse. Applicable and unambiguous meanings have to be given to key terms; exceptions and limitations have to be made explicit; new rules have to be integrated into the corpus of existing legislation.

However, even if the effective implementation of human rights is dependent on satisfying these requirements of positive law, the processes involved give ample opportunity for diluting as well as facilitating the human rights in question. Positivizing human rights is often tantamount to limiting human rights. Crucial exceptions to, and restrictive definitions of, the scope of a right can totally undermine the point of having particular rights. This gives rise to the suspicion that the procedures for translating the uncompromising generality of human rights discourse into the specifics which are required to move effectively against human rights violations is unduly dominated by governments and other compliant organs of the state. This would hardly be surprising given the power of governments to violate rights, and the possibilities of abuse inherent in the legitimate possession of the monopoly of force within a society. Such abuses are rendered more frequent by the fact that states have a legitimate interest in the welfare of the majority of their inhabitants and are in a position to make plausible claims to the effect that they must sometimes sacrifice the interests of minorities to the general good.

Nevertheless, not only is a degree of particularization required if specific human rights are going to have practical force, but the active participation of the state is a prerequisite for the attainment of many human rights objectives. To have effect, human rights must be positivized. That means that they must be cast in a form which can generate both effective executive action and a basis for legal argument concerning their violations. Beyond this, many rights require state commitment to, and finance for, definable policy objectives, particularly in cases where a right requires to be facilitated by law or involves significant state funding. The state is thus the necessary friend, as well as the recurrent enemy, of human rights.

The ambivalence of the state's role in the specification and implementation of human rights, and the inherent difficulty of capturing the moral essence of particular human rights in the legalistic formulae that are required for their attainment, are themes running through this book. No easy solution to the problem of resolving the perennial tension between the beneficial uses and the constant misuses of state power is offered, but it is assumed that the idea and institutions of law have a significant role to play in this sphere. Ways of positivizing without diminishing human rights are explored and suggestions are put forward as to the best ways of guarding against the pitfalls which threaten any attempt to advance from moral rhetoric to social reality.

In this and the subsequent four chapters, some general issues relating to the realization of human rights are considered from different points of view. The remaining chapters deal with specific areas of concern or particular human rights. The contrast is not sharply drawn, since the general issues are illustrated by reference to particular examples of rights violations, and the more specific topics are dealt with in the light of some of the themes which run through the book; particularly the ambivalent role of the state with respect to human rights and the need to identify the essential and inviolable element within each human right.

In chapter 2, Tom Mullen presents the thesis that constitutional interpretation of Bills of Rights may involve a form of moral reasoning which can, on the basis of contemporary theories of moral objectivity, give rise to some confidence in the outcome of such legal processes in the sphere of human rights. Judicial legislation need not be a vehicle for the political prejudices of unelected and unrepresentative persons, nor does it have to follow inappropriately legalistic modes of interpretation, unsuited to the requirements of rapidly changing modern societies. This argument, which goes some way towards defending the Bill of Rights approach to the positivization of human rights, leads the way into many of the subsequent chapters which explore the nature of decisions which have to be made about the content of human rights.

In chapter 3, Esin Örücü argues that an essential aspect of the positivization of human rights is the identification of a 'core' for each right, which encapsulates its inviolable and indefeasible content. Although the concept of the core of rights, which is part of the West German and Turkish systems, has not given rise to any definitive tests for the recognition of particular cores, she argues that it can serve as a device for checking the constant tendency of governments to limit rights, and can heighten popular awareness of the role and significance of human rights.

In chapter 4, Anthony Carty considers a similar issue in connection with states of emergency, in which normal human rights are suspended or modified. Here the issue is whether or not, in states of emergency, some human rights may be put aside so long as other (political) rights are retained. He also explores the prospect of achieving a transcultural consensus as to the content of a broader range of non-derogable rights which places less emphasis on democratic forms. In an effort to break away from the easy application of Western assumptions about the priority of political rights, he argues that we must judge the human rights performance of each state partly in terms of its own political ideology and move towards creating, rather than imposing, a consensus on the non-derogable core of rights.

It may be thought that this semi-relativist position undermines the scope for international law to develop universal standards of human rights. In chapter 5, Noreen Burrows explores this issue in relation to women's rights and pinpoints the reasons why, at the international level, human rights so often fail to get beyond the level of rhetoric. The main reason for the ineffectiveness of international law in this context is that the interpretation and application of these rights is left to the very states whose practices are under challenge. Other reasons include the general absence of concern for the position of women and the lack of precision in the specification of the distinctiveness of the situations in which women typically find themselves. This introduces another recurrent theme of the book: namely the tension between the rhetoric of universality, and the practical need to specify the rights which relate directly to the distinctive oppressions of exploited and deprived groups.

These chapters exemplify the point that the implementation of human rights, which requires the stimulation of governments to legislate and courts to develop appropriate methods of interpretation, is crucially dependent on the task of spelling out the force of human rights in terms of specific freedoms and, where relevant, clearly located duties, correlative to the rights in question. Procedures and formulae are in themselves inadequate for this objective and require supplementation by a living sense of the purposes of the rights in question and the nature of the harms which it is sought to eliminate. These matters are taken up with respect to particular rights and areas of concern in the remaining chapters.

Interestingly, two of these chapters deal with rights in the sphere of medical practice and another deals with human rights whose exercise may be facilitated by medicine, a discipline which has not traditionally been though of as giving rise to human rights problems, but which is attracting increasing attention as a source of contemporary social controversies. This illustrates the general point that the rhetoric of human rights emerges out of the experienced evils and aspirations of the time. In particular, Sheila McLean's examination of the right to reproduce, in chapter 6, indicates the extent to which a concern for human rights emerges in response to specific abuses of governmental power. Claims for rights in this area are by no means a new phenomenon. However, her historical account of the way in which reproduction has developed from a mere capacity to a human right demonstrates the significance of the conjunction of the growth of feminism and the use of the language of rights. She shows how other social and political forces, including the development of high-technology medicine, have also had a considerable impact on individual freedom in this area. She argues forcefully that the right to reproduce is provided by protecting and enlarging freedom of choice in relation to the use of a person's reproductive capacities. In so doing, she strengthens the view that all rights are ultimately related to the protection and development of human choices.

Sheila McLean's analysis of the nature and basis of the right to reproduce has clear and direct implications for the rights of the mentally ill, a group that is particularly vulnerable to rights violations in this sphere. However, in chapter 7, Tom Campbell uses the example of the same group to argue that the element of choice is not always paramount in the determination of the core of a human right. In reaching the tentative conclusion that there may be value in formulating the idea of the right to compulsory treatment, and indicating that this may have application to persons other than the mentally ill, it is pointed out that the rhetoric of human rights may lead us in contradictory directions, between which awkward choices have to be made if we are to progress from generalized statements of rights to specific legislative enactments.

In chapter 8, Sheila McLean, in examining the nature and significance of consent in relation to medical treatment in general, argues that the protection of the autonomy of persons who are vulnerable and relatively powerless through their physical ill-health requires the formulation of a right which involves a quality and degree of disclosure of information that is threatened by the momentum of the therapeutic imperative in modern society. In so doing she demonstrates, through a study of court decisions, the ambivalent role of the state in both fostering and controlling, or failing to control, the practice of medicine. Yet medicine gives rise to some of the most basic choices which human beings are now called upon to make, either for each other or for themselves. In grounding the right to consent to medical treatment in self-determination, she points out that, in terms of the protection of human rights, there is reason to retain the principle that unauthorized medical intervention is a form of (non-criminal) assault on the individual. The recent tendency to use the negligence-based action in this context may result in the undermining of the right to obtain redress for infringement of this fundamental right. Whilst not overtly rights-diminishing, there can be little doubt about its effect on the definition and scope of the right to consent.

The inadequacies of the traditional British approach to human rights are dealt with by Jim Murdoch in chapter 9, which concerns the rights of public assembly and procession. Due to a lack of articulation of the purpose of the rights of those who seek to participate in these activities, and the absence of a clear notion of the role of human rights in limiting the incursion of majority on minority interests, he argues that the problem of public order in contemporary British society is misleadingly presented as a matter of 'balancing' the interests of protestors against the interests of the populace with respect to order and non-violence. This analysis gives substance to his impression that British civil liberties are in a state of crisis.

A comparable impression of the conceptual weakness of contemporary approaches to human rights in the UK emerges from Gerry Maher's treatment of rights in the criminal process in chapter 10. Using material from recent official committee reports, he demonstrates how the absence of an explicit conception of human rights distorts the central issues which have arisen in recent moves to diminish the traditional rights of the accused in the criminal process. In this way, he indicates the practical significance of what some regard as an alien 'rhetoric' in an area which has long been thought of as central to the liberties of the citizen in the UK.

Finally, in chapter 11, Elspeth Attwooll analyses the right to belong to a trade union. This chapter brings out the inherent clash between individual and group interests which is at issue in many contentious human rights. Her main point is that the substance of this right, and the interpretation of the relevant municipal law and international conventions, such as those developed by the International Labour Organisation (ILO) with respect to freedom of association and collective bargaining, depend crucially on the dominant ideology of the states and governments concerned, thus emphasizing the danger of leaving to governments the formulation and implementation of human rights. Her suggestions as to the core of this particular right make clear both the difficulty and the importance of specifying the indefeasible content of those rights which are particularly at the mercy of political trends.

Whilst the contributors operate within their own analytical framework, certain significant distinctions recur through the book. In general, it is held that the central human rights are standardly claim-rights in that they involve others, particularly governments, in having correlative duties to the rights-holders.[6] Pure liberties, which are constituted by no more than the *de facto* absence of obligations on persons in an area of activity, are regarded with some scepticism as putative human rights, unless the absence of obligation is in some way guaranteed by constitutional provisions which forbid inhibiting legislation in that respect, in which case one may speak of a liberty-right.[7] Indeed, in expressing the core content of a right, it is clearly essential to indicate the location and content of the correlative duties and, in particular, to distinguish between those cases where the correlative duty requires only inaction and non-intervention, and those cases which require positive action to safeguard or further the interests of the rights-holders in question. It is this difference between what may be called negative and positive rights which lies at the centre of many problems about the dual function of the rhetoric of human rights in both urging governments on and, at the same time, putting limits to their activities.

The distinctiveness of human rights, however, must lie in their absolute or overriding nature, and it is for this reason that we emphasize the concept of the core of each right as an inviolable element which distinguishes human from other rights.

However, the idea of the core of each human right may be approached from two angles. From one angle, the core may be seen as the absolute and indefeasible element within each right: the irreducible minimum which cannot be subject to any limitation. From another angle, the core may be viewed in a more positive way, as the fundamental purpose or objective of the right in question, which forces us to think not only of the irreducible core but also of those consequential associated rights which are necessary for the realization of the central objectives of a human right. Seen in this second way, the concept of the core leads us to think not so much of where to call a halt to the process of limiting rights as how to work out the necessary mechanisms for attaining their objectives.

These two aspects of the core are closely related, in that it is the objective of the right that will largely determine the irreducible core which is to be protected at all costs. But they must be sharply distinguished in some contexts, since the question of the scope of a right, and what is requisite for its realization, is logically distinct from the question of when, if at all, that right may be set aside or over-ridden by other rights or considerations. To specify the content of a right is not in itself to specify its priority, although the two issues may readily be conflated where the rights in question are alleged to have the absoluteness of human rights.

In identifying the irreducible minimum of a human right, regard must be had to the different factors which make for limiting a right. Specifically, a distinction must be drawn between those limitations which are the outcome of *ad hoc* clashes with other human rights and those which result from giving priority to some alleged wider public good. The former are inherent in any attempt to specify human rights, and are best met by promulgating some general priorities between rights. The latter are more contingent, and more resistable, since they seem to undermine the whole idea that human rights take precedence over the general good. Nevertheless, it is clear that at some point the protections afforded by a human right may have to give way to other non-rights-based considerations, and the purpose of identifying the core of the right will be to help in the determination of when that point has been reached. There may be important differences here between the pressures of utilitarian considerations in normal circumstances, and the allegedly distinctive factors which arise in what are considered to be states of emergency when 'normal' civil life is under threat. The irreducible minimum of a right may not be the same in these differing circumstances. Thus rights which have priority over other rights may have an extensive core which is inviolable even in states of emergency. Other rights, which have a lower priority classification, may have a lesser core more readily threatened even in 'normal' times. Overall, the extent of the core of human rights in relation to considerations of the public interest, whether in situations of emergency or not (although not in relation to each other) will depend in part on what weight is given to the whole idea of human rights as against calculations of aggregate utility.[8]

The pursuit of the core of human rights in the sense of the irreducible minimum is clearly problematic if we are to allow that the core may vary in the different situations outlined above. However, its cohesion may be maintained by concentrating on the notion of the core as the fundamental objective or purpose of the right in question, which can be articulated in relative independence of the priority which such a right may have over other rights or other considerations. Such an approach forces consideration of the experiences which have given rise to the demand for rights, and helps to articulate the values which are threatened by their violations. This aspect of the core also stimulates specific thought about what it is that is morally at stake in a human right, and this in turn will suggest, as Esin Örücü points out, that each fundamental human right must generate a cluster of associated concomitant rights which are necessary for its realization in the social circumstances which pertain at the time.

Although the delineation of the fundamental purposes of a human right should play a part in the process of specifying the irreducible minimum core to be protected in different circumstances, there is inevitably a tension between the assertive idea of the core as a fundamental purpose core, and the more defensive notion of the core as an irreducible minimum. It is suggested that it is the resolution of this tension that is behind many debates about legislating human rights. On the one hand, there are pressures to extend particular positive rights to give reality to the general moral objectives at issue. On the other hand, there is a perceived need to limit human rights to those essentials which rarely conflict with each other, and which it is desired to defend against encroachment in all but the most rigorously defined and circumscribed circumstances. It is in seeking to reconcile these pressures that the concept of the core of human rights has its place.

In exploring the content of the cores of specific rights, a piecemeal approach has been adopted by examining particular rights, rather than by undertaking the more general philosophical task of explicating those elements which are common to the cores of all fundamental rights, and tackling directly the problems of cultural and ideological variations. We have approached the substantive content of rights through the examination of rights in their social context, where there is a direct input from the contemplation of experienced ills and deprivations.

This approach is congruent with the fact that, whilst a great deal of theoretical work has been done in recent years to explicate and refine the idea of human rights,[9] the current vitality of the view that all human beings have certain rights which all others, especially governments, have an absolute duty to respect, owes much to widespread revulsion at recent examples of political and economic repression, and relatively little to the influence of theorists and philosophers.[10] Human rights have emerged since the adoption of the Universal Declaration of Human Rights as a central rallying point for many who seek to champion morality in politics. This has occurred despite the absence of any adequate philosophical vindication of the idea of universal and overriding rights. The human rights movement is based on the need for a counter-ideology to combat the abuses and misuses of political authority by those who invoke, as a justification for their activities, the need to subordinate the particular interests of individuals to the general good. Historically and politically, demands for human rights have been reactions to feelings of moral outrage, rather than products of theoretical conviction.

Nevertheless, the effectiveness of human rights movements depends on the continuing moral force of the idea of human rights. This is, in turn, affected in the long run by its philosophical plausibility, particularly by its clarity and coherence as a concept and its relationship to a distinct, recognizable and persuasive moral outlook. Both the plausibility and the persuasiveness of the general idea of human rights are at once dependent on, and endangered by, efforts to give specific applicable formulations to the raw material of human rights rhetoric, to recruit authoritative political and legal procedures to provide effective protection for such specified rights, and to ensure adequate remedies when they are violated.

That effective human rights require to be particularized and realized in law is clear. What is in question is whether these essential steps to articulate and realize the social cash-value of such rights undermine or underline the persuasive force of generalized declarations of human rights. By exploring this question, the book seeks to contribute to the debate about the intellectual coherence of the idea of human rights, as well as to further the study of its impact on social reality through the medium of legal institutions.

Notes

1   For an analysis of rhetoric in politics see Richard J. Burke, 'Politics as Rhetoric', *Ethics*, 93 (1982), 45–55.

2   For the text of the Universal Declaration of Human Rights, see Ian Brownlie (ed.), *Basic Documents in Human Rights* (Oxford: Clarendon Press, 1977). The Universal Declaration may be taken to exemplify the rhetoric of human rights, or it may be regarded as the first stage towards realizing human rights, since it formulates in general terms a consensus of governments as to the objectives of the political discourse which draws on the language of human rights.

3   See S.A. de Smith, *Constitutional and Administrative Law* (4th edn by H. Street and R. Brazier) (Harmondsworth: Penguin, 1981), 447–51; and K.C. Wheare, *Modern Constitutions* (Oxford: Oxford University Press, 1960).

4   On this and the Bill of Rights debate generally see, for example, Peter Wallington and Jeremy Mcbride (eds), *Civil Liberties and a Bill of Rights* (London: Cobden Trust, 1976); and Colin Campbell (ed.), *Do We Need a Bill of Rights?* (London: Temple Smith, 1980).

5   For a lucid presentation of these elements, see James W. Nickel, 'Are Human Rights Utopian?', *Philosophy and Public Affairs*, 12 (1982), 247–64.

6   This widely used terminology stems from W.H. Hohfeld, *Fundamental Legal Conceptions* (New Haven, Connecticut: Yale University Press, 1919).

7   See Elspeth M.M. Attwooll, 'Liberties, Rights and Power', in E.M.M. Attwooll (ed.), *Perspectives in Jurisprudence* (Glasgow: Glasgow University Press, 1977), 79–97.

8   The nature of the clash between utility and rights is not one which is tackled head on in this book. For some recent contributions on this perennial topic, see E.F. Paul, F.D. Miller and J. Paul (eds), *Human Rights* (Oxford: Basil Blackwell, 1984), and in particular John Gray, 'Indirect Utility and Fundamental Rights', 73–91.

9   Examples include D.D. Raphael (ed.), *Political Theory and the Rights of Man* (London: Macmillan, 1967); Richard E. Flathman, *The Practice of Rights* (Cambridge: Cambridge University Press, 1976); Joel Feinberg, *Rights, Justice and the Bounds of Liberty* (Princeton, New Jersey: Princeton University Press, 1980); J.R. Pennock and John W. Chapman, *Human Rights – Nomos XXIII* (New York: New York University Press, 1981); and Alan Gewirth, *Human Rights* (Chicago: Chicago University Press, 1982).

10 Indeed, in the period when the Universal Declaration of Human Rights was being formulated, analytic philosophy was somewhat sceptical about the natural or human rights tradition; see, for example, Margaret Macdonald, 'Natural Rights', *The Proceedings of the Aristotelian Society*, 47 (1946–7), 225–50.

2

Constitutional Protection of Human Rights

Tom Mullen

The definition and protection of human rights remains one of the major themes of political, philosophical and legal discourse. Although the idea of human rights has been repeatedly and comprehensively criticized,[1] it retains considerable popularity and support. A substantial body of opinion holds that there are such things as human rights and that they ought to have legal protection. This view has, from time to time, received expression in the form of general declarations of the fundamental rights which persons are supposed to have. Clearly the making of such declarations is not sufficient to ensure the actual protection of human rights, and such general declarations of rights have often been dismissed as mere rhetoric. The advocate of human rights must address the issue of how the move from the rhetorical affirmation of rights to the actual protection of human rights is best made. No disparagement of general declarations of rights is intended by this statement, for they have a role to play in the exchange of ideas and the formation of opinion. In that sense, to talk of mere rhetoric is to miss the point because rhetoric undoubtedly has its effect.

What that effect might be is not, however, the principal concern of this chapter. Rather, the concern is to show what implications the choice of mechanism for the protection of rights has, in moving from rhetorical affirmation to real protection of human rights.

Although the notion of human rights has traditionally been less popular amongst lawyers in the UK than it is in other jurisdictions,[2] a significant number of lawyers prefer to analyse the legal system in terms of human rights. Those lawyers who do analyse the legal system in terms of human rights have tended to consider the legal protection

of human rights in isolation from philosophical questions concerning
the definition and elaboration of human rights. They seem to assume
that the definition of human rights at a philosophical level is
unproblematic and that one need only determine the most appropriate
legal mechanism for the protection of human rights. To give but one
example, since the early 1970s a major debate has been taking place
on the desirability of enacting a fundamental guarantee of human rights
into the UK constitution, possibly by incorporating into UK law the
European Convention on Human Rights. Those in favour of a
fundamental guarantee of human rights have pointed to numerous
infringements of, and threats to, liberty in the UK, and lamented the
inability of the British courts, limited as they are by the doctrine of the
Sovereignty of Parliament, to protect the individual from the excesses
of the modern state. A Bill of Rights or some similar instrument
would, they think, provide much better protection.[3]

The opposition to this movement has pointed to the vagueness of
fundamental guarantees of human rights, the numerous qualifications
and exceptions to the absoluteness of such rights which are typically
made, the inflexibility of such mechanisms and their supposedly
undemocratic nature.[4]

There is good reason to be profoundly dissatisfied with this debate.
The opponents of Bills of Rights too readily assume that constitutionally entrenched guarantees of human rights are inimical to
democracy and that severe difficulties in translating general declarations of rights into concrete and specific legal rules make the
enterprise worthless. The supporters of Bills of Rights generally fail to
meet arguments directed against the validity of the concept of human
rights. They also fail to explain the significance of couching
arguments in terms of human rights rather than some other concept.
Last of all, they show no sign of having learned very much from the
experience of other jurisdictions, particularly the USA.

What UK advocates of a Bill of Rights fail to realize is that, if
attention is focussed entirely on legal mechanisms for the protection of
human rights, and theoretical disputes about human rights are left
unresolved, these latter disputes will simply re-emerge when interpretation of legal instruments protecting human rights is required.
The enterprise of protecting human rights through law can only
proceed on the basis of a fully worked out theory of human rights. It is
suggested that legal analysis in this field must, therefore, pay close
attention to moral and philosophical debates about the meaning and

significance of rights, whichever mechanism for the protection of human rights is chosen.

Thus the purpose of this chapter is not so much to argue directly for or against Bills of Rights as to discuss some important implications of the Bill of Rights model for protecting human rights.

There are several variants of the Bill of Rights model. One which has found favour in a number of jurisdictions is the constitutionally entrenched guarantee of human rights accompanied by judicial review of state action. Under this model the constitutional guarantees of rights have overriding authority over other laws and the judiciary has power to declare unconstitutional state legislation or other actions of the state which conflict with the terms of the constitutional guarantees. The principal alternative approach is the piecemeal one of protecting human rights by the enactment of ordinary legislation dealing with individual rights and the development of judge-made case law. This, of course, is the approach which has been adopted in the UK, although it might be more accurate here to speak of the protection of civil liberties rather than of human rights. Intermediate approaches are possible such as enacting a Bill of Rights which has the same constitutional status as a state's other legislation, but space does not permit consideration of such variants, and subsequent references to Bills of Rights or constitutional guarantees of human rights are references to the model described above.

The issues raised by the use of the Bill of Rights model have received very considerable attention in the USA and, given that the USA possesses a highly developed jurisprudence of constitutional protection of human rights, it seems appropriate to draw on the American experience and see what lessons can be learned from it.

In the American Bill of Rights, the enumeration of protected rights includes both fairly specific rights and rights which are expressed at a very high level of generality. Rights in the criminal process are comparatively specific. Other rights are far less specific in their terms, for example, 'Congress shall make no law . . . abridging the freedom of speech, or of the press;'[5] and 'No person shall . . . be deprived of life, liberty or property without due process of law'.[6]

The vagueness and generality of the latter sort of definition is, of course, a serious defect, as far as the opponents of Bills of Rights are concerned. They consider that such general phrases do not give the individual an adequate account of what his or her rights are, do not give courts sufficient guidance to make decisions in concrete cases, and give the judiciary a degree of power that is inappropriate in a democratic society. The language of such provisions is so open-ended that, in any particular case, radically differing views as to whether or not state action is constitutional are possible. This is apparent from such cases as *Buckley* v. *Valeo*[7] in which the US Supreme Court had to consider the constitutionality of limitations on expenditure on political campaigns. The legislation was held to be an unconstitutional abridgement of freedom of speech because it limited the ability of persons to engage in free communication. Yet supporters of the measure had argued that the legislation encouraged freedom of speech by 'equalising the relative abilities of individuals and groups to influence the outcome of elections'[8] and, therefore, protected and furthered First Amendment values.

This sort of case inevitably leads to criticism that judges are making important policy choices which ought to be left to the elected representatives of the people, in the guise of exercising a judicial function of protecting settled legal rights.

The American approach to this predicament has been to look for a method of interpretation of constitutional provisions which can be considered the right method: a method which simultaneously removes the problem of the vagueness of constitutional guarantees and takes proper account of the anti-majoritarian difficulty.

A number of distinct and mutually inconsistent approaches can be discerned in the decided cases and in scholarly writing. This section will attempt briefly to describe and criticize each.

The first approach to be considered is what has been called interpretivism. Interpretivists argue that the answers to constitutional questions can and should be supplied by the actual text of the document or by clear inferences from it. Where simply scrutinizing the text would not provide sufficient guidance, reference is to be made to the intentions of the framers of the Constitution which are to be discovered primarily in the legislative history of the Constitution and its Amendments, and also from other sources such as the history of the political circumstances which gave rise to the provision in question.[9]

Certain Supreme Court Justices, for example, Justice Black,[10] have invoked what appears to be an interpretivist approach but this, more often than not, masks the imposition of value judgements which are neither uncontroversial inferences from the text of the Constitution nor clear applications of the intentions of the framers.

The interpretivist thesis that adjudication should rest on the text and the intentions of the framers solves neither of the twin problems, the vagueness of constitutional provisions and the anti-majoritarian difficulty, which are the principal preoccupations of American constitutional scholarship. Nor does it seem satisfactory as a means of protecting human rights. The difficulties posed by the extreme generality of the terms of the Constitution itself cannot be met by reference to the framer's intent. First, perusal of legislative history shows that different groups and individuals held a variety of views as to the possible meaning and effect of the various positions. Second, the views expressed in debates are, in any event, only an imperfect guide to the actual reasons which motivated votes in favour of particular texts at constitutional conventions. Third, it is not clear why the supposed views of, for example, Congressmen should be preferred to the views of those voting in state legislatures to adopt constitutional amendments. Last of all, an interpretivist is unable to deal with situations which were not, nor could have been, foreseen at the time the constitution or any amendment thereto was adopted. The same point can found the more general criticism that no evolution or growth of constitutional protection of human rights is possible if such a thesis is strictly applied.

The interpretivist thesis solves the problem of legitimacy at one level by apparently restricting the actions of popularly accountable institutions only when such a restriction can be traced to a document which by agreement forms the basis of the political system. However, if the concern is that limiting the freedom of action of elected institutions is undemocratic, then it is not clear why a consensus, or majority, of the past should be able to override a modern consensus or majority.

A further criticism relevant to both vagueness and legitimacy is that the interpretivist thesis does not accord with accepted methods of legal interpretation which include reference to precedent, changing historical and social circumstances, logical consistency and background principles such as a sense of justice, as well as to the original understanding of the meaning of any provision.[11]

One must also have grave misgivings about an interpretivist thesis if one is truly concerned with the protection of human rights. Uncritical acceptance of the (apparent) original understanding may tie constitutional interpretation to views which simply are not protective of human rights. Some interpretivists have taken the view that segregation of the races is not unconstitutional discrimination because the framers of the Fourteenth Amendment did not intend to outlaw segregation.[12] Indeed, not all interpretivists would agree that the Constitution is or should be about the protection of human rights.[13]

The second approach to be considered is that controversies about the meaning of the Constitution's provisions should be settled by reference to tradition. If certain rights have traditionally been seen as fundamental in American political culture then they are deserving of protection. By implication, interpretations of the scope and content of rights which do not have a basis in tradition are to be rejected as undeserving of special constitutional protection.

In *Moore* v. *City of East Cleveland*,[14] the plurality opinion of Justice Powell, in a case invalidating, on due process clause grounds, a city ordinance which limited the class of persons who could live together as a family, stated that 'the Constitution protects the family precisely because the institution of the family is deeply rooted in this Nation's history and tradition'.[15]

A third approach, closely related to the second, is the view that interpretation should be based on some identifiable consensus in society or, in other words, on conventional morality. Those moral principles which can claim to have sufficient weight in conventional morality should guide constitutional interpretation.[16]

In *Breithaupt* v. *Abram*,[17] in which the Court upheld the constitutionality, under the process clause, of taking a blood sample from an unconscious motorist for use as evidence against him in criminal proceedings, the majority referred to 'that "whole community sense of decency and fairness" that has been woven by common experience into the fabric of acceptable conduct'[18] as being the test of constitutionality in this instance. Justice Douglas, although dissenting, appeared to agree that the test of constitutionality was 'the decencies of a civilised state'.[19]

Both these approaches can be dealt with briefly.[20] Appeals to consensus or to tradition are radically indeterminate. Neither the USA nor any other country has a single unambiguous tradition nor shows a consensus of views on such matters as, for example, the rights and wrongs of abortion or the appropriate scope of the freedom of speech. Arguments from these sources can be, and have been, used to support almost any position. Even where it is possible to identify a dominant well-established tradition or widely-inclusive consensus, this may simply amount to the unjustified subordination of the interests and desires of a minority to those of the majority. Neither consensus nor tradition provide plausible answers to the problem of legitimacy. This is so partly because they often do not provide clear guidance, and partly because they involve invoking some alleged will or spirit of the people against the decisions of their elected representatives. References to consensus and tradition also ignore the plausible argument that the enterprise of protecting human rights through constitutional guarantees implies that democracy need not be a purely majoritarian political system. Last of all, it may be said that interpreting constitutional guarantees by reference to consensus or tradition is unlikely to be protective of human rights. There is no necessary connection and, in many political and social circumstances, no actual connection between what tradition or consensus dictates and the human rights persons have.

The fourth approach considers that, whatever may be desirable in the abstract, judges cannot avoid simply substituting their own value judgements for those of the legislature or other branches of the state apparatus, because there is no objective method of adjudication. Judges and commentators should, therefore, admit that this is what is going on. On this view, the only limits that there are on constitutional decision-making are those of prudence and plausibility.[21] The view that judges impose their own values faces the difficulty that there seems little reason to permit unelected judges to replace the choices of accountable political institutions with their own choices. Of course, if one accepts the supposition of this approach that there is no objective judicial method then it inevitably follows that adjudication involves the infusion of the judges' personal beliefs into the process of adjudication.[22] If, however, it can be shown that the 'subjectivist' account of the judicial process is not descriptively correct, then there is little to commend this approach to constitutional interpretation. If there is reason to suppose that an objective judicial method is possible, a matter which will be dealt with shortly, then that supposition should be the basis of any theory of constitutional interpretation.

The fifth approach, usually referred to as process-based theory, is that judicial review should be based on the presuppositions of the democratic system. The decision as to whether or not to invalidate state action depends on whether or not the political process has malfunctioned, in the sense of illegitimately interfering with participation or representation in the political process. This view places particular emphasis on rights of free speech and political participation and the rights of minorities not to be unfairly discriminated against.[23]

The traditional 'double standard' of review in constitutional cases ushered in by the New Deal and summed up in the *Carolene Products* footnote[24] has been interpreted as supporting this view. Under the 'double standard' state action in the economic sphere is presumptively constitutional and will be upheld if it appears to have a rational basis. State action impinging on preferred rights (basically civil and political rights) is subject to more searching constitutional scrutiny.[25]

On this view, the need to make controversial value choices, whether by reference to tradition, consensus or any other source of value, can be obviated by invoking the presuppositions of the democratic system. The judge is concerned not with the rightness or wrongness on substantive grounds of legislative choices, but with the question of whether the democratic system has malfunctioned. Judicial review is orientated towards participation and representation in the political process. The emphasis, in terms of particular rights, is therefore on freedom of expression, voting rights and the rights of minorities not to be discriminated against. If adequate participation and representation can be assured, then there is no reason to interfere with the outcomes of the political process, and every reason to assume that the outcomes generated by the political process will be reasonably fair and just.[26]

On first inspection, this view may seem to go a long way towards dealing with the problem of vagueness and the anti-majoritarian difficulty in that it provides principles of interpretation which are based on the presuppositions of a democratic system.

However, closer examination reveals that it solves neither of these problems. It is not possible to apply this theory to concrete cases without making the substantive value judgements which it claims to eschew. One cannot decide whether a particular minority or person has been unconstitutionally denied effective representation or participation unless one has a substantive ideal of what that minority is entitled to. One can imagine infringements of the rights of minority groups being passed into law after a full debate by a legislature in which that majority has the same voting rights as any other group of persons. It would be odd if the constitutional conclusion to be drawn in that situation was that, because the political process had functioned regularly, they had no grievance. Process-based theory, therefore, rests on substantive moral principles, the nature of which it does not itself explain.[27]

A second criticism is that this theory, being based on the presuppositions of a democratic system, can only hope for acceptance if there is a consensus about the essentials of a fair democratic process. Since there is no consensus about what opportunities for participation and what procedures for representation are most appropriate to a democracy, process-based theory must be seen as based on a particular contestable conception of democracy for which independent justification must be provided.[28] That justification has not yet been forthcoming. Process-based theory, therefore, seems to be neither a clear nor a value-neutral guide to constitutional adjudication.

The third criticism that can be made is that the American Bill of Rights seems to include numerous provisions which are clearly expressions of belief in substantive values, for example, religious liberty and security of property. More generally it can be said that process-based theory does not seem to be a theory of human rights in any meaningful sense. The concentration on the proper functioning of the political process implies that the 'rights' protected by the constitution are simply means towards the end of ensuring that the political process gives opportunities to all to participate, and provides all with some measure of representation. Such 'rights' do not seem to be valued, in themselves, as rights persons possess because they are persons.

The differences between each of these approaches are obvious, yet they do have something in common. With the exception of the fourth option – the 'subjectivist' approach – they seek to provide a neutral method of constitutional interpretation which can evade the charge that judges simply substitute their own view for that of the other branches of government.

The sixth and final approach to be considered is that which bases constitutional adjudication on substantive moral values and, in particular, on a theory of fundamental rights.[29] Using this method of interpretation a judge would reach decisions in, for example, freedom of expression cases by asking whether or not the state action in issue infringed the moral right of freedom of expression. This view is implicit, if not explicit, in many judicial opinions, and has been attacked on the grounds that there is no agreed method of moral philosophy, so that resolving constitutional questions by reference to moral theory really amounts to the imposition of individual beliefs which can claim no superior status over any other beliefs because they are ultimately subjective.

It does, therefore, seem as if attempts to construct value-neutral methods of constitutional interpretation have failed. The various allegedly neutral approaches already discussed either do not provide determinate answers to difficult constitutional questions or provide answers based on concealed value judgements of their own or combine both defects. Nor does it seem likely that any new theories which might be put forward will be both determinate in their outcomes and value-neutral in their outcomes.

This realization might lead some to conclude, in desperation, that constitutional adjudication is inevitably confined to the 'subjective pit of will and power'[30] and that the only improvement which could be made in constitutional adjudication is that the judges be more honest about this. This would, however, be too hasty a conclusion. Similar problems of interpretive method and legitimacy arise in systems without constitutional guarantees of human rights and judicial review, nor are such problems confined to cases involving human rights issues.[31] The American system of government simply raises these issues in a more stark and obvious form, and in a context where they have greater personal significance. These difficulties require attention whatever legal mechanisms are used. It would also be a mistake to assume that these difficulties are incapable of solution. The mistake being made here is the assumption that only a value-neutral method of adjudication can properly be called objective. This is where the sixth view of constitutional interpretation becomes relevant. If it can be shown that the process of moral reasoning can be objective then there seems good reason to allow the process of constitutional interpretation to be guided by substantive moral beliefs. If it is possible for judges, or indeed anyone else concerned with the interpretation of the constitution, to make objective moral judgements, then constitutional interpretation can be rescued from ultimate subjectivity. At least one theorist, in advancing the claim that good constitutional arguments are based on good moral arguments, has explicitly stated that the validity of his thesis depends on there being 'right' answers to moral questions.[32]

It is worth noting that the framers of the American Constitution assumed that there were right answers to moral questions, and this view received expression in the theory of self-evident natural rights which was current at that time. That view of moral objectivity is no longer accepted, nor indeed tenable, but the idea of the transcendent indisputable moral truth does not exhaust the possibility of moral objectivity. Modern moral theories, whilst granting a less exalted status to moral statements, do not deny that they can be objective.

It would not be appropriate in this chapter to embark on a detailed account of contemporary moral theory or to attempt a comprehensive proof of the proposition that moral reasoning can be objective, but it is worth examining briefly some arguments for the objectivity of moral reasoning. The simple statement that moral propositions are ultimately based on value judgements which cannot themselves intelligibly be described as correct or incorrect does not do justice to the complexity of the reasoning processes involved in modern moral theories.

One method of moral reasoning which has a substantial number of adherents has been called 'wide reflective equilibrium'.[33] The method of intuitionism is to reason from basic principles or values which are arrived at solely by intuition, to particular results. The only constraint on the reasoning process is that of logical coherence: the resulting judgements must follow from the principles. Intuitionism clearly implies that moral viewpoints are ultimately subjective. Wide reflective equilibrium goes beyond intuitionism by attempting to achieve coherence amongst three different sets of beliefs a person may hold. These are a set of considered moral judgements, a set of moral principles, and a set of relevant background theories.

One begins by collecting those initial moral judgements of which a person is relatively confident, and which were made under conditions appropriate to avoiding errors of judgement. Next, one proposes various sets of moral principles which might account for those judgements. Having achieved the greatest possible degree of coherence between principles and judgements, one goes on to argue the relative strengths and weaknesses of the alternative sets of principles. This is where some improvement on intuitionism is achieved. Simply settling for the best fit of principles with judgements would not be an essentially different method from intuitionism. The arguments about the strengths of the principles are inferred from a set of relevant background theories, for example, a theory of the person, a theory of the role of morality in society and so on. The background theories must show that the moral principles which are eventually preferred are better than others on grounds other than simple coherence between principles and particular judgements. If this were not so the method would still closely resemble intuitionism. The outcome of the process is that one set of principles is eventually deemed superior. This may, and often will, lead persons to revise particular moral judgements, adopt different principles and possibly also adjust background theories. Once order and coherence amongst particular judgements, principles and background theories have been achieved, a person has arrived at the point of wide reflective equilibrium which gives the theory its name.

Adopting this method of moral reasoning will not, of couse, eliminate disagreements about the correctness of particular moral judgements or the appropriateness of particular moral principles. Individuals may start out with widely differing sets of moral judgements and principles and may employ crucially different background theories. However, it can be argued that it produces fruitful moral debate. By reasoning out fully the implications of shared principles and judgements, and by comparing and evaluating background theories, initial disagreements may be resolved. If disagreements are not resolved it may be possible to identify the precise locus of disagreement such as the terms of a particular background theory, and this may in time lead to resolution of differences. Provided at least some part of the framework is shared, moral debate can advance and can possibly lead to a consensus on moral issues which one might have reason to trust because that consensus is the product of a process of rational inquiry.

Despite the importance which it attaches to consensus, the method of wide reflective equilibrium clearly remains rather individualistic in nature. The emphasis is very much on how individuals should argue and little attention is paid to the conditions under which interpersonal agreement might arise, including the opportunities available to persons to participate in moral discourse. However, these omissions can be supplied, and a more complete idea of the nature of objectivity in moral reasoning arrived at, by reference to another approach, that adopted by Habermas.[34] Habermas has been concerned to refute the claim that moral statements cannot be rationally grounded. He does so by means of an extended critique of the positivist philosophy of science which serves as the starting point of his argument that moral statements can be true. He considers the criteria for the validity of purported statements of fact in science to be based ultimately on conventions and expectations within the scientific community, which cannot themselves be demonstrated to be true. The point is not that scientific statements are ultimately subjective or irrational but that certain assumptions which must be made, for example, that observation statements can be trusted under certain conditions, are the conditions of the possibility of scientific knowledge. A similar approach is taken to the possibility of moral 'knowledge'. The basic question is, what conditions make rational consensus about what is right or true possible? In answer to this question Habermas posits a device called the 'ideal speech situation'[35] which, he considers, provides appropriate criteria for the validation of ethical propositions. Moral truth is found, under this approach, in consensus. However, not all consensus or agreement is considered rational, and it is the function of the ideal speech situation to distinguish between rationally and irrationally grounded moral consensus.

Rational agreement about moral statements is defined as that agreement which has been brought about solely by the force of the arguments used and has not been influenced by any other factors. Moral consensus achieves this ideal of resting only on the force of the arguments used when the two principal requirements of freedom to shift the level of discourse and symmetry are satisfied.

Requiring freedom to shift the level of discourse encourages a completely self-aware, self-critical discourse in which nothing, not even the most basic assumption, is taken for granted. Thus one begins with a particular moral statement or judgement which is disputed. It is in turn supported or refuted by reference to general norms being accepted as binding. The validity of general norms themselves are tested according to their ability to satisfy generally accepted needs and interests. This of course assumes that some human needs or interests can be generalized.

From this point it must be possible to go on to question the total conceptual framework within which moral debate has taken place; for example, participants can question whether the language system used was appropriate, whether different basic assumptions could have been made, and so on. Ultimately it must be possible for participants to reflect on what it is possible for human beings to know and what to do.

Symmetry requires complete equality of participation in the discourse. Everyone has the right to participate and all participants are entitled to make their views known. They are entitled to hear as well as to be heard, and generally to adopt the different possible roles involved in any discussion. The opportunity to do all these things must be given to all equally. If all the requirements described above are satisfied, and consensus is arrived at, that consensus is considered rationally grounded.

It is admitted, however, that the ideal speech situation is a fiction: that such a state of affairs in moral debate never has occurred and never will. Nonetheless, Habermas sees the ideal speech situation as an unavoidable supposition of moral discourse and an ideal which is anticipated in every actual moral discourse. To put it more simply, it functions as a regulative ideal against which actual situations can be measured, but which itself can never be achieved.

Habermas admits that, at the practical level of the creation of political institutions and the formation of societal policy, restrictions will inevitably operate upon discourse. Considerations of time, space, economy and organizational efficiency dictate that. What is crucial, however, is that in specific historical and social circumstances, political and social institutions and their functioning are such that we can reasonably assume that the political and social decisions taken would have been agreed to by all had they had complete freedom to participate in the formation of decisions. In other words, we could reasonably assume that the decisions arrived at would be essentially similar to those that would have been reached in the hypothetical ideal speech situation.[36]

The foregoing account of two related theories of moral reasoning may serve to indicate a plausible approach to constructing the methodology of objectively valid moral judgements. Such theories could be subjected to extensive criticism, and others could have been considered.[37] Space does not permit consideration of all the many possible theories and the counter-arguments to them, but enough has been said to indicate the sort of theoretical approach which can be arrived at by focussing on the rational, informed consensus as a possible condition of the objectivity of moral reasoning. The moral judgements which are arrived at through these processes of reasoning are not represented as timeless and eternal truths, but are considered right because they have been arrived at under the best possible conditions for agreeing on moral truth. To pursue the argument that what is proposed is not true objectivity would, perhaps, be to set too high a standard. After all, when comparisons are made with modern theories of the validity of scientific propositions, it can readily be seen that the concept of objectivity in relation to those propositions has undergone extensive revision. At one stage in intellectual history, it was possible to contrast science as the domain of the indisputably objective with moral discourse as the domain of the irredeemably subjective. Scientific propositions could make sense whereas moral propositions could not. That stage has passed and the status of scientific propositions as reflections of independent reality has increasingly been called into question.[38] Such doubts have not led the questioners to assert that science is not objective or valid; they have simply led to a rethinking of the meaning of objectivity. For propositions to count as scientific they must have been arrived at in a certain way. Objectivity resides in the procedures and the methods adopted and their consensual acceptance by the scientific community rather than in a direct correspondence to independent reality. Given that the objectivity of science is being viewed in a less transcendental or absolute sense, it seems reasonable to apply a similarly qualified standard to moral reasoning. An irrefutable case for the objectivity of moral reasoning has not yet been made but it does seem reasonable to proceed on the basis that objectivity in moral reasoning is possible.

The principal implication of the foregoing discussion of moral theory is that theories of constitutional interpretation based on moral arguments can purport to have some validity and judges can legitimately make decisions which are ultimately based on moral principles. Theories of human rights have, of course, generally been based on moral principles. That does not in itself demonstrate that human rights theories are valid and convincing as moral theories. The theories of moral reasoning already described in this essay do not automatically imply a human rights approach as the answer to the question of what qualities a morally sound society should exhibit. That may seem a serious defect in the argument, but to assume such a thing would be to misunderstand the point which is being made. Such tentative 'proofs' of the objectivity of moral reasoning undermine the principal criticism of the explicitly moral philosophical approach to constitutional interpretation. Furthermore, whilst a human rights approach does not automatically follow from these theories of moral reasoning, clearly such methods of moral reasoning could readily produce moral arguments expressed in terms of human rights.

Having established, albeit tentatively, that there is some justification for basing constitutional interpretation on moral principles it would, of course, be necessary to go on to show that a rights-based approach was preferable to other approaches, for example, a utilitarian approach.[39]

All this may seem far removed from what judges do and can reasonably be expected to do. The judicial process does not closely resemble, for example, Habermas's ideal speech situation (although the use of the *amicus* brief in the Supreme Court effectively increases the number of participants and the range of views canvassed in particular cases). That is not so grave a criticism as might, at first, appear, for it ignores the way in which moral reasoning becomes relevant to, and can be used by, judges. Judges are part of a wider legal and political culture, including practising lawyers, academics, politicians and citizens, all of whom may have something to say about the meaning of the Constitution and all of whom may cast their view of the Constitution in terms of a moral theory of human rights. The views which judges may acquire about the moral demands of human rights are acquired not apart from, but within, this culture, and they are able if they wish to continue to learn from it.

Clearly, it is something of a pipe dream to expect judicial decisions to proceed from exhaustive accounts of moral epistemology, through fully articulated and complex moral theories, to particular decisions. However, the possibility of judges learning from elaboration of such issues in a wider legal and political culture remains. This may not seem an entirely satisfactory answer but, given the absence of a neutral criterion of constitutional interpretation, it is the only real option.

Clearly we cannot assert that judges will be able to deduce from general guarantees of freedom of expression and of other rights, self-evident answers to the problems posed by specific cases. The methods of moral reasoning which have been described have little to say about concrete problems. They are too open-ended to prescribe particular, unarguably correct decisions. But they offer at least the prospect of resolving particular issues in a rational manner. The human rights doctrine that is evolved, when attention is focussed explicitly on the moral requirements of a human rights approach, has more chance of being coherent and properly protective of rights than doctrine which attempts to avoid difficult philosophical issues. The American experience should serve as a warning. Legal doctrine and theory there have been confused by the unhappy combination of a variety of approaches to the problem, of finding guiding considerations. At one time or another, guidance has been sought from the intentions of the framers, from tradition, from societal consensus and from a supposedly value-neutral model of the properly functioning democratic process.

The common element of these approaches is avoidance of difficult moral choices and overt moral reasoning. However, it is only in accepting the need to make such difficult choices and to indulge in moral reasoning that there lies any hope for coherence in doctrine.

The bare injunction to include moral analysis in constitutional interpretation is not, of course, very helpful. At the level of decision-making in concrete cases, analytical techniques must be evolved which can guide judges more fully and still keep faith with the basic moral imperatives of human rights theory.

One such candidate for an analytical technique is the idea of the core. It is not the only possible technique which might be used in adjudicating human rights cases under a constitution but it does illustrate how a more explicit human rights approach might be exemplified in actual doctrine. The idea of the core includes at least two related notions, one of which is the objective or purpose of the right in question. It is useful to focus on the core because asking, in relation to any right, what the purpose of that right is makes it more likely that one will be able to make rational decisions about its application in concrete cases. Incoherent doctrine is partly the product of failure to attend to the question of what the purpose of a right is, or of failure to identify the purpose of a right correctly. Some examples drawn from American Jurisprudence should show this. In evolving constitutional doctrine on freedom of speech, judges have grappled with such unhelpful distinctions as that between speech and conduct,[40] and that between protected and unprotected speech, for example, obscenity,[41] rather than getting to grips with the real issues.

The lack of sympathy for the 'obscene' ignores the possible role of erotic material as implicit advocacy of an alternative way of life. The speech–conduct distinction unjustifiably favours standard and well-established modes of expressing ideas and emotions over other modes. What the speech–conduct and protected–unprotected speech distinctions have in common is a failure to address the question of what the purpose of a right is.

Each of these strands of doctrine indicates a willingness to make decisions on the basis of assumptions about the proper role of free speech without making a detailed examination of what the point of a human right of freedom of expression is and without critically examining the assumptions which have determined decisions. Nor can assumptions about freedom of expression employed in different doctrinal areas be happily reconciled one with another.

These criticisms should not be seen as an attempt to dictate particular arguable moral propositions about freedom of expression under the guise of a neutral analytical technique. Rational doctrine on free speech could take a number of forms. The point being made is that the Supreme Court is unlikely to achieve a happy resolution of these issues until the issue of the underlying purpose of freedom of expression is clearly addressed. Until then, different strands of doctrine will point in different directions, because underlying differences of outlook never directly confront one another. Identification of the core of the right of freedom of expression carries more hope for coherent doctrine because doctrine could be elaborated in the light of an explicitly stated and well-argued theoretical base.

Similar problems have arisen with the abortion cases. In *Roe* v. *Wade*[42] the Supreme Court held that a woman's right to choose whether or nor to terminate a pregnancy was fundamental. That simple statement, however, conceals the confusion that is evident in Justice Blackmun's majority opinion, which drew on historical beliefs, modern scientific evidence, a principle of freedom of choice in reproductive matters, and the concept of the professional judgement of the physician, without making clear which source of value was more important or how potential conflicts between each rationale for the decision could be resolved. It was not clear whether the fundamental constitutional right to choose to have an abortion was based on a moral principle of reproductive self-determination, or on the view that, since abortion is a health problem, denial of important medical treatment was an infringement of liberty, or on the view that a foetus could not reasonably be said to have rights because it is not a person. The decision, in fact, seems to have been based on each of these ideas but the relationship between them was not made clear. The implications of this for the right to choose an abortion are clear. The different possible rationales for the decision each have different implications for the further development of the right in issue. Thus the emphasis on the medical aspects of abortion [43] may have the effect of changing the content of the right over time. The Court held that the state had a compelling interest in protecting potential life from the point when the foetus became viable, yet viability clearly depends on the state of medical science at a given point. Advances in medical science would logically permit states to proscribe abortion at ever earlier stages of pregnancy. On the other hand, if the rationale of the right is firmly based in a moral principle of complete reproductive self-determination, attempts by states to further limit the right to choose an abortion would remain impermissible. By basing doctrine on such a clear and explicit formulation of moral principle, the content and limits of the right could be made clear.[44]

What the immediately foregoing passage demonstrates is that techniques of analysis can be evolved which give judges more guidance than the simple injunction to introduce overtly moral reasoning into the decision-making process. In this way the task of interpreting broad constitutional guarantees of human rights can be made manageable. This may leave some unconvinced about the utility of Bills of Rights. They might admit that this is the course which judges interpreting a Bill of Rights must follow, whilst asserting that a Bill of Rights should not be introduced into the UK, or any other country which does not already have a Bill of Rights, because the task is one which judges need not perform. This, however, would be to misunderstand the task of judges under a system which preferred the piecemeal legislative approach to protection of human rights.

In the UK, Parliament has dealt with a number of human rights issues by particular enactments, such as the Race Relations Act, 1976, and the Sex Discrimination Act, 1975. Judges interpreting these statutes are not freed from the need to make controversial judgements of value. Both these Acts provide detailed specification of the various situations in which discrimination is forbidden, for example, in the field of employment, in education, in housing, in the provision of goods, facilities and services and so forth. However, whilst the scope of the Act, in terms of areas of human conduct, is clearly delineated, the definition of discrimination itself is framed at a high level of generality. Section 1 of the Sex Discrimination Act, 1975, has a two-part definition of discrimination. It makes clear that indirect discrimination (where *ex facie* neutral requirements have discriminatory impact) is unlawful. So too is direct discrimination. However, the basic definition of direct discrimination is 'a person discriminates against a woman in any circumstances relevant for the purposes of any provisions of this act, if – (a) on the ground of her sex he treats her less favourably than he treats or would treat a man.'[45] The Act does not further define the meaning of less favourable treatment, except in the sense that certain specific declarations are made about differences in treatment which are not to count as discrimination, as where sex is a genuine occupational qualification.[46] Judges are still left with the task of defining the meaning of discrimination in modern society on the basis of an essentially open-ended definition and they will be required to make difficult decisions in many cases where the terms of the statute do not provide a clearly correct legal answer.

Here, the opponent of Bills of Rights might make the more precise criticism that one could accept the need to indulge in moral reasoning in human rights cases whilst still denying the appropriateness of constitutional guarantees of rights. Although judges would face similar difficulties under a piecemeal legislative approach, they would perhaps arise less often and without the consequence of invalidation of democratically enacted legislation. These are persuasive points, but they do not dispose of the issue. The choice of mechanism ultimately depends not only on such questions as whether moral reasoning can be objective and whether human rights is an intelligible philosophical concept, but also on other considerations. The historical, political and social context must, for reasons of prudence, play a large part in the decision, and there may be circumstances in which real protection of human rights requires us to accept the expanded judicial role and the consequences for democratically elected institutions which a Bill of Rights entails.

What can be said is that the objections to the Bill of Rights model are not as great as is often supposed in the UK. Insofar as the objections are based on the view that Bills of Rights raise issues which are incapable of objective judicial resolution, they are misconceived. Both in the UK and in the USA there is a widespread failure to appreciate that the existing differences in constitutional structure create no major differences in the problems of interpretation and of judicial method caused by enacting legal guarantees of human rights. In neither situation is it possible or desirable to separate moral concerns from legal reasoning. The shift from rhetoric to reality in human rights matters must follow the path of moral reasoning.

Notes

1   See e.g. Jeremy Bentham, 'Anarchical Fallacies', in A.I. Melden (ed.), *Human Rights* (Belmont, California: Wadsworth, 1970), 32; D.G. Ritchie, *Natural Rights* (London: Swan Sonnen Schein, 1895); Kai Nielsen, 'Scepticism and Human Rights', in *The Monist*, October 1968, 594.
2   See chapter 10, Gerry Maher, 'Human Rights and the Criminal Process'.
3   See e.g. Sir Leslie Scarman (now Lord Scarman), *English Law – The New Dimension* (London: Steven, 1974), 10–21.

4   See e.g. Lloyd of Hampstead, 'Do We Need a Bill of Rights?', *Modern Law Review*, 39 (1976), 121; J.A.G. Griffith, 'The Political Constitution', *Modern Law Review*, 42 (1979), 1.
5   US Constitution, Amendment I.
6   Ibid., Amendment V.
7   424 U.S. 1 (1976).
8   Ibid., 48.
9   See R. Berger, *Government by Judiciary: The Transformation of The Fourteenth Amendment* (Cambridge, Mass.: Harvard University Press, 1977).
10   Justice Black advanced an interpretivist position in a number of cases e.g. *Pointer* v. *Texas*, 380 U.S. 400 (1965), and (dissenting) in *Griswold* v. *Connecticut*, 381 U.S. 479 (1965).
11   See Thomas C. Grey, 'Do We Have An Unwritten Constitution?', *Stanford Law Review*, 27 (1975), 703.
12   Berger, *Government by Judiciary*, 117–33.
13   See L. Hand, *The Bill of Rights* (Cambridge, Mass.: Harvard University Press, 1958).
14   431 U.S. 494 (1977).
15   Ibid., 503.
16   See H. Wellington, 'Common Law Rules and Constitutional Double Standards: Some Notes of Adjudication', *Yale Law Journal*, 83 (1973), 221.
17   352 U.S. 432 (1957).
18   Ibid., 435.
19   Ibid., 444.
20   For a fuller discussion of consensus and tradition as sources of values, see J.H. Ely, *Democracy and Distrust* (Cambridge, Mass.: Harvard University Press, 1980), 60–9.
21   See M. Tushnet, 'The Dilemmas of Liberal Constitutionalism', *Ohio State Law Journal*, 42 (1981), 410.
22   Ibid., 424–6.
23   See generally Ely, *Democracy*.
24   *United States* v. *Carolene Products Co.*, U.S. 144, at 152 n.4 (1938) The author of the footnote was Justice Stone.

> It is unnecessary to consider now whether legislation which restricts those political processes which can ordinarily be expected to bring about repeal of undesirable legislation, is to be subjected to more exacting judicial scrutiny under the general prohibitions of the Fourteenth Amendment than are most other types of legislation . . .
>   Nor need we enquire whether similar considerations enter into review of statutes directed at particular religious . . . or national . . . or racial minorities . . . ; whether prejudice against discrete and insular minorities may be a special condition which tends seriously to curtail the operation of those processes ordinarily to be relied upon to protect minorities, and which may call for a correspondingly more searching judicial enquiry.

25   On the 'double standard' generally see H.J. Abraham, *Freedom and the Court* (4th edn) (New York: Oxford University Press, 1977), 13–27.
26   Ely, *Democracy*, 73–179.
27   See also L. Tribe, 'The Puzzling Persistence of Process-Based Constitutional Theories', *Yale Law Journal*, 89 (1980), 1063.
28   See M. Perry, *The Constitution, The Courts, and Human Rights* (New Haven, Connecticut: Yale University Press, 1982), 79–80.

29　See generally L. Tribe, *American Constitutional Law* (New York: The Foundation Press, 1978); R. Dworkin, *Taking Rights Seriously* (London: Duckworth, 1978).

30　The phrase is taken from Tribe, *Constitutional Law*, 11.

31　See *Bromley London Borough Council* v. *Greater London Council* [1982] 1 All E.R., 129.

32　Perry, *The Constitution*, x.

33　A more detailed account of this method can be found in N. Daniels, 'Wide Reflective Equilibrium and Theory Acceptance in Ethics', *Journal of Philosophy*, 76 (1970), 256. See also J. Rawls, 'The Independence of Moral Theory', *Proceedings and Addresses of the American Philosophical Association*, 47 (1974/5), 5.

34　Habermas's approach to these and other matters is well summarized in T. McCarthy, *The Critical Theory of Jurgen Habermas* (Cambridge, Mass.: MIT Press, 1978).

35　McCarthy, *Critical Theory*, 306–10.

36　McCarthy, *Critical Theory*, 309–10 and 331–3.

37　See, e.g., R. Unger, *Knowledge and Politics* (New York: Free Press, 1975). Unger attempts to show that the ends men hold in common can give us knowledge of the good in certain circumstances. See especially 242–4.

38　See generally P. Feyerabend, *Against Method: Outline of an Anarchistic Theory of Knowledge* (London: New Left Books, 1975); N. Cartwright, *How the Laws of Physics Lie* (Oxford: Clarendon Press, 1983); T.S. Kuhn, *The Structure of Scientific Revolutions* (Chicago: University of Chicago Press, 1962); McCarthy, *Critical Theory*.

39　Gerry Maher, in chapter 10, discusses the significance of adopting an approach based on human rights rather than on utilitarianism in respect of the criminal process, and shows the special and useful role that the notion of human rights can play in moral argument.

40　See *Cox* v. *Louisiana*, 379 U.S. 559 (1965), 563, and *United States* v. *O'Brien*, 391 U.S. 367 (1968), 376.

41　See *Roth* v. *United States*, 354 U.S. 476 (1957), 485, and *Miller* v. *California*, 413 U.S. 15 (1973).

42　410 U.S. 113 (1973).

43　Ibid., 163 and 165–166; see also *Doe* v. *Bolton*, 410 U.S. 179, 192.

44　Sheila McLean analyses the rights involved in the abortion situation in terms of freedom of choice in reproductive matters in chapter 6, 'The Right to Reproduce'.

45　Section 2 of the Act makes it clear that references to discrimination against women are to be read as applying equally to the treatment of men.

46　Sex Discrimination Act, 1975, Section 7.

3

The Core of Rights and Freedoms: the Limit of Limits

Esin Örücü

This chapter inquires into the extent and limits of the regulation of basic rights in a world where human rights are positivized. It is concerned less with basic philosophical assumptions about rights than with the critique of practice. The fact that rights are expressed in a rhetorical form in international documents, where they appear as ultimate aspirations embodying objectives felt to be generally desirable, and also at a more practical level within individual legal systems, makes it imperative that rights are studied as they actually are: regulated and limited. Moving from rhetoric to reality requires that human rights are examined as they are positivized and concretized.

How human rights are to be protected in their positivized form as basic legal rights in the process of their identification, specification and concretization through legal provisions is a crucial practical problem. Its solution does not involve settling such questions as whether human rights are rights that all persons equally have simply by being human, or whether such rights exist only within a normative order and are therefore culturally relative. Nevertheless, any human rights discourse assumes that some human interests require special legal or political protection.

A number of logically related key questions will be considered. First, does positivization and concretization of a right necessarily entail a limitation of that right? In other words, is every regulation a limitation? Second, is the law-maker free to limit a right without restriction in the process of concretization? If not, what can legitimately be imposed by the law-maker? What tests have been developed by courts to measure and evaluate the presence and extent of these conditions? Third, even when legitimate reasons for limitations exist, how far can a right be limited before it is reduced to a mere semantic right? That is, may the law-maker impose a limitation in the normative scope of a right so long as the tests for legitimate requirements and conditions are satisfied, or is there in every right an area into which no law-maker may go? If so, what is the limit of limitations and how can it be determined and defined? In this connection, it will be asked whether courts have succeeded in developing criteria for determining an irreducible minimum, that is a nucleus or core, for every right, which can be universally acceptable and used by all courts to protect the minimum content of a right? Also, the question of whether a right can be taken on its own or must be taken with its concomitant rights will be considered.

In taking up these issues, the concept of a right will be analysed in terms of a normative scope with three distinct parts: a core,[1] a circumjacence, and an outer edge, the core being that part of a right which is essential to its definition. Using this analysis, the main question to be answered is whether, in a world of qualified rights, we require the concept of the core as the one area in the normative scope of a right which must be protected absolutely?

The Concretization of Rights and Freedoms

When rights discourse operates at the level of moral or natural rights, the rights require respect only; when rights are considered as basic legal rights, they require positive action for their realization.

These rights are either guaranteed as *Grundrechte* in written constitutions or, as in the British legal system, regarded as freedoms whose existence is evidenced only by the absence of legal restraints. In both cases these basic legal rights are subject to specification and regulation. Even the seemingly absolute guarantees of the First Amendment to the US Constitution are considerably limited in practice by, for example, the clear and present danger test.

Legal systems with general constitutions or catalogues of fundamental rights are explicit about which rights shall receive protection. This specification of rights is, in effect, a declaration of which rights are regarded as worthy of guaranteeing at the higher level of a Bill of Rights or a constitutional document in an individual legal system. For example, the French Declaration of the Rights of Man of 1789 specifies liberty, property, security and resistance to oppression. The Basic Law of the German Republic of 1949 specifies and guarantees a wide range of rights, such as human dignity, free development of personality, freedoms of conscience, faith, religion, speech, the press, teaching, petition, assembly, association, occupation and movement, privacy of mail and telecommunications, protection against arbitrary searches and seizures, citizenship, functional equivalents of *habeas corpus* and due process and so on.

The specification process is the first step in the move to positivization and is the moment in rights discourse when a natural or moral right takes the form of a basic or fundamental legal right. The specification is not in itself, however, a concretization, that is, it is not directly applicable to specific circumstances.

A written constitution, as the supreme law of the land, is legally the clearest embodiment of principles and rights. The inevitable abstraction in the specification of rights at this level is compensated for by further legislative enactments which can be seen as the concretization of constitutional norms. It is noteworthy that through the process of enacting constitutional guarantees of rights, even pure liberties[2] are converted into civil rights and further positive rights. These positive rights are again concretized at lower levels of law-making by the executive and appear in their ultimate concrete form in court decisions where a single individual's right is protected. This process of the concretization of a right is in accordance with Kelsen's account of the unfolding of the normative order.[3] In a legal system, which is a normative hierarchy, superior rules remain incomplete as rules of law until concretized by lower norms, that is, regulated. Every concretizing norm is a link in the chain of progressive individualization of law, which is itself a continuing process. In the terms of this chapter, a fundamental rule is one where a right has been specified and the process of concretization which follows specification is a process of regulation.

In a system such as the British, where freedoms are regarded as understood or taken for granted, so that, 'the citizen may do as he likes unless he clashes with some specific restriction on his freedom',[4] and arrangements for the protection of human rights are quite different from those in most other countries, freedoms, when specified, are specified in statutes or common law. Although the British Parliament has never attempted to formulate a catalogue of basic rights, it has taken direct account of, for instance, the safeguarding of personal liberty (*habeas corpus*) and preserving the rule of law. This kind of specification, converting a freedom into a basic legal right, is in effect a regulation which fundamentally is also a limitation of a pure liberty. In the process of positivization the right will further be subject to executive concretization in its implementation. Thus, the positivization of human rights is a fact, not only within systems with written constitutions and Bills of Rights, but also in the UK.

Regulating a specific right involves enacting rules. Some of these rules facilitate the achievement of the objectives of the right and enable the right-holder to exercise his or her right, and others narrow the normative scope of that right and therefore limit the right-holder. Though every limitation is born out of a regulation, not all regulations impose limitation. Regulations tend to be general; limitations are normally required to be concrete, narrow and technical. Regulating a right can be related to its mode of utilization. For example, in order to exercise the right to travel abroad one needs a passport. Limiting a right relates to its scope, as when one is only permitted to travel to certain countries. This distinction between the two concepts of limitation and regulation is not just one of semantics. It is of specific importance in the debate about the 'prohibition on touching the core of a right in the process of regulating it',[5] since a regulation applies to the totality of a right, whereas a limitation can only be introduced into the circumjacence of the right and has to stop at its core. A limitation, being an external intervention, must also be differentiated from the inherent limitations of a right sometimes encountered in the specification of that right in the constitutional text. For example, the Basic Law of the Federal Republic of Germany specifies in Article 8 that, 'all Germans shall have the right to assemble peaceably and unarmed without prior notification or permission.'

It has been claimed that for human rights to exist in reality, their scope and the ways in which they can be utilized have to be determined and shown; in other words, they have to be regulated. In this approach regulating a right defines and strengthens it.[6] However, there are certain basic legal rights the regulation of which does entail a limitation, such as the rights to life, freedom of thought, freedom of conscience and freedom of expression. Here regulation is synonymous with limitation. There are certain basic legal rights where a regulation in the form of a legislative enactment is the creator of the right, as in the case of the right to enter into collective agreements.

In sum, in the process of positivization of human rights, the normative scope of the specified rights is concretized by regulations, since rights can only be used when regulated. For all basic rights regulations provide facilitations, and for most basic rights regulations will carry limitations. It is also true that some basic rights are specified with inherent limitations.

The next question to be dealt with is when and how basic legal rights can be limited. A two-fold approach will be adopted. The first will review some constitutional enactments in order to ascertain concepts introduced to circumscribe legitimate grounds for limitations. The second will look at tests employed by courts in their efforts to protect rights, asking whether these inroads into the normative scope of a right are always legitimate.

Legitimate Limitations

The United Nations Universal Declaration of Human Rights (1948) which says in Article 1: 'All human beings are born free and equal in dignity and rights', admits in Article 29 that rights are balanced by, and correlative with, duties. Thus human rights, even when conceived of as natural rights, are not boundless. Also, the escape clause, Article 29/2, indicates that the exercise of a person's rights and freedoms may be restricted for the purpose of meeting the 'just requirements of morality, public order and general welfare in a democratic society'.

In another supra-national document, the European Convention on Human Rights (1950), there is, for example, in Article 8 the statement of a right: 'everyone has the right to respect for his private and family life, his home and his correspondence', and the recognition of legitimate limitations:

> there shall be no interference by a public authority with the exercise of this right except such as is in accordance with the law and is necessary in a democratic society in the interests of national security, public safety or the economic well-being of the country, for the prevention of disorder or crime, for the protection of health and morals, or for the protection of the rights and freedoms of others.

This pattern can also be seen in other articles of the Convention.

The same approach can be found in the Basic Law of the Federal Republic of Germany of 1949. For example in Article 2, there is the statement of a right: 'Everyone shall have the right to the free development of his personality', and the recognition of legitimate limitations; 'in so far as he does not violate the rights of others, or offend against the constitutional order or the moral code'. Again in Article 11, there is the statement of a right: '[a]ll Germans shall enjoy freedom of movement throughout the federal territory', and also of legitimate limitations;

> this right may be restricted only by or pursuant to a law and only in cases in which an adequate basis of existence is lacking and special burdens would arise to the community as a result thereof, or in which such restriction is necessary to avert an imminent danger to the existence or the free democratic basic order of the Federation or a Land, to combat the danger of epidemics, to deal with natural disasters or particularly grave accidents, to protect young people from neglect or to prevent crime.

A similar pattern can be seen in other articles of the Constitution. There is no general clause for qualifications and each right and freedom has to be considered separately for the specific limitations in its relevant article.

Similarly the 1961 Constitution of the Turkish Republic[7] has a number of articles guaranteeing specific rights or freedoms and stating limitations, such as Article 18:

> Everyone has freedom of movement: this freedom may be restricted only by law and only to ensure national security and to combat epidemics. Everyone has freedom of settlement wherever he chooses. This freedom may be restricted only by law and only to ensure national security, to combat epidemics, to protect eminent domain, to realise social, economic and agricultural developments. Turks enjoy the freedom to enter and leave the country. The freedom to leave the country is to be regulated by law.

The same pattern can be seen in other articles of the Constitution.

In contrast to the above, the US Constitution lays down certain rights and freedoms without mentioning any requirements or conditions either in individual articles or in a general limitation article. The First Amendment reads:

> Congress shall make no law respecting an establishment of religion, or prohibiting the free exercise thereof; or abridging the freedom of

speech, or of the press; or the right of the people peaceably to assemble
and to petition the government for a redress of grievances. . .

However, in practice, an elaborate series of tests for legitimate
limitations has been developed, particularly the doctrine of preferred
rights and balancing of competing interests.

In the Canadian Charter of Rights and Freedoms of 1982 there is
yet another picture. The rights and freedoms guaranteed are in seven
separate areas: fundamental freedoms, democratic rights, mobility
rights, legal rights, equality rights, rights relating to the two official
languages and the minority language educational rights. These rights
are not absolute, but are subject to two different kinds of exceptions or
limitations. Section 33 provides that the Parliament or a provincial
legislature can opt out with regard to the guarantees of fundamental
freedoms, legal and equality rights, by expressly declaring within a
statute that it shall operate notwithstanding any specified provision in
the Charter. Section 1 of the Charter further provides that the
condition is 'subject only to such reasonable limits prescribed by law
as can be demonstrably justified in a free and democratic society'.

In their different ways each operative system of rights can be
described as a system of qualified rights or as a system of qualified
guarantees. Certain concepts appear to be generally acceptable as
qualifications and legitimate limitations. These qualifying concepts,
which must be within reasonable limits that can be demonstrably
justified and determined by law within a democratic society, include
public safety, public health, public order, public policy, general
morality, general or public welfare, public interest, defence, the
protection of youth, the national interest and the common good.

Without entering into a discussion of the necessity or the merits of
constitutional review of ordinary legislation, it is clear that, in the long
run, either by direct mandate or via legal control of executive
decisions, the courts of law are the final arbiters of whether these
requirements or qualifications are present and are reasonably
employed. It is in general the courts (ordinary, administrative or
constitutional), in their efforts to control governmental power vis-à-
vis the individual, which have attempted to create or formulate the
tests and standards which they use as touchstones every time a
complaint reaches them that a right has been violated. This is within
the normal scope of their duty.[8]

The first step taken by a court is to see whether public power has been used arbitrarily and the second is to see whether it has been used, under the guise of one of the qualifying concepts, to curb a basic legal right unreasonably. Among the tests used by courts in this process are a number developed by the US Supreme Court which, in the absence of constitutional qualifications of rights and freedoms, is under a strong duty to protect the individual.

One of the most important of these tests is strict scrutiny. This requires that the challenged classification be narrowly drawn and be necessary to promote a compelling state interest. The Court evaluates the importance of the government's objective in order to determine whether it is significant enough to justify an infringement upon constitutional values. If the objective is found to be compelling, the Court then independently examines the necessity of the classification for achieving that objective, as well as the existence of any less burdensome alternative for reaching that end. Fundamental rights subject to strict scrutiny have their source either explicitly or implicitly in the Constitution or they are those rights designated by the Supreme Court as fundamental.[9]

The compelling state interest standard and the reasonableness standard were, for example, used in *Shapiro* v. *Thompson*,[10] where the Court felt that the classification of state residency burdened a constitutional right, and the denial of a welfare aid was seen as a penalty on the right of movement. The Court has also used tests such as minimal rationality, heightened scrutiny and substantial rationality.[11]

In the context of proportionality the other important tests developed by the Supreme Court are the balancing test,[12] the alternative means test,[13] and the clear and present danger test.[14] These tests involve the Court in balancing the interest to be protected in limiting a certain right with the interest inherent in upholding the right in question. Sometimes it is two competing public interests which have to be balanced. The final aim is to determine whether the law strikes a fair balance overall.

The test of proportionality widely used on the continent is a test originally developed by the French Conseil d'Etat in its control of administrative legality. In determining the limit of administrative actions by the necessity of the situation, the Court applies tests such as manifest error (*erreur manifeste d'appréciation des faits*), disproportionality and the balance sheet (*le bilan*). The Federal Constitutional Court in Germany also uses this administrative law test of proportionality (*Verhältnismässigkeit*) or disproportionality extensively, to determine whether the limitations to individual right referred to in the provisions of the Constitution are adhered to. The law-maker cannot go beyond these, though any one, or more than one, of the limitations can be used. The Federal Constitutional Court uses the test of proportionality by asking whether the means used is suitable (*Geeignetheit*) for realizing the objective of the limitation,[15] whether the means used is necessary (*Erforderlichkeit*) for the objective of the limitation,[16] and whether the means and the end are in a relationship which is proportionate (*Proportionalitaet*).[17] These questions are asked in relation to the facts of every individual case and every right when there is a limitation and a challenge.

It could be claimed that the test of proportionality is an ultimate test for justice and a requisite concretization of the rule of law or *Rechtsstaat* and thus immanent in the concept of basic rights.

To sum up, the process of enacting constitutional guarantees of rights converts even pure or understood liberties into civil rights and further into basic positive rights. These basic rights cannot be absolute; they are qualified. There seems to be a general consensus on these qualifications in international documents and individual constitutions. The courts, in protecting basic rights and judging the validity of acts of restraint, are asking the same sorts of questions, applying similar tests and developing parallel doctrines to keep public power within the framework of the legal qualifications.

Even when no qualification is mentioned, a right is limited by its own normative scope.[18] Every regulation narrowing the normative scope of a right must be imposed by, or pursuant to, a law. Beyond this, a right may only be limited when it collides with another.

A fundamental question remains. Is it the case that, as long as a public power keeps within the legitimate limitations, and rights are qualified by these limitations, and the public power passes the tests of the courts, it necessarily follows that the scope of a right can be indefinitely narrowed, or is there a duty to protect an irreducible minimum, the essential content of a right, absolutely? Is this irreducible minimum the limit to limitations?

The Core of Rights, The Limits of Limits

In seeking to clarify the essential content of a right, it is important to note that having a right must mean having the necessary conditions for exercising that right. Arguably a right is meaningless when it is impossible for the right-holder to exercise it. The normative scope of a right tells the right-holders what should be available to them.

The exercising of a right often depends on the availability of other rights. For example, the right to travel, if unaccompanied by the right to a passport, may not be exercisable. Within the European Community, there is an enforceable right to move from one member state to another to take up employment (Article 48), necessarily involving the right to hold the document which makes that movement possible. The refusal to issue a passport has been judged by the Supreme Court of India[19] also to be an infringement of the fundamental right to travel abroad which, in its turn, was stated to be an integral part of the right to personal liberty. In such a situation one can talk of concomitant or connected rights. The concept of peripheral rights have been introduced into discussions of electronic eaves-dropping in the US.[20] The freedom of circulation is seen as an ancillary to liberty of publishing by the US Supreme Court.[21] Similarily the right to disseminate the products of the printing press is regarded by the Hoge Raad (The Supreme Ordinary Court in the Netherlands) as ancillary to the right to free publication, protected by Article 7 of the Dutch Constitution.[22]

Although concomitant rights may not be included in the actual scope of the ordinary or primary right, they should be viewed together. Rights can be thought of as clusters of primary and concomitant rights.

When a right is subjected to formalities, conditions, restrictions or penalties prescribed by law and judged as valid and acceptable in the individual instance by a court, a further question arises as to the extent of these limitations. It is possible that a limitation of a right or its concomitant right may reduce that right to an unusable conceptual form. For example, if limitations are permanent rather than temporary, or general rather than specific, a mere semantic right would remain. So how far can a right be regulated and limited before it becomes vacuous or even illusory? How far can one go before one rubs up against the core of the right? In analysing and answering these questions one must introduce into the discourse the concept of the 'guaranteed core'. Only then can a distinction be made between the circumjacence of a right, which is defeasible, and the core of the right and the essential concomitant rights, which are indefeasible.

In Germany[23] and Turkey in particular, the concept of the core of a right has been the subject of a large number of jurisprudential discussions, the metaphor of a right with a core, a circumjacence and an outer edge being very much in the forefront. The main reason is that in both countries the prohibition on encroaching upon or touching the core of a right is positivized in their Constitutions. This is because both Constitutions are historically products of a reaction to periods of governmental suppression, and positive regulation in this area was seen as a necessity. The guaranteed core in these systems should be viewed as more than a declaratory provision and be regarded as a constitutive one.

The concept of the core as part of a constitutional norm in Germany appears as the essential content which acts to limit legitimate limitations in Article 19/2 of the Basic Law: '[i]n no case may the essential content (*Wesengehalt*) of a basic right be encroached upon.' This Constitution was very influential in the preparation of the Turkish Constitution of 1961,[24] and the German Article 19/2 corresponds to the Turkish Article 11/2: '[l]aw cannot touch the core of a right or a freedom even on such grounds as public interest, general morality, public order, social justice and national security'.[25]

In addition to these two Constitutions, this concept occurs only in the recent Portuguese Constitution of 1976, Article 18/3 (as amended in 1982): '[l]aws restricting rights, liberties and guarantees must assume a general and abstract nature and cannot be retroactive nor can they reduce the extent or scope of the essential content of constitutional provisions.' Similarly the draft Swiss Constitution (1979) has introduced the core concept. Draft Article 23/1 reads: '[f]undamental rights can be limited only if a preponderant public interest justifies it. Their essence is inviolable.'

There is one interesting variant in use of this concept in the Netherlands. Article 131/2 of the Dutch Constitution reads: 'Acts of Parliament are inviolable.' Legally, there can be no challenge of unconstitutionality. Although there are scattered provisions on human rights and freedoms, few provisions contain an actual guarantee against invasion by Parliament. Courts scrutinize subordinate legislation, so discussion of constitutionality only occurs in relation to the local authorities' application of the law.[26] Neither the concept of the core (*kernrechten*), the nucleus of a right, nor other rights necessary in the exercise of a right (*connexe rechten*) give rise to extra protection by the courts. The governmental proposal for constitutional amendment in 1976[27] pointed out that, as no definition of a nucleus can be given, this claim borders on arbitrariness since it has to be decided in each individual instance. However, though the theory of *kernrechten* is rejected by the government, a mass of case law has developed around Article 7 of the Dutch Constitution using the concepts of both *kernrechten* and *connexe rechten*.[28] The idea of *kernrechten* is developed by the Hoge Raad in interpreting the Constitution and conventions (since rights are posited, and their scope, and therefore core, is determined by the Constitution), and the idea of *connexe rechten* has been developed solely by the Hoge Raad (and therefore relies on case law).

The right protected by Article 7 is freedom of information and the press: '[n]o person shall require previous permission to publish thoughts or feelings by means of the printing press, without prejudice to every person's responsibility according to law.' In 1950, the Hoge Raad distinguished two elements in Article 7.[29] The first was the core to be protected, that is 'the right of the mind, the right to express one's mind through the press', the exercise of which could not be subject to prior restraint. The second was the ancillary right, that is 'the right to disseminate the product of the printing press', which could not be completely prohibited, or made conditional upon a licence, lest the nucleus of Article 7 be rendered completely illusory. Then, extending the scope of the ancillary right, the Hoge Raad further protected the distribution of handbills in the streets, distribution of printed matter with simultaneous oral presentation, signs in neon letters, picketing with sandwich-boards, demonstrations, posterhanging and advertisements, including political advertisements.[30]

In the German and Turkish systems, limitations can be introduced only into the area circumjacent to the core of the right, and the limit of limitations is the membrane dividing the one from the other. Every limitation advances from the outer edge of the right towards its core, but at this membrane it has to stop. Where the core starts or ends cannot be determined in the abstract. This determination is discretionary, and both in German and Turkish law is left to the independent judiciary.

It has already been seen that the German Federal Constitutional Court uses various forms of disproportionality as tests to protect the scope of a right circumjacent to its core, which appear to be effective. Therefore the Court has developed only a very limited number of criteria to determine the core, as most violations render the law void before the core itself is touched, and encroachment upon the core will not even be a matter for discussion.

In the Turkish legal system, however, where there is a very extensive section on rights and freedoms in the Constitution, where the Constitutional Court has not developed many refined tests to protect the scope of a right circumjacent to its core,[31] and where there are extensive claims of violation of rights, the Constitutional Court frequently refers to the core concept and has developed a number of criteria to discover, define and determine the scope of the core. It first determines whether the objective and grounds for legitimate limitations exist; if so it then looks into the core itself. When the Court arrives at a negative conclusion at the first stage, it will find the limitation unconstitutional in any case and therefore will not discuss the core. Some examples of this will be examined.

In a system of qualified rights and freedoms, the first consideration is that the qualifications do not extend so far as to render the exercise of the right or freedom difficult beyond a reasonable measure; yet the determination of this measure of reasonableness is difficult and often not sufficient to clarify the guaranteed core.

Sometimes the core of a right is the exercise of it.[32] In this case, concomitant rights must be considered to be part of the core of that primary right and the guaranteed core must embrace all the cores of the relevant cluster of rights. Sometimes, in determining the content of the core, recourse is made to supplementary guarantees provided in individual constitutional provisions. There are, for example, four groups of such supplementary guarantees in a number of articles in the Turkish Constitution of 1961: 'the prohibition of prior authorisation', 'the prohibition of censorship', 'where restraints have to be specified by law and be pursuant to a decision duly rendered by a court', and 'guarantees inherent in the scope of the rights'. These may be seen as positivized elements of the cores of those particular rights.[33]

In relation to specific rights, for example freedom of thought (Article 20), the core of the freedom is the thought itself;[34] for the right of property, the core is the concrete relationship between the owner and the thing,[35] and so on.

If limitations, which are in themselves legitimate, go beyond the circumjacence of the right to touch the core, then they are regarded as unreasonable or demonstrably unjustifiable. Whether this has taken place has to be determined in relation to every individual right or right-cluster and used in structuring the discretionary power of the judiciary.

The Turkish Constitutional Court in the period 1961–81 developed various criteria applicable to instances of claims of encroachment upon the core of a right. The Court did not define the core as a concept, but in a large number of cases referred to this concept as the limit beyond which limitations could not be justified. If one identifies criteria which have been used in various decisions, it is apparent that these are immensely varied. A limitation is regarded as an encroachment upon the core when (a) it makes the exercise of a right or freedom, according to its purpose, extremely difficult or even impossible,[36] (b) it binds a right to such conditions as to make it impotent,[37] (c) it is explicitly prohibitive,[38] (d) it is implicitly prohibitive,[39] (e) it makes the use of the right extremely difficult,[40] (f) it hinders the realization of its purpose,[41] (g) it takes away its efficacy,[42] (h) it makes benefitting from the right dependent on prior general licensing or permission,[43] (i) it is introduced by very vague provisions open to a number of interpretations,[44] (j) it removes a right generally,[45] (k) it is so extensive that the exercise of the right becomes impossible or directly or indirectly impeded,[46] (l) it creates an unjustifiable inequality,[47] (m) it is permanent,[48] (n) it introduces qualifications above and beyond the legitimate ones,[49] or (o) it imposes obligations on an unqualified right.[50] These criteria have sometimes been used simultaneously in the same case.

When the Court finds that the limitation touches the core, legitimate limitations, such as the public interest (which is the one most frequently referred to), or social need, are not regarded as relevant. Apparently, the Court regards as absolute the prohibition on touching the core of a right.

In the period 1970–80 the Turkish Constitutional Court repeated, in relation to all rights and freedoms, a formula along the following lines: provisions explicitly prohibiting the exercise of a right or implicitly making a right impotent or making the use of it extremely difficult and preventing the realization of its objective and taking away its efficacy, touch the core of that right or freedom. The years from 1975 to 1980 in particular seem to be an unproductive period for the Court in further developing the concept of the core. It is interesting to note that, in the political climate of the time when Turkey saw extremist terrorist activities in the streets and educational establishments in the large cities, the Court chose to extend the scope of the concept of public interest and, by giving a wide meaning to this qualification, permitted a limitation by stating that 'in times of social crisis, public interest expands, therefore there is no encroachment on the core of the right relating to the inviolability of the individual.' (Article 14)[51] The Court also referred to a hierarchy of rights and preferred interests and stated that: 'to preserve secularism which is of the utmost importance, freedom of expression can be limited. This regulation [limiting religious propaganda] deemed essential by the Constitution cannot be connected in any way with being contrary to freedom of expression.'[52] This indicates that the existence of a positivized concept of the core of rights may not in itself set clear limits to the limitation of rights.

The practical question for Turkey today is whether or not the Court will continue in the same way and use its precedents in implementing the 1982 Constitution even though this Constitution does not have a provision prohibiting encroachment upon the core, but has more or less kept the 1961 catalogue of rights and freedoms, with additional qualifications. There is also a new article, Article 15, relating to the suspension of the exercise of rights, making it possible to take measures contrary to the guarantees in the Constitution in times of war, martial law or exceptional circumstances.[53] The limit here arises from the obligations imposed by international law. Even in the above circumstances, the right to life and basic material and spiritual well-being cannot be touched. No one can be forced to reveal his or her faith, conscience, thoughts and beliefs, or be punished for these. Offences and punishment cannot be retroactive and nobody can be considered guilty until proven so by a court decision. In relation to these limitations the Court might very well use the concept of the core.

In German legal literature there are those who claim that the guaranteed core is limited to the objective normative area of the right. Thus limitations may not, in concrete and specific instances, be regarded as encroaching upon this core.[54] This view relies on a 1953 Federal Constitutional Court decision,[55] where it was stated that determining whether the core has been touched or not will be dependent upon the legal decision as to whether the specific right still retains its importance in society after the limitation. In this determination, 'the regulated relationship', 'the regulation itself', and 'public opinion on this point' all play a part. Thus the subjective normative area of a right cannot be the decisive factor in such decisions. Yet later, the Court developed another approach:

> [l]aw cannot restrain the intellectual, political, and economic freedoms of man to the extent of encroaching upon the core of those freedoms. Therefore the Constitution holds immune an area within which every citizen can shape his private life. Hence, there is a last untouchable area of human freedom which is protected from every intervention by public power.[56]

This approach extends the guaranteed core to the individual subjective normative area of the right, to the cluster of norms, the legal institutions from which innumerable subjective public rights arise. Thus the 'guaranteed' core protects both the objective and the subjective norm.

However, the whole of a right is not protected with the same intensity. The guarantee becomes meaningless when that part of the right which cannot be relinquished is touched. This unrelinquishable nucleus is the raison d'être of the basic legal norm, essential to its definition, and surrounded by the less securely guarded elements. These notions gain a concrete content as each individual right is analysed. Within the core, the exercise of the right is absolute. What is crucial is what is left after the limitation, and what can be achieved with it. If a basic right is reduced to such an extent that, for instance, the right-holder cannot pursue that right in the courts, this indicates that the core of this right has been touched.[57]

It is claimed that the core of the basic rights enables Man to participate freely in public life,[58] and that the core guarantees the dignity of Man, whichever right is concerned.[59] This is an approach which tries to determine the lowest common denominator for all basic rights. Although this is an important exercise, it is vital to establish the content of the core of each right by determining what are the unrelinquishable minima within the normative scope of that right. Those concomitant rights embraced by the 'guaranteed core' must also be determined at this stage. Only after that might a common denominator for all rights be created.

At this point it is necessary to examine how the three German Courts, the Federal Court of Appeal, the Federal Administrative Court and the Federal Constitutional Court, have separately developed distinct criteria to determine the core.

The Federal Court of Appeal, in one decision, gave this formula:

'[l]imitations not absolutely necessary to achieve the objective should be considered touching the core.'[60] This may be criticized because the test of necessary limitations should only apply to the circumjacence. In any case, touching the core is the result of a disproportionate limitation.[61] The Federal Court of Appeal relates proportionality to the prohibition on touching the core and, instead of looking at the impact or weight of the limitation, looks at the necessity and proportionality of the intervention. The Court concludes that the limitation can be introduced only when absolutely necessary, and should be as narrow as possible, otherwise it will constitute a violation of the core.[62] Although this decision creates a protective membrane around the core by introducing proportionality as an additional concept, it may very well lead to the view that if a limitation is proportionate then it can touch the core. Yet later in 1955 the Court added that a limitation cannot be introduced for any objective except when 'higher values are concerned'.[63]

The Federal Administrative Court says that the determining factor in touching the core is not the objective or the reason of the limitation, but rather what is left of the right after the limitation. One would expect this to be an absolute criterion, yet it has been relativized by the introduction of a further concern, the inherent limitations of a right.[64] Thus, if a limitation is seen as essential for the public interest, violation of the core is allowed, by saying that this is immanent in the scope of the basic right. Theories of inherent or immanent limitations have been developed in German jurisprudence specifically related to Article 21/1: '[t]he right to the free development of personality', the immanent limitations of which are 'rights of others', 'the constitutional order' and 'the moral code'.

Finally the Federal Constitutional Court regards the core as an absolute limit to limits and does not uphold either of the views above. According to this Court there is nothing that can justify touching the core. The Court has pointed out in various decisions that the guaranteed core is an unrelinquishable principle of the Constitution,[65] that it blocks the intervention of public power,[66] that it is an absolute[67] and an ultimate[68] limit. The Court has also affirmed that the content of each guaranteed core must be determined for every basic right in view of its specific importance within the whole system of basic rights.[69]

Concluding Reflections

In the real world of qualified rights and qualified guarantees, the best that can be offered, perhaps, is simply the concept of the guaranteed core. The core concept can only move into the realm of reality, and thus have significant impact, by positivization, that is by the legal recognition that there is a guaranteed core for each right. In legal systems without Bills of Rights, the concept of the core should become part of legislative enactments related to specific rights and freedoms, or be utilized by courts as the ultimate limit beyond which public power cannot go. In legal systems with Bills of Rights, the concept of the core should be inserted into the provisions of the Bills and upheld by the courts. Yet at this moment the great majority of legal systems are working on strengthening the circumjacence by elaborating on the legitimate limitations rather than working to identify the cores.

The most significant contribution of the concept of the guaranteed core is the extra awareness of the status of human rights that it creates; an awareness not only on the part of the public power, the courts and legal scholars, but also, and perhaps even more important, on the part of the ordinary person, who thereby gains insight into the essential content of his or her rights.

Some evidence for this can be seen from the impact of the concept of the core in the short existence of the Turkish Constitutional Court which was set up in 1961. Twenty-four years is not a sufficient period of time to establish lasting traditions. Yet even in this time the most significant achievement of the Court has been the creation of an awareness that there are impervious cores in rights, and that there is a limit to limitations. This is obvious when one looks at the number of cases challenging legislation, and containing claims of encroachment upon the core, which have been brought to the attention of the Court. The Turkish Constitutional Court has provided certain criteria and a formula, albeit somewhat vague, for determining instances of encroachment, but it has not defined the core as a concept. Although much thought has been given to the matter, a guaranteed core for each basic legal right has not yet been defined.

Alongside this positive development can also be observed a tendency on the part of the Court to employ the historical method of interpretation so that its discussions sometimes get caught up in the old debates of the Constituent Assembly that 'the core cannot be defined, but an encroachment would be detected and understood by the courts and public opinion – the particular conception of law and legality in the populace.'[70]

Unfortunately, the Court has also tended to widen the scope, increase the weight and expand the meaning of legitimate limitations, especially the public interest, and to use rather general and vague definitions of crucial concepts. These trends could prove very significant for the future as they could very well lead to an enlargement of the circumjacence at the expense of the core.

The same trend can be detected in Germany over a longer period. But there, tests to curb the unreasonable and unnecessary extension of limitations have been very carefully worked out and used for over 40 years and control within the circumjacence is more vigorous. It is true that the German Federal Constitutional Court has not developed a formula for determining encroachments, but then the German Basic Law does not have a general limitation article as does the Turkish Constitution of 1961, although the guaranteed core is held to be an absolute limit in both systems.

Looking into the question of whether the criteria developed by the courts and the literature can be refined to become universally acceptable and generalized to encompass all rights, it is clear that much work is yet to be done. Every basic right requires a defined core and precise criteria for identifying encroachments. Only then would cores have solid contents and each right an essential definition. Further, the relationship between the primary rights and their concomitants should be worked out, and the whole idea of the guaranteed core must be strengthened if it is to be really effective. The criteria must be concretized in relation to the normative scope of each basic right, and the essential definition of each right must be given. The scope of each right must be analysed in terms of an outer edge, a circumjacence and a core. The essential elements of the norm which are unrelinquishable and unchangeable for the guaranteed core must be determined. This would need extensive multi-disciplinary work. Once meaningful criteria for every right have been established which can be concretized for every right, it should be possible to formulate a lowest common denominator, and perhaps even the average, or ideally the highest, common denominator of all guaranteed cores. If these could be upheld universally, and if governments and courts actively preserved these cores as impervious, then we might begin to talk of rights in an absolute and universal manner. This will only be possible when the concept of the guaranteed core is widely adopted in legal practice and doctrine, and in the political institutions within any given jurisdiction.

The feasibility of this programme at this stage is an open question. It still remains to be seen whether there is, or ever could be, a constancy or universality in these efforts to safeguard the core and prescribe the limits of such acceptable qualifications as may be introduced into the circumjacence. At the moment, the courts lead the way. However, the theoretical development of legal doctrine should help the courts to strengthen the core concept and to create this common denominator of guaranteed cores. Ultimately the rhetoric of the core concept will not become effectively embodied in the reality of human rights practices in particular legal systems simply through philosophical and legal developments. It will only become a reality through the emergence of a public awareness that fundamental interests are better safeguarded by the identification of basic human rights with indefeasible cores.

Notes

1 The core of a right is not to be confused with the concept of core rights used to refer to a few select basic rights as having special status. See also C. Wellman, 'A new conception of Human Rights', in E. Kamenka and A. Ehr-Soon Tay (eds), *Human Rights* (London: Edward Arnold, 1978), 48–53.

2 See p. 10.

3 H. Kelsen, *General Theory of Law and State* (New York: Russell & Russell, 1945), 115–30.

4 H. Street, *Freedom, the Individual, and the Law* (5th edn) (Harmondsworth: Penguin, 1982), 12.

5 Both the 1949 German Basic Law and the 1961 Turkish Constitution take account of this prohibition and therefore there is extensive discussion of these concepts in the legal literature of both countries. For a discussion of various stances see Fazil Saglam, *Temel Haklarin Sinirlanmasi ve Ozu* (Ankara: Ankara Universitesi SBF Yayinlari, 1982), 17–52.

6 See S.I. Benn and R.S. Peters, *Social Principles and the Democratic State* (5th imp.), (London: George Allen & Unwin, 1966), 213: 'law may be a necessary condition for liberty, since one man's freedom depends on the law's restraint on others.'

7 This Constitution was replaced in 1982.

8 See p.3.

9 Interstate travel was held to be a constitutional right by the Supreme Court (*Griffin* v. *Breckenridge*, 403 U.S. 88 (1971)), as was the right to access to the judicial system (*Griffin* v. *Illinois*, 351 U.S. 12 (1956)) and the right of privacy (*Griswold* v. *Connecticut*, 381 U.S. 479 (1965)) and *Roe* v. *Wade*, 410 U.S. 113 (1973). All these rights trigger strict scrutiny.

10 394 U.S. 618, 634 (1969). The Supreme Court invalidated statutory prohibition of welfare benefits to otherwise eligible recipients who had not been state residents for a year. The one-year waiting period penalized the exercise of the constitutional right of interstate movement.

11 The substantial rationality standard was employed, for example, in *Sosna* v. *Iowa*, 419 U.S. 393 (1975), *Martinez* v. *Bynum*, 103 Supreme Court 1838 (1983), and *Plyer* v. *Doe*, 457 U.S. 202 (1982).
12 *NAACP* v. *Button*, 371 U.S. 415 (1963), *Bryan* v. *Zimmerman*, 278 U.S. 63 (1928), and *Barenblatt* v. *U.S.*, 360 U.S. 109 (1959).
13 *Shelton* v. *Tucker*, 364 U.S. 479 (1960).
14 *Schenck* v. *U.S.*, 249 U.S. 47 (1919).
15 BVerfGE 30, 316 : 33, 187, BVerfGE 35, 12 : 30, 263, BVerfGE 17, 315.
16 BVerfGE 30, 316 : 25, 17 : 33, 187. 17, 279. This case is concerned with a ban imposed on the taking of orders by pedlars for a drug normally prescribed by vets. The court, in finding the limitation unnecessary, stated that the aim of the limitation, to protect health, could have been realized by a less restrictive limitation on the freedom of profession, namely the requirement of a prescription.
17 BVerfGE 7, 405. BVerfGE 7, 407 : 16, 202. For example in BVerfGE 11, 44 the court found a limitation, which imposed a restriction on the medical profession by requiring that there should be one practising doctor in the social security services for every 500 social security patients, to be disproportionate.
18 See J.W. Nickel, 'Are Human Rights Utopian?', *Philosophy and Public Affairs*, 12 (1982), 248, 256. He defines 'scope' as 'what a right is to', and 'weight' as 'its rank in relation to other norms'.
19 *Satwant Sing Sawhney* v. *The Government of India* (Supreme Court of India, 10 April, 1967).
20 *Griswold* v. *Connecticut*, 381 U.S. 479, 484 (1965): *Berger* v. *New York* 388 U.S. 41 (1967), and *United States* v. *United States District Council* 407 U.S. 297 (1972).
21 *Lovell* v. *City of Griffin*, 303 U.S. 444 (1938).
22 See S.B. Ybema, *Constitutionalism and Civil Liberties* (Leiden: Universitaire Pers, 1973) 264–5.
23 The most important development of German theory is the work of Haeberle, *Die Wesengehaltgarantie des Art. 19 Abs. 2 Grundgesetz, zugleich ein Beitrag zum institutionellen Verstandnis der Grundrechte und zur Lehre vom Gesetzesvorbehalt* (Karlsruhe: 1962).
24 In the 1982 Constitution, which was promulgated as a reaction to internal problems, the system is different, more elaborate and the core concept has been eliminated as a constitutional norm. Yet Article 12 states: 'Everyone enjoys fundamental rights and freedoms which are inviolable, inalienable and cannot be relinquished', and the general limitation article, Article 13, says: 'the general and specific limitations of fundamental rights and freedoms cannot be contrary to the necessities of the democratic social order and cannot be used outside this aim'.
25 In the amended Article of 1971, Article 11/2 reads simply: '[l]aw cannot touch the core of fundamental rights and freedoms.'
26 See generally, Ybema, *Constitutionalism*.
27 Zitting 1975–6/13, 872, 9–11.
28 See M.C.B. Burkens, *Beperking van Grondrechten* (Deveter: Kleuwer, 1971), 141–6, and D.H.M. Meuwissen, *De Europese Conventie en het Nederlanse recht*, dissertation (Leiden: A.W. Sijthoff, 1968).
29 HR 28 Nov. 1950, NJ 1951, 137.
30 HR 27 Feb. 1951, NJ 1951, 472; HR 10 June 1952, NJ 1952, 688; HR 24 Jan. 1967, NJ 1967, 270; HR 30 May 1967, NJ 1968, 4 and HR 14 Jan. 1969, NJ 1969, 191; HR 17 Feb. 1981, NJ 1981, 299; HR 13 Jan. 1981, NJ 1981, 254; HR 15 June 1982, NJ 1983, 121 and HR 28 June 1983, NJ 1984, 64; HR 30 Oct. 1980, NJ 1981, 422; HR 6 Dec. 1983, NJ 1984, 601 respectively.
31 Although this Court also views first the legitimate limitations for validity (most

public interest and public order), before discussing the encroachment onto the core. The Turkish Constitutional Court mostly uses test of suitability (e.g. 8, 9 Feb. 1972, 70/48, 72/3 AMKD X 111–15) and proportionality (e.g. 18 Feb. 1971, 70/22, 71/20 AMKD X 3–27; 9 March 1971, 70/42, 71/30 AMKD IX 338–58), 8 Feb. 1979, 78/54, 79/9 RG 24 April 1979; 16618 is a case where the Court uses this latter test, in combination with the core, for a limitation on the press and saves the limitation.

32 S. Guran, *Ifade Hurriyeti Uzerinde Idarenin Yetkileri* (Istanbul: Istanbul Universitesi Yayinlari, 1969), 416–17. In this work he is specifically analysing freedom of expression.

33 Saglam, *Temel Haklarin*, 156–60.

34 B. Tanor, *Siyasi Dusunce Hurriyeti ve 1961 Anayasasi* (Istanbul: Oncu Kitabevi Yayini, 1969), 167–8.

35 Esin Örücü, *Tasinmaz Mulkiyetine Bir Kamu Hukuku Yaklasimi – Mulkiyet Hakkinin Sinirlanmasi* (Istanbul: Istanbul Universitesi Yayinlari, 1976), 61–3, and E. Örücü, '1961 Anayasasi ve Anayasa Mahkemesine gore Hakkin Ozu Kavrami ve Mulkiyet Hakkinin Ozu', 41, no. 3–4 *Istanbul Universitesi Hukuk Fakultesi Mecmuasi* (Istanbul: Istanbul Universitesi Yayinin, 1976).

36 8 April 1963, 63/16, 63/83, AMKD I 1971, 194–210; 8 April 1963, 63/17, 63/84, AMKD I 1971, 210–20. (Both related to freedom of expression.) 2 June 1977, 77/43, 77/84, RG 5 Dec. 1977: 16, 130 (on equality). 8–9 Feb. 1972, 70/48, 72/3, RG 19 Oct. 1972: 14, 341 (on trade union membership).

37 8 April 1963, 63/16, 63/83, AMKD I 1971, 194–210 (on freedom of expression).

38 4 Jan. 1963, 62/208, 63/1 AMKD I 1971, 70–6 (on the right to assemble and participate in demonstrations).

39 Ibid., and 18–22 Nov. 1976, 76/27, 76/51, RG 16 May 77:15, 939 (also on the right to demonstrate and participate in marches).

40 4 Jan. 1963, 62/208, 63/1 AMKD I 1964, 70–6 (on the right to assemble and participate in marches).

41 26 March 1963, 63/3, 63/67 AMKD I 1964, 147–60 (on the right of property). 18–22 Nov. 1976, 76/27, 76/51 RG 16 March 77: 5, 939 (on the right to demonstrate).

42 4 Jan. 1963, 62/208, 63/1 AMKD I 1964, 70–6 (on the right to assemble . . .). 28 Jan. 1964, 63/128, 64/8 AMKD II 1965, 43–56 (on the right to form associations).

43 4 Jan. 1963, 62/208, 63/1 AMKD I 1964, 70–6 (on the right to assemble . . .); 25 April 1974, 73/41, 74/13 AMKD XII 1974, 152 (on due process and the right of privacy); 18–22 Nov. 1976, 76/27, 76/51 AMKD XIV 1976, 364 (on the right to assemble . . .).

44 4 Jan. 1963, 63/208, 63/1 AMKD I 1964, 70–6 (on the right to assemble . . .).

45 11 Oct. 1963, 63/124, 63/243 AMKD I 1971, 422–39 (on the right of property).

46 26 Sept. 1965, 63/173, 65/40 AMKD IV 1967, 266 (freedom of expression, right to form associations). The Court also notes that if a limitation is very narrow there is no touching of the core. See, 10 Dec. 1976, 75/200, 76/9 RG 10 March 76: 15, 583 (right of petition): 20 Jan. 1970, 69/56, 70/4 RG 21 July 70: 13, 555 (freedom of work and contract and the right to social security).

47 10 Feb. 1970, 69/60, 70/8 AMKD VIII, 1971, 202–10 (on the right of property).

48 18–19 June 1968, 66/19, 68/25 AMKD VII, 1970, 18–48 (on the right of property).

49 25 April 1974, 73/41, 74/13 RG 14 Sept. 74: 15,006 (on due process and the right of privacy).

50 3 Nov. 1964, 63/152, 64/66 RG 17 March 65: 11,955 (on the right to education).

51 4 Dec. 1980, 80/43, 80/64 RG April 1981; 17, 297.
52 3 July 1980, 80/19, 80/48 RG 3 Nov. 1980; 17, 149.
53 See p. 60–79.
54 F. Klein, *Das Bonner Grundgesetz*, Kommentar, vol. 1 (2nd edn) (Berlin and Frankfurt, 1955).
55 BVerfGE 2, 285.
56 BVerfGE 6, 41.
57 H. Kruger, 'Der Wesensgehalt der Grundrechte', in *DOV* (1955), 599.
58 Ibid. (1976 edn), 51.
59 G. Durig, 'Der Grundsatz von der Menschenwürde', in *AOR*, 81 (1956), 117.
60 BGHSt 4, 392 and BGHZ 6, 270.
61 P. Lerche, *Übermass im Verfassungsrecht* (Koln, 1961), 79.
62 BGHSt 4, 377.
63 See *DOV* (1955), 730.
64 BVerfGE 2, 87 : 7, 171.
65 BVerfGE 4, 170.
66 BVerfGE 8, 329.
67 BVerfGE 16, 201.
68 BVerfGE 31, 69.
69 BVerfGE 22, 180.
70 28 Jan. 1964, 63/128, 64/8, RG 17 April 64: 11,685..

4

Human Rights in a State of Exception: the ILA and the Third World

Anthony Carty

Introduction

The International Law Association (ILA) Minimum Standards of Human Rights Norms in a State of Exception appears to indicate a great professional confidence among international lawyers concerning the usefulness of adding substantially to the existing rules of human rights law. The Paris Conference adopted a Report of the Committee on the Enforcement of Human Rights Law which is remarkable for its immense detail and sophistication. The preparation of the Standards went through three conferences in Belgrade (1980), Montreal (1982) and Paris (1984), the commentaries at each stage helping to indicate how the thought of the ILA had developed. The original concern of the Committee was with what were called regional problems in the implementation of human rights, that is, their implementation in Africa, Asia and Latin America.[1] The standards are couched in universal terms and the commentary shows how far the Committee has been influenced by the experience of Western Europe and Latin America. Nonetheless the problem of the state of emergency,[2] that is, the willingness of states to invoke it as a justification for derogation from human rights law, is primarily a Third World one. In its recent report on the subject, the International Commission of Jurists (ICJ) points to almost 30 states in the Third World, outside Latin America, in order to demonstrate that the problem is not exclusive to Latin America. Indeed it boasts that it offers the first survey of how it arises in Eastern Europe.[3]

So it is primarily within a Third World context that it will be asked whether the ILA Committee's work is convincing. In this context the point will be made that the ILA attempts to preserve the core of human rights by treating the political human rights of the major international conventions as non-derogable. That is to say, if there are free general elections resulting in democratically elected legislatures, if these remain in permanent session, and if the judiciary is allowed to test the conformity of the latter's emergency legislation with the constitution, then there will be a very significant decline in serious human rights violations.

It does appear that the ILA sees states of emergency in terms of the suspension of the doctrine of the separation of powers in favour of the Executive. A reaffirmation of the doctrine in the strictest possible terms is seen as the most direct way to put an end to the human rights violations which typically accompany states of emergency. This approach has been criticized by Valades as amounting to no more than a denial of the problem. He objects to any response to the undermining of the rule of law which is nothing more than a reaffirmation of the nominal constitution and a call for its more rigorous application.[4]

In this Latin American view the challenge posed to legal theory is that it is impossible to find positive legal standards to define the circumstances which justify the imposition of a state of exception. Constitutions make a casuistic reference to circumstances justifying the emergency. That is to say a criterion is provided, but its meaning depends entirely upon a judgement as to the significance of concrete circumstances. Such a judgement will be political in the sense that the causes which give rise to the state of emergency cannot be incorporated in juridical concepts. It is a matter of the extent to which legal forms do or do not find roots in social processes which appear far removed from normative considerations. In purely nominal legal terms a full state of emergency means the complete abolition of the separation of powers, with all power concentrated in one sole organ. This does not have to be the Executive; the final authority could be a wider collegiality. Yet the vital point to grasp is that the rule of law places the state within the law, while a state of emergency puts the 'supreme power' outside the law.

Clearly this model is extreme and there can be degrees of movement from one point to the other. Yet its essential feature is that it equates normality with law and emergency with non-law. It makes no sense to try to judge the one in terms of the other. Some measure of theoretical analysis has to address the relationship between social disorganization and the collapse of mechanical institutions.[5] In other words the ILA appears to have no theoretical understanding of the state, particularly in the Third World.

In this chapter a statement of the ILA proposals is followed by a suggestion that the ILA perspective is perhaps too much shaped by the experience of Latin American states, where abrogation of a liberal constitution has been followed by massive human rights violations. There follows a discussion of states of exception in Argentina and Algeria. These examples show that there is no necessary connection between the absence of a liberal constitution and extensive human rights violations. Instead it is suggested that one may in the examples considered more usefully look to the ideology of the governing regime, that is, its system of values, to find the reasons for the human rights violations which occur. Given this standpoint, the concluding section of the study asks how far the legal method at present employed by the ILA is suited to the critical analysis of the ideologies of governing regimes in developing countries which do not rest their legitimacy on liberal constitutions. It is argued that the purported value-neutrality of the ILA analysis, the logically deductive application of general legal standards to factually clear situations, is impossible. Instead the lawyer has to make a break with this traditional method of analysis. One possible way forward, which is very briefly outlined here, is a form of cultural anthropology. Vague and abstract human rights standards are accepted at a global level. For instance, most Arab states are parties to the UN Covenant on Civil and Political Rights. There is need for a hermeneutic of such human rights standards which takes full account of the cultural diversity of the states which are parties to them, while at the same time not abandoning the quest for a universal consensus as to their meaning.

The ILA, States of Emergency and the Place for Political Human Rights

There is a consensus that the state does not have an unqualified right to declare that a state of emergency exists which justifies derogations from human rights. A public emergency has to exist as a matter of objective fact, which is reviewable where the state submits to the jurisdiction of an international body. Article 15 of the European

Human Rights Convention and Article 4 of the UN Covenant on Civil and Political Rights define these objective facts in virtually identical terms. In times of public emergency threatening the life of the nation, the state may take measures in derogation of some of its human rights obligations, to the extent strictly required by the exigencies of the situation.

There is no doubt that the ILA adds considerably to these terse provisions. It insists that 'public emergency' means an exceptional situation of crisis or public danger, actual or imminent, which affects the whole population of the country or that of the area to which the emergency applies, and constitutes a threat to the organized life of the community of which the state is composed.

Neither article says anything about who exactly may declare the emergency. The ILA requires the constitution of every state to define the procedure for declaring a state of exception providing, as a minimum, that wherever the Executive has the power to declare a state of exception, it shall always be subject to confirmation by the people's representatives, and the legislature, within the shortest possible time. If the legislature is dissolved, it shall be re-elected as soon as practicable, in accordance with a constitution which shall ensure that it is freely chosen and representative of the entire nation. In any case, a declaration of emergency shall never exceed the period strictly required to restore normal conditions, and each extension shall be subject to the prior approval of the legislature.

At the regional or international level, the declaration of emergency will be subject to such review as the terms of the particular treaty shall provide. At the national level, review will be exercised in terms of the legal tradition of the state concerned.[6] Such provisions may appear to leave little scope to the judiciary; however, it is given the power to decide whether emergency legislation is in conformity with the constitution, and whether any particular exercise of the emergency power is in conformity with the emergency legislation. This is within a context in which legislation is supposed to play a large role. The fundamental functions of the legislature must remain intact, and it has to provide general guidelines to regulate executive discretion.

In any case no measure taken may discriminate solely on grounds of race, religion, colour, nationality, sex or social origin. The judiciary retains the power to ensure that there is no encroachment upon non-derogable rights, and that measures affecting derogable rights are in accordance with the principle of proportionality. As an institutional

safeguard the constitution must prohibit the use of emergency powers
to remove judges or otherwise to restrict their independence.[7]

The Influence of a Latin American Perspective on the Approach of International Lawyers

In their study on states of emergency, the International Commission
of Jurists (ICJ) note the complaint of Latin Americans that the
attention given to states of emergency and human rights problems in
Latin America is disproportionate. It surmises that Latin American
emergencies are better known, probably because of greater government commitment to human rights in the region, and because of the
large number of efficient non-governmental human rights organizations working there.[8] They are nonetheless no more serious than
emergencies in other parts of the world.

It is possible that the Latin American experience has had a
significant effect upon the approach of international lawyers to the
problem of states of emergency. The Latin American countries are all
societies with something like a Western concept of the rule of law and
the separation of powers enshrined in a written constitution. Such a
starting point may well encourage lawyers to see states of emergency
analytically as deviations from this formal model.

For instance, the ICJ considers possible justifications of the
Argentinian military coup of 1976 in terms of the 1853 Constitution,
as amended, even though there had been only one election in the
country in the previous 14 years. The military interventions are seen
as justified by 'pretexts' which do nothing to change the fact that the
regime was unlawful 'in form and in essence'.[9]

The analysis of the problem in terms of deviation from formal
constitutional norms is even clearer in the study by Questiaux which
was requested by the UN Human Rights Commission. She considers
many states outside Latin America, although mostly ones with a long
Western tradition of legal formalism, for example Turkey, Liberia and
South Africa. The heart of her report concerns the pattern of
constitution abrogation in Latin America, particularly in Chile,
Argentina, Uruguay and Brazil. That her analysis is in terms of
deviation from formal constitutional norms can be seen most of all in
two features of states of emergency which she stresses. The first is the
institutionalization of emergency regimes in which the doctrine of the

separation of powers is replaced by a hierarchization of authority. That is to say the legislative power is subordinated to the executive, and the latter to the military. The example given is Chile.[10] The second is the form of repression which is supposed inevitably to follow. This is characterized as a fanning out of the net for victims. On the basis of apparently loose definitions of crimes such as political and other activities in opposition to national aims, the regime will widen its circle of victims beyond 'terrorists' to include political activists and those whose democratic opinions are well known in the liberal professions. This pattern of repression is particularly Latin American, and was especially characteristic of Argentina in the years following the 1976 military coup.[11]

It is the excessive concentration of interest on the Latin American situation which leads international lawyers to believe that treating political rights as non-derogable will ensure, as a matter of actual state practice, that massive violations of non-derogable rights will no longer occur. In fact, widespread instances of torture and political murder do not necessarily occur in states where guarantees of Western-style democracy do not exist. It is quite possible to construct the legitimacy of a state on other grounds, and to find relatively little evidence of human rights violations of these two most serious kinds.

A comparison of the military coups in Argentina and Algeria shows what little significance the absence of a formal concept of the state and the rule of law had in both cases. In the former torture and political killing were widespread, whilst in the latter they were virtually non-existent. The reason for the difference between the two experiences is to be found in the nature of the legitimacy which each *de facto* regime has claimed, and not the measure of the presence or absence of legal guarantees of political rights.

A non-derogable human right is one which a state may not revoke in a state of emergency. If it appears that a number of states exist in permanent 'states of emergency' and yet such rights are not violated, then there appears to be no object in requiring observation of non-derogable rights to protect persons in states of emergency. Indeed it can be said that the language of human rights is not appropriate to describe the quality of political life in such developing countries. Furthermore, there is a danger that it may actually be used to justify interventions in the internal affairs of countries which do not satisfy Western-style formal criteria of democracy.

*The 'State of Emergency' in Argentina: the Relevance of the
Absence of Political Human Rights*

The ICJ's criticism of the Inter-American Commission on Human
Rights (IACHR) Report on the Situation of Human Rights in
Argentina is a reflection of the impossibility of grasping the
Argentinian crisis simply in terms of the absence of political human
rights, particularly the absence of a functioning legislature.[12] This is a
matter of debate among international lawyers and the striking
contrast between the two approaches is that the ICJ simply insists
upon the formal maintenance of political democracy, whereas the
IACHR recognizes the discrepancy between political institutions and
political reality, but has nothing useful to say about it.

The ICJ finds remarkable the fact that the IACHR does not enter
into the question of the legitimacy of the military government of
Argentina and its imposition of a state of emergency. It does not
examine whether any of the restrictions which the military imposed
upon derogable human rights were necessary. It does not comment
upon the international legal implications of the military's avowed
intention of permanently eliminating certain ideologies and political
formations. Indeed the IACHR claims, in a non-committal tone, that
it has come to an adequate understanding of the violence and unrest
which devastated Argentina in the years immediately prior to the
military coup.

None of this is to deny the value of the findings of fact which the
IACHR made with respect to tortures and deaths, particularly deaths
following the disappearance of the persons concerned. It is accepted
that the intergovernmental nature of the Report was a reason why its
findings of fact could not be ignored by the Argentine government.[13]
The question is whether the 'lapses' on the other matters have
implications for the existence or viability of specifically political
human rights, especially the right to participation in government. The
IACHR merely states that steps should be taken such 'as are
necessary to restore the activity and participation of political parties
in the public life of the nation.' This position is based upon
Argentina's participation in the drafting of the Universal and the
American Declarations of Human Rights.[14] Beyond this, the IACHR
gave a detailed presentation of the document, *Terrorism in Argentina*,
with which the military justified the coup. The document pointed to

the virtually indiscriminate killing of major personalities from 1970 onwards, and concluded that the coup was necessary to contain 'the progressive disintegration of the State, the general chaos and the situation of extreme social indifference'.[15] On this basis the IACHR itself said that it had an adequate understanding of the situation in Argentina at the time of the coup.

The military set out a vision of the political future of Argentina in its document, a *Political Basis of the Armed Forces for the National Reorganization Process*, which the IACHR notes without any comment at all. This is where the IACHR might have intervened to trace the historical and cultural roots of the ideology of the Argentinian regime as a possible explanation for the extraordinary measure of violence for which it was responsible.

For instance, the document describes features of the situation which appear to be common to other Latin American states such as Brazil and Chile in which similar human rights violations have occurred. The Argentinian Constitution of 1853 is not as such abrogated. Yet the military insist that any decree of theirs which is incompatible with the Constitution takes precedence. They claim the right to intervene at any time to ensure that there is sufficient national strategic leadership to ensure the fulfilment of national goals.[16] The latter are defined as the restoration of the essential values which are the foundation of state action, the eradication of subversion, the validity of Christian moral values, the revitalization of constitutional institutions, and the dignity of the Argentinian person.[17] There is still a place for dialogue with political parties to see how responsible participation in government can be achieved. Yet the fact remains that the armed forces, 'in their institutionalized intervention in the Government, will be competent to adopt decisions for the national strategic leadership.'[18]

These are essentially fascist legal theories having their roots in the writings of Carl Schmitt, particularly those concerning the nature of dictatorship.[19] Such views have been widespread in Latin America and they represent not a deviation from liberal constitutional theory, but a quite opposing conception of the nature of the state.[20] It is this fascist ideology which is itself the cause, in the sense of an intellectual justification, for the human rights violations which have been so systematic and so clearly an integral part of official policy. The concept of the enemy is central to the Schmitt theory of dictatorship as a state of permanent emergency. The distinction between friend and enemy is borrowed from the language of international conflict and treated as central to the resolution of internal differences. The denial of liberal pluralism in this context means the suppression of dialogue between those engaged in social conflict. The *dictator* simply treats those with whom he disagrees as the *enemy* and hence to be eliminated. The ideology itself helps explain the massive human rights violations.[21]

However, not every conceivable aspect of this ideology is central to the question of human rights conflicts. In the Latin American context, this ideology has to be seen as opposing itself to the Marxist ideology of the class struggle. Any element of the population which can be seen as encouraging a wider Marxist war of subversion, whether inside or beyond the national frontier, is a threat which has to be eliminated at all costs.[22] In such a context, a conflict between two ideologies neither of which accepts the liberal presuppositions of political human rights, it is not enough simply to deplore the non-observance of the latter. One has to try to understand the context which appears to render the liberal language irrelevant.

The Algerian Military Coup of 1965: the Irrelevance of Military Authoritarianism to Human Rights Violations

Algeria's political system has been widely defined as a 'no-party state'. In fact legality is argued in terms of a struggling group's more or less faithful adherence to the principles of the Algerian Revolution. The principles of socialism and democracy, in the sense of workers' management of industry and agrarian reform through pea... cooperatives, have been very largely uncontested. The argument is whether leaders are truly dedicated to these principles or whether they backslide because of a desire for personal advantage, incompetence in organization, or any possible inclination towards private capitalist motivation.

For these reasons the coup of June 1965 was never recognized as such by its authors. The military alleged that the 'constitutional' President, Ben Bella, was trying to incorporate in one person a revolution which belonged to the whole people, all of whom were militant revolutionaries.[23] The 'state' taken over by the military had always had to function without a party, and inevitably the military themselves did not have the capacity to administer any state. Hence the military entered into partnership with technocrats, sometimes characterized as having 'petit bourgeois' origins, with whom they had no clearly defined ideological differences. Indeed a French constitutional law specialist of the Magreb considers this ambience equally damaging for any clear development of the notion of the state itself as autonomous. Given that situation, the state could not be the bearer of all the expectations placed in it.[24]

Official legitimacy is bound to be a reflection of the contradictions in society. However, at the time of independence in 1962, there was no social force in a position to direct Algerian society. The elections which took place in 1962 were themselves required by the Accords d'Evian concluded with the French, and were not rooted in a principle of legitimacy which expressed itself in relatively stable norms and procedures. This was inevitable given the colonial and immediate pre-independence history of Algeria.[25]

The war of independence began because the road to peaceful constitutional development was blocked: a very common feature of colonial societies. The repression of the civilian Algerian population by the French during the war, between 1954 and 1962, was such that the leaders of the Front de Libération Nationale (FLN) were either imprisoned or in exile. The FLN was itself a movement and not a party able to hold annual congresses based on delegates chosen from the population as a whole. This was so at least partly because of the physical constraints under which it operated.

In the course of the struggle the military leaders gained a material ascendancy in terms of the organized supporters upon whom they could count. Even within the military the so-called army of the frontiers, that is, with Tunisia and Morocco, was many times larger than the scattered underground forces operating in the interior of the country. The former could rely upon a wide measure of shelter from the neighbouring (and themselves recently independent) governments.

At the point of independence, a majority of the civilian leaders of the FLN tried to persuade the French to keep the frontiers closed against the 'armies of the frontiers', but the latter declined to accept such a responsibility. When the same majority tried to relieve the military leaders of their posts, the only effect was that a minority of civilians led by Ben Bella, who had most of the time been in exile, formed an alliance with military officers, the leader of whom was Boumedienne. They proceeded to have general elections with candidates from a list selected by Ben Bella. The National Assembly elected an Executive Council with Ben Bella at its head. The former did declare itself, in the autumn of 1962, the sole depository and

guardian of the sovereignty of the Algerian people, but the composition
of the Commission which drafted the Constitution was determined by
Ben Bella.

Article 59 of the constitution had given the President the authority
to take exceptional measures in cases of imminent peril. Ben Bella
invoked this article at first because of disturbances in one of the
military regions. However, he continued to invoke the Article against
other opposition and gradually removed other civilian leaders of the
FLN and the Executive Council. Such a use of the emergency power
led one specialist in the Algerian political system to say that it was
'comme si l'article 59 constituait moins une procédure exceptionnelle
qu'un mécanisme normal conforme à la logique du régime'.[26] So it
could be said that the military coup itself did no more than bring a
clandestine absence of constitutionality out into the open.[27] The coup
gave authority to the Council of the Revolution which was to be understood as an historic force much as were the founders of the FLN itself.[28]

The immediate context of the coup was a struggle within the very
small circle of the governing elite. When Ben Bella tried to interfere
with the hierarchy of military personnel, Boumedienne had Ben Bella
removed. The latter could not have resisted. In three years he had
been able to establish some public identity. However, the only
organization in the country remained the army. The President had
not tried to reform the inchoate character of the FLN and its
hierarchical nature; instead he had been engaged in a process of
marginalization of the remaining civilian leaders.[29]

In the years which followed the coup the 'state' could claim
legitimacy to the extent that it realized the principles of the
revolution, bringing concrete benefits to society. The National
Charter and Constitution of 1976, presented as the culmination of the
Algerian Revolution, do not alter the terms of the main debate or
opposition inside and outside Algeria. That debate is about the social
and economic oppressiveness of development organized from above
by a technocratic elite which is allied to a privileged military class.
The consequence has been that there has been little opportunity to
develop truly grass-root democracy, whether in agriculture, industry
or in the more formal municipal and provincial assemblies. There is
widespread apathy in the population at large and a considerable
measure of privilege, which has led to allegations of corruption, has
been enjoyed by the governing elite.[30]

There is no doubt that the considerable dissatisfaction with the political system which exists does not have a coherent means of expressing itself. Yet one cannot force the development of clearly defined social forces capable of insisting that disputes be resolved through a pluralist dialogue. Perhaps if that stage is reached one might look to a party-based legislative system or to other institutions which could be more appropriate.

However, this much is certain. Where in a colonial war of independence a minority take the lead, clandestinely in large part, using military force to drive out the colonial power, the conditions for Western-style democracy will be unlikely to exist afterwards. Indeed there will be little in the way of socio-economic infrastructure to support stably organized political groupings if the colonial power has made more than a superficial occupation of the country. Yet none of these factors, very typical of the Third World, make inevitable any brutal oppression of the majority of the population by those who have taken responsibility to drive their countries towards independence.

The Algerian and Argentinian experiences are similar in a number of respects. They reflect very weak political and administrative institutions. The governing military elites have recourse to an ideological programme to give them legitimacy. Needless to say the regimes engage in an auto-interpretation of these programmes which is only open to review if the regimes collapse. However, one has to look further than the structure of the regimes to find the causes of human rights violations. This is where Argentina and Algeria differ. The former was caught in a socio-economic crisis which led to a fascist response from a significant sector of the country. The latter was faced with the virtual collapse of socio-economic structures following the mass exodus of the colonial French.

In this context there is a great danger in trying to insist that international law already imposes upon states a duty to guarantee political human rights in the terms which the ILA suggests. This can only provide Western societies with a means to criticize, possibly to the point of intervention, the conduct of the internal affairs of countries, many of which owe their structural difficulties to a former Western presence.

States of Exception and the Task of the Human Rights Lawyer

The ILA is the most widely-based professional association of international lawyers, so it is appropriate to take their report on states

of exception as a starting point for a critique of the role of the human
rights lawyer in the face of the challenge to basic human rights which
the absence of Western liberal constitutions in Third World states is
thought to present. It is clear that their report assumes a positivist,
empiricist approach to the problem of states of emergencies. The facts
are there to be ascertained, provided an impartial fact-finding
mechanism exists. The 'crisis', as seen by the international lawyers,
can be subsumed under legal norms which are clear, although their
application calls for a casuistic method of interpretation.

The question of the existence of a state of exception is by its very
nature not merely factual. It implies a notion of necessity which itself
presupposes a choice of the lesser of two evils which is a judgement of
value. As such it is almost inevitable, particularly in a democratic
society, that the lawyer, and particularly the judiciary, with whose
role the international lawyer identifies as much as would a municipal
law colleague, will lean towards deference to the discretion of the
political branch of government, rather than towards balancing the
rights of the authorities against the rights of the individual.[31]

It is more realistic to recognize that at an international level the
concepts of democracy, public safety and national security are
meaningful, if at all, only in a particular ideological and cultural
context.[32] It is this complexity which the lawyer should endeavour to
unravel, taking fully into account the significance of the fact that
international law formulations of the political human rights which the
ILA would champion seem to be breached more often than observed.
There has to be a cultural and ideological examination of issues which
are far too intractable to be reduced to the illusory lucidity of liberal
concepts of political human rights norms.

The legal method of the ILA

What has the ILA offered in the way of background analysis of the
causes of states of emergency in the Third World? The first stage of
the ILA's work, the Belgrade Report, sets out very fully the usual
grounds given to justify their existence. It appears to treat these
grounds as merely attempts made by certain groups in power to pass
off as threats to the nation as a whole what are only threats to the
power-holders for the time being. Articles 4 of the UN Covenant and
13 of the European Convention both require the factual existence of
the circumstances justifying the assumption of power.[33] Although the

Belgrade Report is not categorical as to the justiciability of the issue,[34] it offers no 'uncloaking mechanism' other than the desirability of adequate fact-finding mechanisms, such as supposedly exist under the system of the European Convention.

The Montreal Report accepts the casuistic nature of the concept of state of emergency. It acknowledges that the specification of the circumstances which give rise to the state of exception cannot be limited to a description of their nature, such as war, internal subversion, etc. It is a matter of an appropriate degree of seriousness. The notion that it is a matter of searching out adequate facts reappears. If the deciding organ has to withstand public opinion, national and international scrutiny, it will have to provide an adequate statement of facts to justify its action.[35] This approach does not point towards any particular institution as the deciding organ, although it is remakable in supposing that assessment of facts has no political, in the sense of ideological or value-laden, dimension.

The definition of public emergency which the ILA minimum standards propose is itself taken from the Lawless Case[36] and the Greek Case (a Commission Case). The phrase 'an exceptional situation of crisis or public danger, actual or imminent, a threat to the organized life of the community' may sound more elaborate than 'threatening the life of the nation'. Nonetheless the Paris Report states categorically that:

> It is neither desirable nor possible to stipulate in abstracto what particular type or types of events will automatically constitute a public emergency within the meaning of the term: each case has to be judged on its own merits, taking into account the overriding concern for the continuance of a democratic society.[37]

The question is, how to reach such a judgment? Concerning the measures to be taken, the ILA's commentary merely quotes one particular European case virtually without comment. It does not appear to concern itself with whether there is a regional dimension to the problem of implementation of human rights. Indeed the word 'Regional' has been dropped from its title. The 'tests' which the European Court, in *Ireland* v. *United Kingdom*, is supposed to provide are the following. First, the measures should at least apparently make it possible to abate the specific danger. Second, the application of the ordinary law must be insufficient to meet the present danger. Third, the undue severity of extraordinary measures may be offset by adequate safeguards. The underlying principle of these 'tests' is quoted from the judgment of the Court itself: 'It is certainly not the Court's function to substitute for the British Government's assessment any other assessment of what might be the most prudent or most expedient policy to combat terrorism.'[38]

The primary issue in dispute was whether it was necessary for the British government to introduce internment, that is, detention without trial, to respond to the activities of the Irish Republican Army (IRA). It was one possible way to isolate suspected IRA members and to extract information about their activities. However, it could also be argued that its potentially random character, and its use exclusively against the Roman Catholic population, could only serve to antagonize the latter. The Irish government pointed to an increase in IRA activity after internment was imposed. It was eventually withdrawn as a means to combat the IRA.

Nonetheless, the Court insisted that it fell in the first place to each state, by reason of direct and continuous contact with the pressing needs of the moment, to take the necessary decisions. The state is in principle in a better position than an international judge to decide on the presence of an emergency and on the nature of the steps required to avert it. This leaves the state a wide, although not unlimited, margin of appreciation.[39] In stressing that it must not substitute its own judgment for the state's, nor engage in wisdom after the event about decisions taken, the Court said that a state struggling against a public emergency would be rendered defenceless if it were required to accomplish at once each of its chosen means of action with each of the accompanying safeguards.[40]

A very strong impression is given in the critical literature, not considered by the ILA, that the European Commission and Court made political value judgements which they did not disclose and discuss. In Green's view, the consequence of the Court's decision is 'that unless the action resorted to amounted to so blatant a disregard of all humanitarian principles as to resemble the practices of the Nazi regime involving an evident risk of genocide' a state could not fall foul of the requirements of Article 15 of the European Convention.[41] Another view is that the Court did not refute the Irish argument that if ordinary courts were enough for Protestant violence, they should equally be enough for Catholic violence.[42]

It is difficult to see what lawyers stand to gain from continued analysis of this type of jurisprudence whether at a national or international level. One is left with exhortations to balance human rights with the reasonable needs of the state, to find a delicate balance between the rights of the individual and those of the state and so forth.[43] Where it is said that the question of whether a threat to the life of a nation exists can be objectively determined, one might still ask how this is to be done. If all that is said is that there is a margin of appreciation open to national authorities in the first place, one has not clarified any legal limits and can have no basis for being satisfied with the outcome of international reviews which have taken place.[44] More fundamentally, the search for guidance in the jurisprudence is itself a reflection of the same sterile juridical positivism which Valades deplores. To advocate balancing of the reasonable needs of the state and the requirements of human rights presupposes that the jurist has some conception, however feeble, of what these are and mean.

The most usual dilemma which faces the judge in the Third World is a *de facto* seizure of power, incompatible with the previous legal order, however interpreted. The question is simply how judges are to respond to a situation of naked power, which of course deprives them of their own authority in a legal positivist sense. Should they accept a *de facto* situation or should they render a critical response in terms of some supra-positivist standard? The question is whether effectiveness alone, to the exclusion of all considerations of morality and justice, can be made the sole condition of the validity of the new legal order. If the answer is negative, there is a clear role or necessity for value judgements about the implications of the *de facto* revolutionary action. That necessity becomes clear in this context because the very absence of the state makes it impossible for the judiciary to argue its way to a solution in terms of formal legal concepts.

The approach of the ILA to this general issue is to propose that political human rights be non-derogable under international law. At present only the American Convention of Human Rights, Articles 23 and 27(2), treats the right to participate in government as non-derogable. Consistently with its overall argument the ILA considers that such non-derogability should be generalized. All human rights should be subject only to such limitations as are strictly necessary for the general welfare in a democratic society. This is taken to mean that restrictions may only be imposed by laws passed by democratic law-making processes,[45] which is merely a restatement of the problem.

Once again the ILA assumes that a clear norm of positive law can be applied to facts which can themselves be understood free from value judgements. This is perhaps clearest in the Montreal stage of the ILA's proceedings. There it is asserted that the basis for the legitimacy of a declaration of a state of emergency is:

> the fulfilment of the norm that the will of the people shall be the basis of the authority of every government functioning in every state, normal or exceptional . . . (the) fact that in many parts of the world the aforesaid norms are breached more than they are observed does not in any way diminish the value of those norms. On the contrary, such norms provide important signposts for measuring the manner and extent of departures in practice.[46]

The question then arises, much more clearly than in the Paris Report's commentary to Article 15, what authority uses the above-mentioned measure to see whether a particular declaration of a state of exception is valid. There appears to be no indication that the ILA has taken cognizance of the hazards of judgments which treat values as objectively existing facts. For instance, how is the will of the people to be objectively determined? The Algerian case study indicates that it is highly problematic for an international review agency to answer this question, and even more dangerous if one or two states try to answer it unilaterally, albeit ostensibly in the name of the international community.

A possible task for the human rights lawyer

If the rule of law, in the Western liberal sense, is something which exists in a state of 'normalcy', the question which theoretical analysis has to address is how to understand what appears to be a widespread phenomenon of deinstitutionalization in Third World countries. Reasons have been given for suggesting that the language of liberal constitutional law may not be an appropriate means to describe the quality of political life in developing countries. It accentuates their divergence from the developed West, but does not explain it, nor does it indicate just how serious the situation may be, either in the perspective of the particular society or in the light of a somehow absolute international standard, if such exists. It is suggested that the comparison between Algeria and Argentina bears this out.

Instead what is called for is a hermeneutic of international norms which have received virtually universal assent, but which are nonetheless open to very differing interpretations. By way of illustration one might take further the example of Arab states given the consideration of the case of Algeria in this study. These states have nearly all ratified the UN Civil and Political Covenant. Article 25 guarantees the right of participation in government. This includes the right to participate in the conduct of public affairs either directly or through freely chosen representatives. It means that genuine periodic elections must be held, guaranteeing the free expression of the will of the electors.

Authoritarian government is a recurrent feature of Arab societies; it is not simply the mark of Algeria. Even from an unashamedly Western perspective, it is perfectly clear that Arab societies could satisfy the letter of Article 25 without satisfying its spirit. For instance, it does not exclude a one-party state or a Presidential system of government which is virtually a periodic ratification of dictatorship. Yet it should still be the task of the lawyer to ask what are the justifications given by the powers in place in Arab societies for regimes which almost consistently represent a form of personalized leadership.

The lawyer's task is then to treat these pretensions critically in terms of the qualitatively most impressive Arab and Muslim traditions of authority in government. What this exercise might involve is shown by the Algerian case study. The exercise does not have to be exclusively intellectual in a cultural sense. Clearly there is a place for the types of sociological analysis undertaken by Max Weber distinguishing the rationalist legal orders of developed capitalist societies from the apparently charismatic leadership of pre- or semi-capitalist societies.[47] The former conceptual aspect of the human rights lawyer's work is concerned with the development of generally agreed and clearly understood human rights standards. It is this level of analysis which will bring home to such lawyers rudely the relativity of their own perspective and the limitations of their own under-standing.[48] A more sociological approach, admitting of course, a Western bias, will help one to retain a realistic awareness of what types of institutions are actually possible at a given point in time.

Notes

1   'Report of the Subcommittee on the Study of Regional Problems in the Implementation of Human Rights', in *Report of the 59th Conference of the International Law Association* (Belgrade Report) (London: ILA, 1982), 89–90.
2   The terms 'state of exception' and 'state of emergency' are used interchangeably in international law.
3   ICJ, *States of Emergency, Their Impact on Human Rights* (Geneva: ICJ, 1983), 413.
4   D. Valades, *Dictadura constitutional en America Latina* (Mexico: UNAM, 1974), 36.
5   Ibid., 25, 31, 41–8.
6   'Report of the International Committee on the Enforcement of Human Rights Law', (Paris Report), in *Report of the 61st Conference of the International Law Association* (London: ILA, 1984), Section A, Emergency Declaration, Duration and Control.
7   Ibid., Section B, Emergency Powers and Protection of the Individual: General Principles.
8   ICJ, *States of Emergency*, 465.
9   Ibid., 4–5.
10 N. Questiaux, *Study of the Implications for Human Rights of Recent Developments Concerning Situations Known as States of Siege or Emergency*, UN Doc. E/CN 4/Sub, 2/432 Rev. 2 (1982) 31, 34.
11 Ibid., 36, 39–40.
12 OEA/Ser L/V/11.49 doc. 19 corr. 1 11 April 1980.
13 ICJ, *States of Emergency*, 449–50.
14 IACHR Report 21, 266 (Washington: IACHR, OEA/Ser. L/V/II. 49. doc. 19 corr. 1 11 April 1980).
15 Ibid., 22–3.
16 Ibid., 248–50.
17 Ibid., 16.
18 Ibid., 250.
19 *Die Diktatur, von den Anfängen des modernen Souveränitätsgedankens bis zum proletarischen Klassenkampf* (2nd edn) (München: Dunker & Humblot, 1928); *Der Huter der Verfassung* (2nd edn) (Tübingen: Mohr, 1961): for an introduction, see M. Stolleis, 'Carl Schmidt', in M.J. Sattler (ed.), *Staat und Recht, Die deutsche Staatslehre im 19. und 20. Jahrhundert* (München: List Verlag, 1972), 123–46.
20 J. Tapia Valdes, 'Estado, Derecho y Doctrina de la Seguridad Nacional', in *El Terrorismo de Estado* (Mexico: Neuva Imagen, 1980), 164. See also 8–44. Tapia Valdes was Professor of Constitutional Law in the University of Chile and Minister of Education in the Allende Government.
21 Valdes, 'Estado, Derecho y Doctrina', esp. 210.
22 Ibid.
23 This analysis relies primarily upon A. Yefsah, *Le processus de légitimation du pouvoir militaire et la construction de l'état en Algérie* (Paris: Anthropos, 1982), in particular pp. 115–16 quoting at length a speech by Boumedienne.
24 M. Camau, *Pouvoirs et Institutions au Magreb* (Tunis: Ceres, 1978), esp. 123.
25 Ibid., 126.
26 'As if Article 59 amounted to a normal mechanism, conforming to the logic of the regime, instead of being an exceptional procedure.' Ibid., 132–3, quoting Jean Leca.
27 Ibid., 133.
28 Ibid., 134–5.

29 Yefsah, *Le processus de légitimation*, chs 1–3; also B. Tilbi, *Militär und Socialismus in der Dritten Welt* (Frankfurt am Main: Suhrkampf, 1973), 163–90, stressing a sociology of the military, before and after independence, as a cohesive and inevitably hierarchical and privileged force.

30 Yefsah, *Le processus de légitimation*, ch. 4, and esp. Tilbi, *Militär und Socialismus*, 186–90; more generally Dersa, *L'Algérie en débat* (Paris: Maspero, 1981), and Kuider Sami Nair, 'Algérie, 1954–1982: forces sociales et blocs au pouvoirs', in *Les Temps Modernes* (July–Aug., 1982), 11–13.

31 See in particular C.J. Alexander, 'The Illusory Protection of Human Rights by National Courts during Periods of Emergency', *Human Rights Law Journal*, 1 (1984), 2–3, 12–13; conclusions based on a review of the US, UK, Australia, New Zealand, Canada, India, South America and Ireland.

32 See the comments of UNESCO relating to the limitations on the exercise of human rights and fundamental freedoms, in E.I. Daes, *The Individual's Duties to the Community and the Limitations on Human Rights and Freedoms under article 29 of the UDHR* (New York: UN, 1983). The Rapporteur herself has no doubt as to the meaning of democracy, see 177–8.

33 The Belgrade Report, paras 11 and 26–7.

34 Ibid., para. 32.

35 'The Report of the Subcommittee on the Study of Regional Problems in the Implementation of Human Rights Norms in a State of Exception' (Montreal Report), in *Report to the 60th Conference of the ILA* (London: ILA, 1983), paras 16, 18.

36 *Lawless* v. *Ireland*, Eur. Court HR, Series A, No. 4.

37 Paris Report, Section a, para. 1.

38 Ibid., paras 6–7.

39 *Ireland* v. *United Kingdom*, Eur. Court HR, Series A, No. 25, Judgment, para. 207.

40 Ibid., paras 214, 220.

41 L.C. Green, 'Derogations of Human Rights in Emergency Situations', *Canadian Yearbook of International Law* 92 (1978) 100.

42 J.F. Hartman, 'Derogations from Human Rights in Public Emergency', *Harvard International Law Journal*, 1 (1981), 33–5, 37–9.

43 See for instance R. Higgins, 'Derogations under Human Rights Treaties', *British Yearbook of International Law* 281 (1978), particularly 289, 319.

44 Ibid., 300, 304, 319; also C. Warbrick, 'The Protection of Human Rights in National Emergencies', in F.E. Dowrick (ed.), *Human Rights* (Westmead: Saxon House, 1979), 96.

45 Paris Report, Section c, comment to Article 15.

46 Montreal Report, paras 11, 13.

47 See Max Weber, *The Theory of Social and Economic Organisation*, ed. Talcott Parsons, tr. A.M. Henderson and Talcott Parsons (London: Free Press, 1947), especially ch. 3.

48 See, for instance, H. Enayat, *Modern Islamic Political Thought* (London: Macmillan, 1982), 125–39, for a recent discussion of Islamic theories of democracy. Enayat suggests that theoretical attempts to reconcile Islam and democracy have failed. See esp. 135–6.

5

International Law and Human Rights: the Case of Women's Rights

Noreen Burrows

In the context of public international law it is perhaps misleading to speak of women's rights, because throughout the substantial body of law which relates to the status of women there has been no attempt to define the exact sphere of women's rights nor to enumerate those rights which might be said to be peculiar to women. Existing international declarations and covenants concentrate on the problem of outlawing discrimination in law and in practice, providing that the rights which the international community recognizes as being human rights, that is, those provided for in the 1966 International Covenants on Civil and Political Rights, and on Economic, Social and Cultural Rights shall be available to all irrespective of their sex. Thus the same conditions should be imposed on all persons when exercising, for example, their right to vote, to work, or to education.

It was the perception that there exists widespread discrimination against women throughout the world which led the states which make up the membership of the UN to adopt in 1967 the Declaration on the Elimination of All Forms of Discrimination Against Women (the Declaration),[1] which was translated into legal form in the 1979 Convention on the Elimination of All Forms of Discrimination Against Women (the Convention): this Convention was opened for signature and ratification in 1980.[2] This chapter examines that Convention and in so doing concentrates on three areas: the rationale underlying the international instruments which have been adopted relating to the status of women; the motivation of states in the adoption of such texts; and the likely success or otherwise of international law as a means of providing women with solutions to the problems which they face in playing their full role in society.

The Rationale Underlying International Legislation

Human rights discourse has traditionally been male dominated in the sense that, in what is essentially a man's world, men have struggled to assert their dignity and common humanity against an overbearing state apparatus. Attempts to define a body of civil and political rights were made from the eighteenth century onwards in societies that were organized by men and, predominantly, for men. Women played an insignificant role in the determination of political, legal and institutional structures both in the USA and in Europe where much of the human rights debate was pursued. Lone voices, such as that of Mary Wollstonecroft, did attempt to vindicate the rights of women[3] and a certain philosophical tradition did develop in which pleas were made for the emancipation of women to allow them to escape their traditional domestic role and to enter more fully into society.[4] However, such attempts as were made were unsuccessful in including women in the human rights debate.

This is not to claim that the area of civil and political rights is necessarily sex-specific and, in particular, specific to men; rather that the rights typically claimed were designed to regulate the relations between men and the state. In some cases the law did specifically exclude women from the exercise of human rights, but more generally they were excluded from holding rights due to the fact that society undervalued their importance and to some extent ignored their existence. Declarations of the rights of man reflected exactly that perspective.

The extension of the rights of men to include women came about by a gradual process of change in societies, as the part which women played in society changed and they increasingly entered into public life. Such developments depended on the society in question, of course, as well as on changing economic conditions. Women's own struggle to extend the franchise led to a recognition of women's right to vote. The entrance of women into the work force led to demands for equal pay. The aim of the women's movement was mainly to achieve a place for women in a man's world, and in order successfully to accomplish this task there was a need to extend the legal recognition of rights to women. Thus the emphasis in both municipal and international law came to be on the elimination of discrimination.

At the international level, the UN Charter was the first international instrument to recognize 'the equal rights of men and women'[5] and since the foundation of the UN sex has been a forbidden ground of discrimination for all states which subscribe to the aims and principles of that organization. Therefore, in the international context, what has been developed is a set of legislative reforms which seek to place women in the same situation as men. In this context women's rights are not therefore rights which are specific to women, but are rather universally recognized rights held by all people by virtue of their common humanity and regardless of their sex.

Whilst there was an evident need for such a recognition it does ignore the real differences which exist in the worlds which divide women and men. Such differences are two-fold; those largely defined by the structure of society, and those based on the biological distinction between sexes. The former relate to the fact that typically certain functions are performed by women, such as child-care, housework, subsistence farming. The latter relates to the exclusive performance by women of bearing and suckling children. These areas, which have been defined by states as being areas of private life, are often thought not to be areas where the discourse of human rights is relevant, yet they are areas in which the majority of the world's women live out their days. A definition of rights which omits to take on board the needs and aspirations of half the human race cannot thereby lay claim to universality nor can it be seen to have an overriding moral authority. For most women, what it is to be human is to work long hours in agriculture or in the home, to receive little or no remuneration, and to be faced with political and legal processes which ignore their contribution to society and accord no recognition of their particular needs.

To some extent the failure of states to translate the needs of women into protected rights has been due to the failure of women to specify the rights to which they may justifiably lay claim. However, existing structures do not take into account factors such as the high degree of illiteracy among women, nor their inability to formulate policy due to their exclusion from public life. More importantly, women have not grasped the fact that the distinction drawn by states between public and private areas of life, which roughly corresponds to the world of men and that of women, allowing for the existence of rights in the former but not in the latter, is a distinction drawn for political reasons. It is not one which is inherent in the nature of society, neither is it natural, nor necessary.

In the international setting the ambivalence of states in this matter has been demonstrated by their reluctance to take on board the crucial question of the role of the family in determining the status of women. The Declaration, whilst proclaiming the equal rights of women in civil matters, states that this equality is '[w]ithout prejudice to the safeguarding of the unity and harmony of the family, which remains the basic unit of society'.[6] Attempts to include an equivalent statement in the Convention were quashed and there is now some evidence to suggest that states are becoming more willing to open up to scrutiny the role of men and women in the family. The preamble to the Convention recalls the contribution of women to the welfare of the family, the social significance of maternity, and the contribution of both parents to the care of children. It affirms that change is required 'in the traditional role of men as well as the role of women in society and in the family'.[7] However, in the text of the Convention there is no attempt to translate the private relations in the family into a system which is governed by a set of rights.

It can be argued that attempting to define a body of rights for women is in itself discriminatory, in that women would be accorded rights which would not be available to men. If discrimination *per se* is illegal it would be invidious to claim a specially protected status for women. However, the international community has accepted that certain activities which seek to remove the historical legacy of the inferior position of women are permissible. Discrimination, in the context of international law, has a pejorative connotation and is said to mean 'any distinction, exclusion, or restriction . . . which has the effect or purpose of impairing or nullifying the recognition, enjoyment or exercise by women' of their rights (Article 1 of the Convention). Thus special measures aimed at achieving equality are permitted provided that they do not allow for the maintenance of unequal or separate standards (Article 4 of the Convention).

In reality men and women rarely occupy the same situations. Those women who, by choice or necessity, live in a man's world cannot expect to have a specially privileged status. However, those women who occupy a place in the women's world can legitimately claim rights which are typically theirs. This is not to deny the same rights to men who might, by choice or necessity, enter the women's world, excepting of course any rights surrounding child-birth. The former are not necessarily sex-specific but are rights which apply in concrete economic and social settings.

States, acting in concert, have so far made only small steps in defining a body of rights which could apply in the women's world or the private sphere. They have defined as private relationships in the home and in domestic labour. They have defined as private the sexual relations between a man and his wife, and the economic consequences of matrimony. The decision as to whether to have children is defined as consensual, thus ignoring the primary role of women in the care of such offspring.

However, within certain states women have begun to demand rights in some of these areas. Pattullo,[8] for example, describes the ways in which the personal rights of women are coming to be recognized in the UK. She cites as examples the right of women to be protected by law from violence inside marriage, or the more easy availability of abortion under the 1967 Abortion Act. However, recognition of the rights of women is by no means universal throughout the international community and, as she points out, moves towards the recognition of rights of women in the UK can be easily jeopardized when faced with government which is hostile, for whatever reasons, to the necessary changes in the law which would arise from the recognition of these rights. Furthermore, such legal provisions as have been developed in the UK are not presented in terms of rights of women. Protection from violence inside marriage extends to both partners and the law has failed to protect women from marital rape.[9] Moreover, the right to terminate a pregnancy is either limited by qualifying legal conditions or by the competing interest of the state in foetal life, or 'maternal health'.[10]

The Convention does provide some indicators as to what might constitute a body of rights for women. It commits states to endeavouring to eliminate sex-role stereotyping (Article 5); to eliminating traffic in women and the exploitation of the prostitution of women (Article 6); to providing rights surrounding maternity such as protection from dismissal on the grounds of pregnancy, the right to maternity leave, and the right to special protection for women in types of work proved harmful to them (Article 11). For women in rural areas, the Convention encourages states to permit them to organize self-help groups and agricultural cooperatives in order to help them obtain access to paid employment and to have 'access to agricultural credit and loans, marketing facilities, appropriate technology and equal treatment in land and agrarian reforms' (Article 14). In family law, women are to be accorded equal rights with men to enter marriage, to divorce, in respect of matrimonial property, in respect of children and of personal rights (Article 16). However, the main thrust of the Convention is the elimination of discrimination and it is not intended to provide a list of rights for women.

An international definition of the rights of women would of course not be easy to achieve. Opponents of 'radical universalism' argue that universalist definitions of rights imply 'a priority to the demands of cosmopolitan community' and fail to take into account 'cross cultural variations in human rights'.[11] Given the diversity in the forms of interpersonal relations and cultural variations which exist, say in the structure of the family, it may prove difficult to specify with sufficient precision those rights which the international community would recognize as being the rights of women. However, there are certain patterns of women's existence which point to the types of rights which they may claim. Certain of these rights would be those exclusive to women, whilst others would be those typically claimed by women.

Rights exclusive to women are those centred on child-birth and would be accorded to women before, during and after the confinement. The Convention provides for some of these rights, for example the right to maternity leave with pay, or to special protection for women during pregnancy in types of work proved to be harmful to them. Other rights which might be said to be exclusive to women are those which enable her to protect her person, such as the right to abortion, and to choose the time and spacing of her children.[12] Other rights need not be sex-specific in their general formulation but could be particularized to situations in which women would be the main beneficiaries were such rights recognized by the state. Thus, the right to a minimum wage for child-care or for work performed in the home or in subsistence farming would acknowledge the protected status of such tasks, and the applicability of human rights standards to them and to the persons who predominately perform them. The right to literacy would also benefit women who make up the bulk of the world's illiterates.[13]

In defining such rights, and the examples given above are by no means exhaustive or definitive, states would be committed to recognizing that improvements in the status of women are not merely dependent on the elimination of discrimination in areas which have traditionally been seen as coming within the sphere of human rights, important though this is, but also on recognizing that women should have rights in areas which have been designated as the private domain. This is not to argue that women and men should necessarily remain within their traditional roles, but merely that women should not remain without rights in the role which has traditionally been seen as female. If this is approved, then women will be free to assert their dignity and worth as human beings.

The Role of the State in the Adoption of International Legal Texts

An examination of international legal texts relating to women shows that states have defined the problem of failure to respect women's rights solely in terms of discrimination, rather than recognizing that there is in fact a distinct body of rights which are primarily applicable to women. That they have done so arises out of the context in which the international agreements which relate to the status of women have been adopted. The concentration on the elimination of discrimination and the absence of an approach which takes into consideration the undervaluation of women and their activities, both of which are prevalent in all societies, demonstrate that states have not taken on board the idea of the rights of women. If discrimination is eliminated in areas such as the workplace, or in the political process, that would be a move towards a society which would value to some extent women and womanhood. However, there would still be a need to recognize the particular rights of women. It is unlikely that societies will fundamentally restructure themselves so as to place men in the home-centred environment or that domestic tasks will be shared equitably between the sexes. Even were women to have unlimited access to what is at present the male environment, they would still occupy their own particular sphere. There would still be a need to develop a body of women's rights.

The international law of human rights is a phenomenon of the twentieth century. With the creation of the UN and its family of organizations in 1946, and particularly with the adoption of the Universal Declaration of Human Rights in 1948, a process of law creation was initiated which resulted in the adoption of several international treaties seeking to particularize the rights which the international community endeavours to protect.

Attempts to eliminate discrimination on racial grounds provided the pattern for subsequent international attempts to outlaw discrimination based on sex. In 1965 the UN opened for signature and ratification the Internation Convention on the Elimination of All Forms of Racial Discrimination.[14] As McKean points out, this was part of the decolonization ethic current in the UN in the 1960s. It followed on from the declarations relating to the elimination of colonialism and the granting of independence to colonial peoples and territories.[15] Following the adoption of this Convention it was suggested that a similar international treaty be established to eliminate discrimination against women. In this way, emphasis came to be placed not on defining women's rights as such, but on the elimination of discrimination against them within the conservative context of already accepted, male-dominated, norms.

A further factor which influenced the way in which the international community approached the status of women is the institutional nature of the UN itself. In 1947 the UN established a Commission on the Status of Women whose task was 'to prepare recommendations on women's rights in the political, economic, social and educational fields'.[16] The Commission subsequently worked to define areas where women were perceived to be disadvantaged, and produced literally hundreds of recommendations which were forwarded to the Economic and Social Council of the UN. However, it worked in somewhat splendid isolation until the General Assembly propelled the work of the UN into the area of development, which has subsequently become the overwhelming interest of that organization. As part of the first UN Development Decade the General Assembly requested the Commission on the Status of Women to prepare a Declaration on the Elimination of All Forms of Discrimination Against Women as part of the UN Programme of Concerted International Action for Women. Thus the Commission was swept into the programmatic activities of the UN in the area of development.

In many ways, the UN has been effectively deprived of much of its authority over its members. Its role in the maintenance of international peace has been significantly weakened and it is increasingly seen as having only limited importance. This is particularly true as far as the rich and powerful nations of the Western world are concerned. One result of this has been the increasing bureaucratization of the UN itself but, more importantly, its member states have tended to substitute institutional goals for a commitment to real action. Thus the UN has embarked on a series of exercises in long-term planning which, in an institutional setting, have become an end in themselves. In the context of the UN, such programmes are beneficial in that they provide the international community with an opportunity to be seen to be working harmoniously and with the maximum of cooperation, yet the real struggles between states continue elsewhere.

The human rights debate is caught up in this process and nowhere is this more true than in the work of the Commission on the Status of Women. Observers of the UN will note in the years 1965–85 there has been a welter of activity which relates to women. The General Assembly has adopted a World Plan of Action, Regional Plans of Action, has held three international conferences, several regional conferences, adopted many resolutions and declarations, and, arising out of these activities, adopted the Convention on the Elimination of All Forms of Discrimination Against Women in 1979 in time for the world conference for the review of the Decade for the Advancement of Women. Work on the preparation of the Convention, particularly in the Third Committee of the General Assembly, was kept to a minimum in order to meet the deadline of this conference. Indeed it would seem that the motivation for the adoption of the Convention was to provide a focus for the conference, rather than representing a sincere attempt to define the rights of women. It was simpler to follow established patterns than to initiate new ones.

That states have followed the path of the elimination of discrimination to the neglect of other possible options is perhaps due to the fact that, as yet, demands emanating from within states have not been on such a scale as to demonstrate a need to take action at the international level to define women's rights. International consideration of the status of women in society is relatively new, and very often demands for state action have been made in the form of demands for equality of rights. Even then, states have been faced with competing claims from men. It is only recently, for example, that the feminist debate in the USA and the UK has turned its attention to the role of women in the family.[17] Those women who were educated and articulate enough to formulate demands for action have usually been women who have wanted to assert their rights to move into the man's world. The feminist debate has therefore omitted to take into consideration those women who, by choice or necessity, live in a very different world. Furthermore, feminist claims have had to compete with conservative elements within states in order to achieve any kind of recognition and, typically, it is the strongest claims which win out in the political process. The equality of rights movement has suffered setbacks in the USA, for example, when the Equal Rights Amendment was eventually defeated: and that in a country with a powerful feminist lobby. It is unlikely that states as such will set out to recognize rights for women when women themselves have not presented a coherent argument for rights particular to them. International action to date has been a continuation of the national debate and, as such, has a great deal of merit. What needs to be emphasized, however, is that the adoption of the Convention is not a solution to the problem of denying fundamental rights to women but can only be a step in the direction of valuing women's potential and actual contribution.

International Law and Human Rights

International human rights law has only recently come to be accepted as part of international law in general. Historically, international law was a mechanism which could be used to afford protection to certain groups of persons or to individuals only in very limited circumstances. Thus the rights of minorities living in certain geographical areas, or under certain political systems, were protected by international treaties, the rights of consular and diplomatic personnel were recognized by customary international law, and slavery and analogous practices were outlawed. However, the development of a comprehensive body of international human rights law had to await the twentieth century and in particular the foundation of the UN and its family of organizations. The reason for this lies in the nature of international law itself, which has traditionally been defined as the law governing the behaviour of states in their relations with each other, rather than as a body of law which prescribes the ways in which states, and their institutions, should behave towards persons who are their nationals or subject to their jurisdiction. Indeed, international law is grounded on the principle of legal sovereignty, one aspect of which, territorial sovereignty, gives to the state the complete and exclusive authority over all persons on and above its territory. Furthermore, the legal principle of the non-intervention in the domestic affairs of another state would seem, taken together with the principle of sovereignty, to preclude any development of an international law of human rights in which an organ other than the state itself would determine the legality of its activities in respect of persons within its jurisdiction. However, since 1945 it has come to be accepted that states may not use the argument of domestic jurisdiction to mask gross violations of human rights.[18]

International treaties relating to human rights which are adopted do not of themselves confer rights on individuals except in those countries which accept that international treaties are part of domestic law, for example, the Netherlands. The obligation assumed by the state is therefore towards other states who are parties to the treaty. The obligation is to afford protection of the rights enumerated in the text of the treaty, and failure to do so is a breach of an obligation which is owed, not to the individual whose rights have been violated, but to the other parties to the treaty. In other words, the duty imposed by international law is one owed to other states and not to the victim of an alleged violation. The obligation assumed by the state thereafter is to make available to its citizens the rights provided in the treaty. It may do this in one of two ways, either by legislating to recognize such rights in its own legal system or by subscribing to an international enforcement mechanism. If international law, as a system, is to provide effective supervision of the behaviour of states, the latter option is preferable. To this end, various types of enforcement mechanisms have been created providing for the right of complaint by one state about the behaviour of another, or requiring that states report to an international committee on the extent of their compliance with the terms of the treaty, or according to individuals the right of petition to an international forum to make a complaint against their own state. International enforcement mechanisms are, however, very weak when confronted with an intransigent state and one of the main problems for international human rights law is the inability to enforce compliance.

A further problem for international law is the absence of a legislative body which may adopt texts for the whole international community. International treaties create legal obligations for the states which are parties to them and for those states only. The status of an international treaty for a state which is not a party to it is at best a moral one. It is under no obligation to act. International human rights treaties may have, of course, a persuasive influence on non-parties, and may be used by the individual to persuade his or her government to act in a particular way. It can be argued that the existence of a body of international legal rules which create obligations for a number of states is in itself a powerful moral force in the international community, providing a moral yardstick to which other states may aspire, or to which individuals may point if they seek to influence their own state, whether or not that state has ratified the treaty in question. This is an attractive view for those who champion morality in international relations. However, it does not satisfy critics who argue that without a translation of the rhetoric of human rights into enforceable legal rules the individual is in a very weak position in respect of a very powerful state. To such a critic, the main attraction of international law is that it purports to subject states to international obligations and fetters their discretion in their approach to their citizens. However, the translation of rhetoric into reality would remove their doubts as to the utility of international law.

The Convention on the Elimination of All Forms of Discrimination Against Women provides a useful model for an analysis of the problems of international law and the international legal process. The Convention was opened for signature and ratification on 1 March 1980 and came into force on 3 September 1981. As of 2 January 1984 it had attracted a total of 90 signatures and 54 ratifications. In such a short space of time this rate of ratification is apparently impressive. Nonetheless, it is only in force for one-third of the international community and at least one major power, the USA, is not bound by the legal rules contained therein. The obligations accepted by parties to the Convention are contained in Article 2. States party to it agree to condemn discrimination. As Egon Schwelb argued in his analysis of the Convention on the Elimination of All Forms of Racial Discrimination, 'it is not easy to establish the normative content of this treaty commitment'.[19] The obligation to condemn may well be satisfied by ratification of the Convention. In the context of sex discrimination it should perhaps be read in the light of the obligation which follows: 'to pursue by all appropriate means and without delay a policy of eliminating discrimination against women' (Article 2). The pursuit of such a policy would provide the normative content of the obligation to condemn. Article 2 goes on to provide that states must give effect in law to the obligations undertaken under the Convention and create the legal means whereby women claim their rights. Article 24 provides that states will adopt all the necessary measures to achieve a full realization of the rights recognized. Thus the parties to the Convention agree to give force in the municipal sphere to the rights outlined in the Convention. This extends their commitment beyond mere ratification and requires positive enforcement action at the national, and therefore accountable, level. It could, if acted upon, minimize the difficulty outlined above as to the nature of international agreements. The inter-state relationship would then be a check on the behaviour of the ratifying state, rather than the sole mechanism for enforcing compliance with the terms of the treaty.

The obligation so to act is not an immediate one. Like the Covenant on Economic, Social and Cultural Rights of 1966, the 1979 Convention provides for its progressive implementation. Thus a margin of discretion is left to each state as to when it will fulfil the obligations assumed. In the case of the 1966 Covenant, rights were divided into categories: hence the two separate Covenants. Civil and political rights are recognized as requiring immediate implementation, whereas social, cultural and economic rights are to be afforded protection whenever the state finds it in its power to do so. No such distinction is drawn in the 1979 Convention and thus it might be said that the recognition of women's civil and political rights may also be deferred. However, in practice this may not prove to be important. There are only a handful of states which do not recognize women's right to vote[20] and to hold public office and many of the rights contained in the 1966 Covenant are not covered by the 1979 Convention. In addition, the 1966 Covenant provides that the rights contained therein are to be protected irrespective of sex. However, the progressive implementation of the 1979 Convention does allow a certain flexibility to states which could ratify the Convention, thus demonstrating their commitment to the advancement of women, without the necessity for immediate action. For women in such a state the Convention would then provide valuable ammunition in their task of persuading their own government to extend legislation to permit women the full enjoyment of their rights, but by the nature of the Convention would not provide them with an enforcement mechanism.

Progressive implementation may be used to defer action by those states which do not feel the pressure for change from within. The Convention obliges states to change attitudes yet, as Galey points out, the permanent representative of the Philippines, in his report to the Committee on the Elimination of Discrimination Against Women (established under the Convention), expressed the view that 'women complemented men but were not equal to them and that men preferred their women to remain feminine and gentle'.[21] The Philippines ratified the Convention on 5 August 1981, one of the first states to do so. Ratification would not seem therefore in all cases to demand positive action. Indeed ratification might be used by a state to suggest an apparent commitment to the views of the cosmopolitan society, masking its real position. The nature and extent of state compliance with the terms of the Convention are beyond the scope of the present chapter, and one anecdote is not sufficient evidence, but there is an obvious danger that human rights instruments may be used as a smokescreen for domestic inactivity, rather than as a basis for positive action.

One way to avoid this is to provide an international mechanism whereby the activity (or inactivity) of a state may be assessed. Enforcement machinery at the international level can be of several kinds, and the international community has experimented with different types of mechanisms. Probably the most effective is where provision is made for an individual who claims that his or her rights have been violated to bring the case directly before a court or tribunal. Such a court may be an international one, like the European Court of Human Rights, or it may be a domestic court; for example, individuals may invoke 'enforceable Community rights' in UK courts under the 1972 European Communities Act which gave effect to European Community Law in the UK.[22] The effectiveness of such a procedure lies in the interest which the individual has in the protection of his or her own rights. In another context,[23] the European Court of Justice has indicated that it is the vigilance of the individual in the protection of the rights which are conferred upon him or her by the Treaties establishing the European Communities which will ensure the functioning of a European law and legal system.

This is given added force when one examines the operation of the system of human rights law operating under the 1950 European Convention on Human Rights. Comparing the vast number of complaints made by individuals against their own state with the number of complaints brought by one state against another, it can be seen that, where provision is made for individuals to enforce their rights directly, then they will use the international mechanisms which are provided. Such vigilance on the part of individuals must then be matched by the vigilance of the state in ensuring that it is not forever to be seen as the pariah of the international community.

Another international form of enforcement mechanism is the complaints system by which one state may bring a complaint against another. As noted above, the effectiveness of such a system depends on the willingness of states to become involved in a dispute with their neighbours. Experience shows that states are not willing to do this except under extreme circumstances, and that the motivation for the complaint is more likely to be connected with wider political considerations than with a concern for the individuals whose rights have been violated. Furthermore, the outcome of this type of procedure, whether before a tribunal established under international law or before a committee of experts, is merely a declaration to the effect that a state is in breach of its treaty obligations. International law has not yet developed a method of ensuring compliance with international standards beyond the bad publicity surrounding a finding of a breach of international law.

The most common, and the least effective, method devised by international law to try to enforce human rights standards is the reports procedure. This is a method of self-monitoring by states whereby each state reports on its success or failure in the implementation of international standards. Only one of these procedures has been declared successful by international lawyers.[24] However, any likely success is dependent on several factors. The first is the existence of an independent committee of experts who request the information and who vet the replies: for example, the Group of Experts of the ILO. Second in importance is the ability to define the exact form in which states must reply to the request for information. Simple questions along the lines of the extent to which the state complies with an obligation result in simple answers that the state does comply in every respect with that obligation. Experience within the Commission on the Status of Women has shown that reporting procedures which are not adequately prepared become useless exercises.[25] Furthermore, they undermine the ability of the international community to enforce human rights standards, in that neither international organizations nor third states have the authority to question the replies given by states under these procedures. States need not necessarily furnish incorrect information: mere selectivity in the type of information provided will subvert the operation of the system.

The Convention on the Elimination of All Forms of Discrimination Against Women is modelled on the 1965 Convention on the Elimination of All Forms of Racial Discrimination. This latter Convention establishes three types of machinery for the protection of ethnic groups. One state may complain of a violation of the Convention carried out by another state (Articles 11–13), or an individual who claims to have suffered racial discrimination at the hands of a state may bring a complaint against that state (Article 14).

These two are the strongest mechanisms of international law for ensuring compliance with the provisions of the Convention. In addition the Convention provides for a reporting procedure (Article 16). It is unfortunate, therefore, that, when the women's Convention was being prepared, only one enforcement mechanism was included, and even more unfortunate that this mechanism is the weak system of the reports procedures established by Article 21.

The Convention establishes a Committee on the Elimination of Discrimination Against Women to consist of initially 18, and later 35, 'experts of high moral standing and competence in the field covered by the Convention' (Article 17). The Committee is to consider reports submitted to it by the parties to the Convention on 'the legislative, judicial, administrative or other measures which they have adopted to give effect to the provisions [of the Convention]' (Article 18). These reports are to be submitted once every four years or whenever the Committee requests them. The Committee is empowered to make 'suggestions and recommendations' based on the reports (Article 21). It is not clear to whom these suggestions and recommendations are to be addressed, but presumably they will be addressed to the international community at large and to specific states where necessary.

The work of the Committee to date is described by Galey who points to some of the problems which have arisen.[26] The first problem is in the composition of the Committee. The Convention provides that the Committee be composed of a group of independent experts. From the biographies of at least some of the members it is clear that they have been drawn straight from government service. Thus the integrity of the Committee as an independent body must be called into question. Membership of the Committee is to be on the basis of equitable geographical distribution. Again a problem has arisen, as the number of states ratifying the Convention is small compared with the number of states in the international community. The Committee has become therefore unduly weighted in favour of the Eastern European states. As it was these states which were originally opposed to the establishment of an independent committee in the discussions leading to the adoption of the Convention, Galey suggests that this might be a problem for its operation. However, there is no concrete evidence to suggest that the Eastern European members have tried to subvert its operation.

In the procedure of the Committee, Galey indicates several

problem areas. The first is the failure of the ratifying state to report on time. The second is the lack of time devoted to each report (the Committee meets for two weeks every year), and the backlog of reports which has developed due to the infrequency of meetings. More importantly, the Committee has failed to agree as to the exact nature of the recommendations and suggestions which it is entitled to make. Its report is transmitted to the Economic and Social Council and the General Assembly for consideration, but as yet neither of these bodies has developed particular mechanisms for dealing with the reports of the Committee.

The international enforcement machinery provided for in the Convention is therefore very weak, and it does not inspire a great deal of optimism as to its ability to encourage compliance by recalcitrant states. Bearing in mind that the machinery operates only for parties to the Convention, who might be supposed to have a commitment to the elimination of discrimination, and does not cover two-thirds of the international community, hopes that international law, as a legal system, may make a significant contribution to the elimination of discrimination against women may be ill-founded.

This view, of course, ignores the moral value of international law and the persuasive influence which that law can have on states which have not assumed legal obligations under international treaties. The very existence of such treaties relating to the elimination of discrimination against women may preclude the possibility that in the future sex may again become a permissible ground for discrimination. The Convention has set out the ethic of the cosmopolitan community and, whilst some states may refuse to accept it on grounds such as religion, it remains nonetheless the prevalent international ethic.[27]

Women's Rights in the Future

The industry of the international community in developing a set of rules which seek to outlaw discrimination against women has, to date, been quite impressive. The Convention is potentially a useful instrument for women to use as a means of leverage on their own particular state. It bolsters their claim to equality of treatment in all the areas covered by the text. However, the Convention must be translated into specific legislation to be enforced at the domestic level if it is to have a real impact on the lives of women. Some states are willing to undertake the type of activity required, others may become willing in the future. Without such commitment on the part of states, the Convention, in real terms, remains a dead-letter, for the international legal system is incapable of forcing states' hands where they are unwilling to act.

Moreover, concentration on the elimination of discrimination obfuscates the central issues in respect of the status of women. These are that women occupy a different place in society from men and that their role is undervalued or discounted. Traditional human rights discourse is based on a moral commitment to the dignity and equality of persons, yet it has neglected to take into consideration the particular situation of women. There *are* some rights which are exclusive to women (for example, relating to child-birth) and some which are predominantly required by women (for example, in the contribution of their unpaid labour). A recognition of women's rights in these areas would demonstrate a moral commitment to acceptance of the dignity and worth of women.

States in the international community have not taken this issue on board, and their commitment to recognizing the status of women must be seriously called into question until they do so. The path of non-discrimination, even if it were followed vigorously and with political good-will, would satisfy only a part of women's legitimate claims. At the moment there is little evidence to suggest that states are actively pursuing policies of non-discrimination, and no evidence whatsoever to suggest that they are making efforts to extend the discourse of human rights to include the particular needs of women.

Notes

1 GA Res. 2263, 22 GAOR, UN Doc. A/6555 and Corr. 1 (1967).
2 GA Res. 34/180, UN Doc. A/RES/34/180 (XXXIV) 1980.
3 M. Wollstonecroft, *A Vindication of the Rights of Women*, (Harmondsworth: Penguin, 1975).
4 See, for example, J.S. Mill, *The Subjection of Women* (London: Dent, 1929); F. Engels, *The Origin of the Family, Private Property and the State* (London: Lawrence & Wishart, 1968); A. Bebel, *Women Under Socialism* (New York: Schocken, 1975).
5 Charter of the United Nations, Preamble; and see Article 55.
6 Article 6.
7 Preamble.
8 P. Pattullo, 'Women's Rights', in P. Wallington, *Civil Liberties 1984* (Oxford: Martin Robertson, 1984).
9 For example in *H.M.A.* v. *Duffy* 1983, S.L.T. 7, the success of the charge of rape of a wife by her husband depended on the existence of *de facto* or *de iure* separation. Thus the only sex-specific violence within marriage does not amount

to rape, although in some cases less serious charges of assault may be upheld.
10 Abortion Act 1967, Section 1 (UK); *Roe* v. *Wade*, 410 US 113 (1973) (USA).
11 J. Donnelly, 'Cultural Relativism and Universal Human Rights', *Human Rights Quarterly*, 6 (1984), 400.
12 For further discussion, see chapter 6 below.
13 C. Jeffries, *Illiteracy: A World Problem* (London: Pall Mall, 1967); E. Boulding, S. Nuss, D. Carson and M. Greenstein, *Handbook of International Data on Women* (New York: Sage, 1967).
14 GA Res. 2106 (XX) UN Doc. A/RES/2106 (XX) 1966.
15 W. McKean, *Equality and Discrimination under International Law* (Oxford: Clarendon Press, 1983).
16 Resolution of the Economic and Social Council 48 (IV).
17 See, for example, J.B. Elshtain, *Public Man, Private Woman* (Oxford: Martin Robertson, 1981). Certain issues about reproduction and fertility had been discussed from the nineteenth century onwards. However, see chapter 6 below.
18 See, for example, M. Akehurst, *A Modern Introduction to International Law* (London: George Allen & Unwin, 1977).
19 E. Schwelb, 'The International Convention on the Elimination of All Forms of Racial Discrimination', *International and Comparative Law Quarterly* 15 (1966), 996.
20 Bahrain, Kuwait, Oman, Qatar, Saudi Arabia and United Arab Emirates.
21 M. Galey, 'International Enforcement of Women's Rights', *Human Rights Quarterly* 6 (1984), 463–90, esp. p. 485.
22 European Communities Act, 1972, Section 2(1).
23 26/62 *Van Gend en Loos* v. *Nederlandse Administratie der Bellastingen*, (1963) CMLR 105; 9 Rec. 1.
24 E.A. Landy, *The Effectiveness of International Supervision* (London: Stevens, 1966).
25 N. Burrows, 'Monitoring Compliance with Human Rights Standards', *Netherlands International Law Review*, 31 (1984), 332.
26 M. Galey, 'International Enforcement'.
27 Certain states, for example those quoted in note 20 above, voted against adoption of the 1967 Declaration and are unlikely to become parties to the 1979 Convention.

6

The Right to Reproduce

Sheila McLean

If we are appropriately to use the language of rights in respect of reproduction, it is essential that we identify the nature and extent of any right which exists. If, as some would argue, existence of a right entails a corresponding duty, then in talking of a right to reproduce we may merely mean that no person or organization has a right to interfere with an individual's existing capacity to procreate. Perhaps this view may even imply that there is some duty, for example on states, to facilitate reproduction. Historically, reference to the right to reproduce has been generated by the former of these propositions, but seldom by the latter. However, as will be argued below, the second many now have some relevance. To take such a restricted view of the scope of the right to which reference may be made would, however, limit both the extent of the discussion and the nature of the protection which the language of rights and its translation into reality can afford.

Reproduction may also be seen as an interest worthy of special consideration: a perspective on human rights which would elevate the protection of procreative capacities to the status of a principle of morality, exceptions to which would require particular justification. Moreover, if reproduction is an interest worthy of special protection, then emphasis could legitimately be placed on assisting reproduction by, for example, the use of modern technology. However, no matter which of the above views on the scope of this right is taken, the outcome will seldom vary significantly, although the latter may lend some weight to the facilitation of reproduction whilst the former does not so obviously stress or require this.

However, are these options all that is meant when talking of there being a right to reproduce? While non-interference by the state may be a genuine and important value in itself, is it our sole concern in this area of human behaviour? Merely not interfering with existing capacities admittedly permits of reproduction, but does not tackle the fundamental issue. Is the production of offspring the overriding moral good which demands the protection of the terminology of human rights? Might not the debate equally focus on the individual's right to self-determination, which – whilst still acknowledging an inherent value in freedom from intervention and the importance of reproduction or parenting – none the less also depends on freedom of choice? To adopt such a perspective can expand our consideration of reproduction and ultimately render any right more meaningful.

In any event, it can be seen that the history of the debate in this area has depended on the elevation of procreation from a mere capacity which cannot be interfered with, to the kind of right which depends on an element of choice, albeit that such choices may be closely linked with freedom from intervention. As will be seen below, the use of the language of rights in relation to this aspect of human behaviour arose initially from the claims of early feminists that there was a right to control reproduction, vested in the individual and subject to his or her control.[1] Moreover, state intervention in procreative practices generated its own debate on the question as to whether or not there was a right to reproduce.[2] This discourse was based not merely on the rights/duties concept, but also on the view that the decision whether or not to procreate was a protected choice analogous to a right of privacy, guaranteed constitutionally in some countries. International concern about state intervention was generated not merely by the assumption of authority over another human being, but also by the fact that such assumption of authority resulted in the removal of choices about reproduction, thus minimizing the individual's right to self-determination.

Whilst the major debate in the twentieth century has revolved around the morality and legality of compulsory non-procreation[3] – primarily through the device of compulsory sterilization – it was not merely the question of bodily integrity which was at issue. For example, bodily integrity can be protected in medical situations by the existence of rules concerning the type of consent which renders medical intervention lawful.[4] If this were all that the debate was about, then it would be possible to argue that the compulsory sterilization of, for example, the mentally ill, who lack legal capacity to consent, would not be unlawful or distasteful. However, although the groups on whom compulsory sterilization was practised were primarily those whose capacity was in doubt, the compulsory removal of their reproductive capacities was nonetheless ultimately condemned. It is necessary therefore to search more deeply for the core of this right. Indeed, even although it might be thought undesirable that these same groups should reproduce, either because of the potential to pass on genetic problems or because they might be deemed unfit for parenting, the practice of preventing reproduction was nonetheless seen as morally opprobrious.

It is submitted that the compulsion not to reproduce was distasteful partly because of the discriminatory way in which it occurred, but primarily because the freedom to reproduce, if one so desired, was regarded as an aspect of being human which should not be denied. In other words, freedom of choice was vital to the protection of the individual's right. Moreover, the question of reproductive rights also has its roots firmly entrenched in the individual's freedom *not* to reproduce. Just as it is seen as offensive that people should be precluded from having the freedom to choose *to* reproduce, so it would be offensive should people be forced to reproduce. It is thus the liberty to make free choices about whether or not to reproduce which forms the core of this right. Quite apart from the use of force on the citizen which was involved in non-consensual sterilization – the main mechanism used compulsorily to limit procreation – removal of the capacity to procreate also precluded choices about procreation and was worthy of concern on this ground also.

Of course, the existence of a right to reproduce does not also imply a duty to reproduce. Indeed, as a recent English case put it:

> The policy of the state . . . is to provide the widest freedom of choice. It makes available to the public the means of planning their families or planning to have no family. If plans go awry, it provides for the possibility of abortion. *But there is no pressure on couples either to have children or not to have children or to have only a limited number of children.*[5] (emphasis added)

It is logical, therefore, to assume that the use of the terminology of rights in this area implies that the fundamental good is that people have protected choices about the exercise of existing capacities, and not that they should be forced to breed whenever chance dictates. Viewed in this way, it can reasonably be assumed that the state interference which contributed to the reference to human rights in this area was condemned not only because it constituted unlawful use of force against the individual, nor merely because it denied the pleasures of parenthood to those involved, but also because it removed from them the freedom to make choices about whether or not, and when, to procreate. Indeed, interference by states with the freedom *not* to reproduce has itself generated considerable debate in relation, for example, to the legalization of voluntary sterilization,[6] abortion[7] and the free and legal availability of access to birth control.[8] Although the element of choice remains crucial in these areas, the state may ultimately limit its availability by denying it where other important interests compete: as it may with all human rights. Thus, if it is accepted that the core of the right to reproduce is the individual's choice about when or whether to breed, state interference by limiting access to birth control or outlawing voluntary sterilization would amount to the kind of interference which is challengeable as a denial of fundamental rights. However, limiting the availability of abortions where the right to life of the foetus is regarded as paramount – for example, where the foetus is capable of life outside the womb – could be argued not to be a fundamental intrusion on the right to reproduce since it is merely a balancing of competing interests. In these circumstances, the right to reproduce may be defeasible, owing to an overriding state interest in protecting the life of viable foetuses. In practice, where the decision about termination encompasses real or equal risks to mother and foetus, the principle of double effect[9] is routinely applied to facilitate decision-making and to provide a moral framework within which the right to life of one party can be given priority over the right to life of the other.

However, to limit the availability of abortion – as under the British Abortion Act – before viability could be seen as limiting the freedom of choice of the right-holder, and therefore as an infringement of the right itself. Moreover, taking the more positive view of the right to reproduce – that is, highlighting that part of it which relates to the choice *to* reproduce – intervention is also possible. As will be clear below, this has in the past been undertaken by removing the capacity to make choices. However, modern technology generates further problems. Whilst the UK Report of the Committee on Human Fertilization and Embryology[10] proposes methods whereby the availability of procedures such as surrogacy can be limited, it might equally be argued that whereas regulation might be appropriate in order to ensure the safety and efficacy of these procedures, the limitation on commercial contracts and the limited availability of resources in this area of medical practice deny the freedom of choice which is central to the right to reproduce.

In this chapter, it will be implicit that the right to reproduce depends as much on the freedom to control reproduction as it does on the ability to retain existing capacities. In other words, the element of choice is central to the right to reproduce, a claim which will be supported by reference to the historical development of the use of the terminology of rights in this area.

The Social History of the Right to Reproduce

In its early manifestations, state manipulation of reproduction was confined to relatively passive interference with the right to choose whether or not, and when, to reproduce. Interference need not be violent or aggressive in order for it to be meaningful, and early feminists – who introduced the topic of reproduction to the public forum and first used the language of rights in this area – perceived that their lack of control over existing reproductive capacities affected their status and freedom as individuals by rendering them crucially dependent on their vulnerability to biological roulette.[11]

Reproductive choice was, therefore, identified at an early stage as being of central importance in the debate about procreation, although in the case of early feminists the scope of the choice actually sought was relatively limited. Their battle was not for total reproductive self-determination, but rather for the freedom to choose when and how often to reproduce. Their demands, therefore, focussed on free and legal access to effective birth-control methods and made no overt reference to the right to reproduce or any corresponding right not to reproduce. However, their struggle was closely linked to the demand for a right to reproduce in as much as it was implicitly assumed by their claims. Procreation – previously a matter of capacity – became an aspect of the fight for freedom and equal rights for women, all of which were inevitably bound up with freedom of choice. Just as the arguments about equal employment opportunities did not demand that women *should* work, so the debate about reproductive freedom did not imply that all women *should* breed. Feminist arguments were highly influential in the development and content of the debate about reproduction. This has continued throughout the twentieth century which has witnessed in some countries wholesale removal of the capacity to reproduce and the denial of choice.

At this point the importance of freedom of choice can be most clearly seen. If, as has been contended, the right to reproduce implies more than a duty not to interfere with existing capacities, and actually includes the duty not to force reproduction in the same way as not enforcing non-reproduction, then the early feminists – by demanding that reproduction should not be forced on them – were recognizing the kind of right to which reference is being made. Although women's social and financial dependence on the family unit limited initial demands apparently to exclude the option of non-reproduction, the claims which they did make identified the importance of choice, and could by implication have included the right not to reproduce given other social, economic and political freedoms.

However, it was not merely the early feminists who had a major interest in procreative practices. The stage having been set for public discussion of reproduction, other theories were advanced which had a major impact on the development of state attitudes to freedom of choice in reproductive matters and broadened the discussion to include the rights of men as well as women. While women's demands for control over their biological capacities could be argued to have limited men's rights, they did not ultimately deny the existence of such rights; merely they transferred the timing of reproductive choices from Nature to women.

As early feminists fought for the right to control biological capacities by spacing breeding, early genetic knowledge began its own struggle in the area of reproduction: fighting, apparently, for the very antithesis of a right to reproduce. The growth of the eugenics movement in Europe and America, particularly in the early twentieth century, reinforced public concern about, and interest in, reproduction. Eugenics was concerned to improve the genetic stock of Mankind and embraced a number of social and political groups within its theoretical ambit. From 'race suicide' theorists to some feminists, many were drawn to the claims and aspirations of the eugenics movement. Eugenicists argued that compulsory reproductive control was essential if societies were not to be swamped by the unfit, the disabled, the poor and the shiftless. Arguing that the poor (and, almost by definition, the weak and unhealthy) bred too often and the relatively wealthy too seldom, thus apparently implying that the children of the wealthy were biologically superior, the eugenics movement found considerable support, particularly in America. By ignoring the argument that there is no necessary link between wealth and biological soundness, by threatening the development of a 'black America', and by arguing that certain immigrants were biologically inferior, the eugenics movement aroused public fears in the USA. Such genuine genetic logic as there was in their arguments became swamped by an elitist and highly politicized approach to reproduction.

Indeed, such was the influence of this movement that the debate about reproduction became for a time focussed on quality rather than quantity, and the position of many individuals (male and female) became vulnerable to political and medical abuse. Birth control became an issue primarily in as much as it related to forcing those who could or would not voluntarily control their reproductive capacities, not to breed. In fact, the theories of the eugenics movement, incorporated into legislation in most states in America,[12] were surely the clearest example of the non-recognition at that time of a universal right to reproduce. It would deny the existence of such a right in those groups deemed to be unfit, and would render reproduction almost a duty in those groups deemed biologically superior. With its veneer of scientific respectability, the eugenics movement (in both its 'positive' and its 'negative' manifestations) reinforced a class and racial structure which had little to do with individual freedom or human rights and was based rather on confrontation between groups – ethnic and social – within the community. Its espousal demonstrated that a general non-discriminatory right to reproduce most certainly was not thought to exist, and in particular that it did not exist where free reproductive choice might threaten the welfare of the state as understood at any given time. Thanks to the growth of the eugenics movement, and its adoption by various groups, '[r]eproduction was raised from a biological precondition of human striving and achievement to the goal of human life itself.'[13] The struggle for recognition of the right to reproduce (including the right to make reproductive choices), therefore, has its roots in the struggle for women's rights and in scientific and political dogma, each of which lauded motherhood – at least in certain individuals – but the cumulative effect of which clearly bore no resemblance to what would now be understood as recognition of a fundamental human right. Rather, reproduction was viewed either as a duty or as a capacity whose exercise could be controlled by states as they saw fit, and without overwhelming justification.

In view of the constitutional and legal recognition of discriminatory compulsion, even if a view of this right is adopted which would define the core as being merely the duty not to interfere with existing capacities, then it can be seen that the right to reproduce cannot be said to have been accorded the status of a fully human right, unless humanity is redefined to exclude those groups whose breeding is not regarded as 'desirable'. Such redefinition seems both unacceptable and impossible since all people are guaranteed the status of equality by international agreement.[14] State refusal to permit some citizens to procreate must therefore be in violation of any human right to reproduce. Of course, in the face of other more immediate rights, the state may well seek to justify the limitation of procreation where the welfare of the state is threatened by existing practices. It may, for example, indicate that reproduction will be accorded the status of a human right but only within a framework which allows one child per family, as in China. The self-determination of the individual may then be subjugated to the economic welfare of the state.

However, it is also clear that the voluntary nature of procreative practices is central to what is regarded nowadays as being human. Guarantees of freedom from interference here also include freedom from interference in the decision when, or whether, to reproduce, and reinforce the importance of voluntariness. States such as China may provoke international concern when they limit the reproductive capacities of their citizens, but this is not only because thereby people are deprived of the joys of multiple parenting, nor solely because of the element of compulsion involved, although both of these may be relevant. Criticism is also levelled at such state practice because of the removal of the individual's ability to make a free choice about the number or spacing of their children. Even those who do not regard parenthood as a pleasure would argue with enforced removal of existing capacities. Conversely, those who do regard parenting as a positive joy would be likely to argue against states which enforced procreation, again on the basis that choice is central both to the pleasure obtained from parenting and to the freedom of the individual.

The Legal Approach

It can further be shown that reproduction has no lengthy history of being accorded the status of a human right by inquiring what has been the attitude adopted by the law. Indeed, the legal approach may also help to explore the limits of any right which does exist. Were there to be a recognized human right to reproduce, one would anticipate that legal systems – as the primary mechanism for protection in states – would offer support for it, thus rendering competing political, medical or social theories academic or redundant. Moreover, analysis of legal decisions will assist in identifying what it is about the right to reproduce which is fundamentally important.

To use the example of the USA again, it can be seen that the law did have an important role in this area in the twentieth century. Of course, by precluding access to birth control in the past, the law had always played a major part in controlling the struggle for choice in reproductive practices. However, the role adopted by the law in the twentieth century has even been more intrusive in reproductive capacities. Rather than protecting the liberty of the individual, the law – in some states at least – aligned itself with those whose priority was the protection of society from the offspring of certain groups. In short, there was no recognition of a universal right to reproduce in many states in the early part of the twentieth century. Laws rendering the institutionalized and the feeble-minded liable to compulsory sterilization were held to be constitutional, and were acted upon.[15] Meyers, for example, points out that legislation generated a situation which:

> by 1950 had accounted for the sterilisation of over 50,000 persons in America, 20,000 in California alone. By 1964 the accumulative total had reached 63,678. Of these persons, 27,917 were sterilised on grounds of mental illness, 32,374 on grounds of mental deficiency and some 2,387 on other grounds.[16]

Whilst this may not be a startlingly high proportion of the total population of America, it is a higher proportion of the institutionalized and – even if only symbolically – has considerable significance. The legal approach in America to compulsion in this area is amply demonstrated by the following comments from two major cases. In *Buck* v. *Bell*, the court made the following statement:

> We have seen more than once that the public welfare may call upon the best citizens for their lives. It would be strange if it could not call upon those who already sap the strength of the State for these lesser sacrifices, often not felt to be such by those concerned, in order to avoid

our being swamped with incompetence. It is better for all the world, if instead of waiting to execute degenerate offspring for crime, or to let them starve for imbecility, society can prevent those who are manifestly unfit from continuing their kind.[17]

Whilst apparently feeling the need to justify compulsion in this case and a number of others, the courts nonetheless did not recognize any universal human right to reproduce. Moreover, by dismissing the impact of the removal of capacities from certain people on the grounds that they may not in any event recognize their worth, the court also minimized the status of reproduction as a human right. For example, awareness that a human right exists is not necessarily central to the existence of the right, although it may predicate its exercise.[18] Indeed, overt doubt was expressed in some cases as to whether or not such a right could be said to exist, or if it did, what was its status in the hierarchy of competing rights. As the Court in *State* v. *Troutman* said: '*if there be any natural right for natively mental defectives to beget children*, that right gives way to the police power of the State in protecting the common welfare, so far as it can be protected, against this hereditary type of feeble-mindedness'.[19] (emphasis added) There is clearly considerable doubt in this statement that there is a right to reproduce vested in everyone. Whilst it could be taken to imply that other groups *may* have such a right, it is not universal, nor is it given significant status in the competing interests of individuals and groups. As has been seen, many thousands of people were sterilized on a compulsory basis, the justification being the overriding interest of the state and by implication the low status accorded to freedom of choice in reproductive matters. Those whose breeding was seen as likely to produce strong, healthy children were encouraged to do so in the interests of the state, while other groups had their reproductive capacities removed without choice. If there was a right to reproduce recognized and protected by the law, then it was selective and not universal. Moreover, it was unusually vulnerable to perceived state interests.

From prohibiting the spread of birth-control information, the law had then moved into a second stage which simultaneously allowed voluntary control (at least for those with the education and social status to seek and obtain it) and permitted the compulsory removal of reproductive capacities in other groups. There is still at this stage no recognition of a fundamental non-discriminatory right to reproduce vested in individuals. As is the case today, people – and, in particular, women – in certain economic positions were permitted freedom of choice in these matters. For example, while at present the developed and rich countries in the world are free to concentrate on certain aspects of the 'right' to reproduce, and to develop increasingly complex technology to facilitate reproduction, the economic and social situation of many, most notably in developing countries, continues to leave them vulnerable to biological roulette. Control of reproduction (including the right not to reproduce) which is now apparently well established in most developed countries, remains out of the reach of many. Indeed the pressures to reproduce in certain situations continue to reflect not only a lack of information about *how* to control procreative capacity, but relate also to, for example, the economic dependence on producing children capable or working for the family income and providing support for old age.

The Formation of the Right to Reproduce

It can be seen, then, that reproduction became a public, rather than private, issue primarily through a combination of two forces. The growth of feminist demands for limited reproductive self-control generated – by confrontation with traditional social attitudes – public debate on reproductive practices. Whilst early feminists argued for a somewhat limited type of control, and did not threaten existing social norms by questioning what has been called 'the cult of motherhood',[20] they were nonetheless successful in achieving a certain legal and political reinforcement for the view that women in particular should have some control over their own biological capacities. The development of medicine as a 'science' rather than an 'art' coincided with a growth of elitist politics to reinforce state interest in reproductive control. The law served to lend credibility to these social and political movements by supporting compulsory state control of the reproductive practices of some groups, and by justifying such control as being in the interests of the state itself it pandered to the fears of the powerful. The very existence of the state and the quality of that existence were seen to be threatened by reproductive self-determination, and no higher moral authority than the protection of the state's interests was deemed to exist.

Although the most blatant interference with reproductive capacity was that which allowed compulsory sterilization, it should be borne in mind that the state's interests were also served by maintaining a certain type of status for women, thus rendering those whose reproduction was seen as essential vulnerable to the pressure to continue in the traditional role of wife and mother. Moreover, the politicizing of reproductive behaviour was not confined to women. Compulsory sterilization (and occasionally castration) was also undertaken on men. Reproductive choice became not merely a feminist issue, but a more generalized one relating to the individual's rights. The central claims were based, therefore, on choice and not gender. Not only must a right to reproduce apply equally between the sexes, but in fact this was tacitly acknowledged by the condemnation of compulsory programmes which had made no differentiation on the grounds of sex.

Nor can it be central to a right which is dependent on choice that the individual has the physiological capacity to carry a child, although such a facility may have importance in some of the issues arising from reproductive choice. In other words, if a right to reproduce is to be respected then it must be accorded a status which is independent of the gender of the individual, and which can include the right to choose parenting. Indeed, it may also be argued that it should be independent of the sexuality of the individual. If this is accepted – and it must be if the core of the right is freedom of choice and not, for example, perceived suitability for parenting – then the rights of lesbians and homosexuals must also be considered. Whereas, traditionally, their sexual preferences have provided no natural opportunity for exercising existing procreative capacities, it is to be doubted whether they could be denied access to artificial fertilization techniques without this amounting to an infringement of their right to reproduce.

Thus this discussion is moving towards a point where there would seem to be an acknowledgement that a right to reproduce does exist and can be meaningfully described. This right, by using the above example, may be seen as being worthy of protection independently of the basic right to self-determination on which it is predicated. For example, it could be claimed that the right to self-determination is adequately protected by not outlawing homosexuality, and that this is sufficient to protect such a right. However, this will clearly have no impact on that aspect of self-determination which relates to the freedom to use existing biological capacities. If a right to reproduce does exist, then it requires individual status in these, as in other, situations. Thus, whilst the state may have no general duty to facilitate reproduction through technology or the supply of a partner, once facilities are provided – for example through *in vitro* fertilization and surrogacy programmes – to deny access on grounds of sexuality is to infringe the right on a discriminatory basis.

There is little doubt that contemporary language accomodates the use of the language of rights in procreation, but at what stage did this become as closely associated with reproduction as it now is? Despite the already intrusive practices of states such as America, it was the Nazi atrocities of the Second World War which required and generated universal moral outcry. The large-scale abuse of non-combatants which characterized this war made discussion of human rights in general more urgent and more meaningful. Not only was the right to life threatened by the Nazi regime, but more insidious invasions into personal autonomy – such as wholesale human experimentation and sterilization – were central to the behaviour condemned by the world. The UN in reaction promulgated a number of agreements protecting the sanctity of the individual,[21] and states and courts began to review their policies in the light of changing world opinion.

To continue with our example of the USA, policy changes in that country throughout the 1950s and 1960s give clear evidence of the new approach to individual liberty and reflect the first wholesale use of the language of rights in reproduction which is now part of accepted vocabulary. Whilst eugenic arguments still commanded some support, and continued to be put into practice in some states with the authority of the courts, there was a gradual movement away from state interference. Indeed, without referring to a right to reproduce as such, American courts began to treat reproductive choice as an aspect of the constitutionally protected right of privacy, necessarily obtaining the support of the legal system. For example in the case of *Carey* v. *Population Services International* it was said that: 'The decision whether or not to beget or bear a child is at the very heart of . . .[a]. . . cluster of constitutionally protected choices. That decision holds a particularly important place in the history of the right of privacy.'[22] The earlier landmark decision in *Skinner* v. *Oklahoma*[23] had also guaranteed state protection of choices about the potential to procreate. Indeed, *Skinner* made it quite clear that what was being protected was the potential to reproduce (which of course might not be exercised) but that states were not guaranteeing the opportunity to reproduce.[24] These cases make explicit reference to choices in reproduction, and provide the most overt support for the claim that choice is highly significant in what is being protected when reference is made to the right to reproduce.

However, not all states moved quickly to recognize the voluntary exercise of reproductive capacities as fundamental to the human condition. Using the interests of the state as the crucial yardstick, continued interference with the individual's choices about reproductive freedom was justified. In *North Carolina Association for Retarded Children et al.* v. *State of North Carolina et al.*, the court reflected that mental retardation was an identifiable category, and that since 'such persons are in fact different from the general population' they 'may rationally be accorded different treatment for their benefit and the benefit of the public'.[25] The compulsory prevention of the birth of a defective child or of a child whose parents could not properly care for it could be justified as reflecting a compelling state interest and therefore as not breaching the Fourteenth Amendment to the Constitution.

This court at least was not prepared to concede the existence of a general right to reproduce. However, other courts were more concerned with the implications of policies which use the interests of the state as a justification for interfering in the private lives of citizens. For example, in 1974 the District Court in Columbia made reference to the existence of a voluntary right to govern one's own procreation, including the right to choose whether or not to reproduce. The court issued this warning:

> We should not drift into a policy which has unfathomed implications and which permanently deprives unwilling or immature citizens of their ability to procreate without adequate legal safeguards and a legislative determination of the appropriate standards in light of the general welfare and of individual rights.[26]

Whilst debate on the issue of reproductive control has seldom reached the courts in the UK, the issue of non-voluntary sterilization was considered in the case of *Re D (a minor)*.[27] In this case, the right of a child not to be sterilized without her own consent was upheld, but this was at least partly influenced by the impression that the child would – on reaching adulthood – not be sufficiently retarded as to be legally incapable of making other major decisions such as that of getting married. The court referred in its judgment to a fundamental right to reproduce, but it is unclear what would have been the decision had the evidence shown that the girl in question would not have been able legally to consent to marriage at the appropriate age.

Moreover, it has been suggested that the court's reference to the existence of a right to reproduce should be taken in tandem with the rights guaranteed under international and European agreements.[28] Article 12 of the European Convention on Human Rights guarantees the right to 'marry and found a family'. The Universal Declaration of Human Rights guarantees in Article 12 that there shall be no 'arbitrary interference with . . . privacy', and in Article 16 that 'Men and women of full age . . . have the right to marry and found a family.' What is significant about both of these declarations is that they do not *per se* make reference to, or provide for, an individual human right to reproduce. Rather they seem to protect only the rights of those who are married (and those who, by implication, are capable of legally entering into this state). The individual as such is not protected by this: merely the nuclear family, which is 'the natural and fundamental group unit of society and is entitled to protection by society and the State',[29] is accorded special status. Therefore, on a strict interpretation, the individual cannot necessarily anticipate protection of a personal right to reproduce. Protection seems, under these agreements at least, only to be guaranteed to those of a certain age, intellectual capacity and status. This denies the universality which is accorded to, for example, the right to life whose protection is untainted by considerations of age, marital status or intellect. Indeed, the limitations imposed by international agreements may ensure that state intervention can legitimately be undertaken. As Lord Kilbrandon has pointed out, for example:

> It might well be . . . that the European Court would not condemn 'national laws governing the exercise of' the right to found a family if these laws were designed to prohibit the wilful transmitting of genetic defects. Such laws would stand on exactly the same footing as those which, for genetic reasons, forbid marriage and punish sexual intercourse between persons of particular degrees of consanguinity.[30]

However, whilst such apparently limited protection as is offered by those agreements might seem to deny the validity of any claim that choice and not status is central to the right to reproduce, it is submitted that on closer inspection this argument does not work.

The terms of these agreements cannot be, and are not, used to justify compulsorily terminating the pregnancies of those who are unmarried, for example. Whilst laws reinforcing incest taboos may make certain sexual relationships illegal, or proscribe marriage, they do not equally permit the forced termination of incestuous pregnancies. In other words, the agreements may encompass the prevention of certain relationships, and perhaps reinforce the value of traditional family groupings, but do not explicitly deny the right to reproduce itself. On a practical level '[e]ven the one-parent family, whether or not that exists through choice or through misfortune, is given substantial assistance.'[31] The assertion that the right to reproduce is an individual one, dependent on freedom of choice, seems therefore to maintain its force. Recent American decisions seem to have made this clear by their interpretation of reproductive freedom as an aspect of the individual right of privacy. As the Supreme Court said in *Eisenstadt* v. *Baird*:

> the marital couple is not an independent entity with a mind and heart of its own, but an association of two individuals each with a separate intellectual and emotional makeup. If the right to privacy means anything, it is the right of the individual, married or single, to be free from unwarranted governmental intrusion into matters so fundamentally affecting a person as the decision whether to beget or bear a child.[32]

Indeed, international agreements and court decisions made in conformity with them – in recognition of the centrality of freedom of choice – have moved towards a situation where substantial justification is needed before choices about the exercise of reproductive capacities can be interfered with. It is clear from more recent American and other decisions that the justification must reflect a compelling state interest.[33] Of course, this begs the question to some extent, since 'compelling state interests' may be defined in a number of ways which may not be consistent with the priority recognition of a right to reproduce and which may depend on transient political, social, economic or medical theories.

The Role of the State

The language of rights, therefore, has become an integral part of the discussion of reproductive practices for a number of reasons, the most powerful of which has been the practice of some states in interfering with the freedom of certain groups or individuals to make choices. Also important, however, was the preceding struggle for choices about when to procreate. In acknowledging the element of choice as central to both of these arms of the discussion, several things are being implied. First, that the state has a duty not to interfere with the freedom to reproduce, and second that the state should not interfere with choices about reproduction. Only overriding state interest therefore could justify, for example, a limitation on the number of children produced. Indeed, the state's duty not to interfere in the exercise of existing capacities can rationally also be seen as fundamentally a question of choice.

However, what are the implications of the emphasis on choice in this aspect of human behaviour? Does choice, for example, imply total reproductive self-determination? In its most extreme form, of course, total reproductive self-determination must imply that individuals have *complete* freedom of choice in reproductive matters. They must be free to overpopulate or underpopulate. However, as with all human rights, at some point legitimate interests may serve to justify limiting absolute freedom. Indeed, reproduction is so central to the continuation of the species that one can readily imagine the justifications for interference in the unlikely event that this was threatened. Total reproductive control is unlikely to be achieved, therefore, although states may strive to maximize it where it is non-threatening. As Gordon notes: 'Birth control has always been socially regulated in some way. This is because birth control has consequences for two social issues crucial to overall social development: sexual activity and population size.'[34] Whilst it has become accepted terminology to talk of a 'right' to reproduce, it is clear that states may nonetheless reserve the option to limit or remove the freedom to choose whether or not to exercise it: at least in some situations. Indeed, interference with reproductive capacities may only cause public or legal concern because the *nature* of intervention is distasteful rather than because there is an inherent moral objection to limiting or removing this right. In developed countries, the strategies of limitation may relate to factors such as the status of women, 'race suicide' theories, prohibition of parenting in certain sexual groups or eugenic arguments, whereas in developing countries intervention may be based on overpopulation or poverty. Whatever the tactics adopted, limitations of this sort seem to threaten the existence of a general, inalienable right to reproduce vested in the individual.

The struggle for reproductive choice which is central to the existence of a right to reproduce has also been conducted in other ways and may be threatened by relatively undramatic attempts to control the exercise of reproductive capacities. Whilst state discrimination in the area of, for example, compulsory sterilization has generated considerable concern and has contributed to the use of the terminology of rights, true reproductive liberty requires freedom of choice in other less obvious areas.

States, for example, may use the rhetoric of rights while actually interfering in insidious ways with the freedom of the individual to make choices. The clearest example of the denial of reproductive choice arises where competing interests are deemed to be more important. Notably, this conflict arises in the question of termination of pregnancies. Abortion, now regulated in most countries in a manner which makes it permissible under certain circumstances, is a clear example of state control over reproductive self-determination. The permitted ambit of choices in this area reflects a number of limitations on the freedom of people to reproduce or not. Those countries which have legalized abortion have generally done so only in certain circumstances which may relate to the health of the mother, the health of the foetus or the age of the foetus. However, at least in the UK and the USA, no absolute rights to terminate a pregnancy are given.

In America, the rights of the mother to opt for termination are circumscribed after the first trimester of the pregnancy by the interests of the state in maternal health or the right to life of the foetus.[35] In the UK, no practical rights are given to anyone but the doctors, who are required to satisfy themselves that the legal criteria have been met. The mother may request a termination, the father may not prevent it,[36] but the decision whether or not it can be obtained rests solely with the medical profession. Moreover, the individual's rights – such as they are in this area – are constantly subjected to attack from those with religious or other scruples who would seek to enforce their views on those who do not share them, and by political parties seeking the support of these – often powerful – groups in the community.

Freedom of choice in reproductive matters seems to be more obviously protected by the American than by the British approach to abortion. Following the landmark decision in *Roe* v. *Wade*,[37] American courts have offered a clear justification for limiting the mother's freedom of choice. Since competing interests may limit the practical availability of all human rights, there is no special vulnerability here. However, the British legislation makes abortion lawful only on the (somewhat disingenuous) basis of a kind of double-effect principle. That is, the terms of the Abortion Act do not recognize freedom of choice in these matters up to the point at which other rights may become more important, but permit of the harm of abortion in the vaguely defined situation where the mother's life or health are threatened by continuation of the pregnancy. Moreover, because choice is not central to the terms of the legislation, fathers are precluded totally from rights in this area: termination becomes dependent in most cases on the medical assessment of risk.

Access to birth control also remains central to the existence of the right to reproduce. Some states preclude such access on the grounds of religious dogma, whilst others offer it only to those of a certain age. In the recent case of *Gillick* v. *West Norfolk & Wisbech A.H.A.*,[38] the Court of Appeal precluded doctors from providing birth-control advice to girls under the age of sixteen without parental consent except in emergency situations. Not only does this minimize the rights of privacy of such girls, it places them in the invidious position of risking pregnancy when sexually active, and discriminates against them in the sense that contraceptive devices for men are readily available without major restriction. Interestingly, this decision stands in complete contrast to the American decision of *Griswold* v. *Connecticut*[39] in which it was said that 'the right to privacy in connection with decisions affecting procreation extends to minors as well as adults.'

The sum of these controls over reproductive self-determination must generate doubts as to whether or not there is, in fact, a meaningful right to reproduce. If the central part of that right relates to freedom of choice in the exercise of existing capacities, its impact may be substantially reduced even by the nature of these less overt interventions. Tracing the history of debates about choices in reproductive matters demonstrates both the centrality and the vulnerability of choice in this vital area of human behaviour. Even acknowledging that total reproductive self-determination is unlikely to be achieved, states may nonetheless seek to accord the right to reproduce as described above a real rather than a merely symbolic status.

In identifying the fundamentals of the right, and by exposing infringements, validity may also be given to the claim that the right encompasses more than merely the protection of existing capacities, and further that it is more specifically meaningful than the general right to self-determination. To talk of the right to reproduce further implies non-discrimination on grounds of status or sexual preference and demands realization through protection of choice, not only by respecting individual reproductive freedoms but by the consequential facilitation of the status of parenting or non-parenting.

The core of the right to reproduce, therefore, could be identified in two interrelated ways. First, that a person's capacities to reproduce are subject to his or her voluntary exercise and may not be interfered with, and second, that a person may choose whether or not to exercise existing capacities. If there is to be recognition of a right to reproduce, then each of these criteria must be acknowledged and acted upon by states. However, although the language of rights became important in this area largely as a result of active and passive state interference, the paradox is that the state is also the organization presently charged with the protection of rights. Thus, in translating capacity into 'right', ultimate control has inevitably been vested in the very organization whose practices demanded the use of the terminology of rights in the first place. The interest of states in ensuring procreation, in protecting the nuclear family or in ensuring that state resources are not dissipated by caring for the handicapped or disabled child or the child of 'unfit' parents, may still serve to limit the extent and exercise of the right to reproduce.

The benefits of referring to reproduction as a right, however, are that even while the state retains control, it becomes necessary to justify any proposed interference in some strict way. Mere whim will not suffice. States may ultimately interfere with the exercise of all human rights but, as for example with the right to life, it is necessary to have a compelling reason to do so. By using the language of rights in this area, the status of the capacity to procreate is enhanced and afforded some protection through due process of law.

Is, however, facilitation of reproduction by the state also necessarily demanded in recognition of a corresponding duty? Clearly, by depending on the state to protect freedom of choice in these matters, citizens do not necessarily have the status to demand that they are also rendered fertile. However, on the view of rights which emphasizes the special status, and interest in, breeding, the state may in fact be thought to have a duty not merely to protect existing capacities but also to facilitate reproduction. This could take a number of forms, from the facilitation of safe reproduction to legislation protecting men or women from discrimination on the basis of their reproductive capacities in, for example, education and employment. It may take the form of free and ready access to welfare benefits associated with reproduction and facilitation of the parenting process by making choices relatively free from economic or social pressures, it may require that states have a duty to find ways of circumventing infertility in order that those without the pre-existing capacity to procreate can also experience freedom of choice and the joys of parenting.

The first of these has been fought for in particular by women's groups arguing against biological discrimination. The second has depended on political views of the role which should be adopted by the state in providing subsidies for those who require financial assistance, and on economic factors. It is worthy of note at this point, however, that relatively recently courts in America have attempted to reintroduce compulsion in the matter of procreation by seeking to deny access to benefits unless they guarantee that they will not continue to reproduce.[40] The lack of success of such efforts further reinforces the view that it is not only parenting which is important to the right to reproduce: rather the freedom to choose is the core element. Clearly, however, the struggle for recognition of the right to reproduce is by no means concluded.

The last of the above possibilities has become meaningful relatively recently with technological advances in artificial fertilization. Thanks to modern high-technology medicine, some of those who were previously infertile may now be able to have a child or children. However, it is, to say the least, unlikely that the drive to generate such technology arose from the state's perception that implicit in the recognition of a right to reproduce was an inherent guarantee that facilitation of this sort was a duty of the state. Rather, developments reflect the capacity of medicine to expand the categories of people who may make choices about reproduction. Artificial fertilization is therefore a mechanism for creating the capacity to make a free choice, just as legalizing birth control recognizes the same freedom. An interesting side-effect of this facilitation, however, has been that private reproductive practices have once more become the subject of public debate. The current arguments about the morality of artificial fertilization, the legality or morality of surrogacy agreements and so on, have revitalized public debate about private practices, and once again have rendered the choices of some vulnerable to the moral, religious or political views of others.

Conclusion

It has been argued in this chapter that the use of the language of rights in this area of interest is a reaction to two main political thrusts. In its earliest stages, the rhetoric of rights was used to insist on a limited reproductive self-control. In the second phase, wholesale removal of existing capacities generated the use of the language of rights to reinforce arguments against such practices by reference to the kinds of overriding moral considerations which often characterize the discussion of human rights. An appeal to human rights rendered protection of these interests more likely in a century dominated by discussion of human rights, and the mechanisms for protection more efficient. The paradox remains, however, that it is primarily the behaviour of states which generated the need to make reference to reproduction in terms of human rights – either by removing capacities or by limiting freedom of choice – but it is also states which are now in the role of guarantors and limiters of the right itself. Indeed, perhaps the ultimate paradox is that these same states – by regarding orthodox medicine as a good in itself, and by not overtly scrutinizing the aims of medical and scientific research – have once more generated a situation in which the language of rights may become a necessary and integral part of the arsenal of those arguing for choice in reproductive practices. If states limit the availability of existing technology, they may once again leave themselves vulnerable to accusations of discrimination and denial of choice. The debate may have moved from the negative to the positive – that is from preventing conception to creating it – but the crucial question of freedom of choice remains at the forefront.

It may, therefore, be concluded that there can be identified the core and the scope of a right to reproduce, and that its status as a human right demands respect. The reality, however, is that the rhetoric of rights has limited practical value in this as in other areas. It is as a method of highlighting the problems of removing existing capacities that the language of rights has been most functional, demanding rationalization and justification. However, in other aspects of freedom of choice, the rhetoric of rights may have had less impact on reality.

Notes

1 For an excellent discussion of the development of the birth control movement in the USA, see Linda Gordon, *Woman's Body, Woman's Right* (Harmondsworth: Penguin, 1977).

2 Ibid., particularly ch. 5.

3 For a discussion of compulsory sterilization programmes in the USA, see David Meyers, *The Human Body and the Law* (Edinburgh: Edinburgh University Press, 1971), ch. 2.

4 For further discussion, see ch. 8 below; see also S.A.M. McLean and A.J. MacKay, 'Consent to Medical Treatment', in S.A.M. McLean (ed.), *Legal Issues in Medicine* (Aldershot: Gower, 1981).

5 *Thake* v. *Maurice* [1984] 2 All E.R. 513, 526.

6 See, for example, Lord Denning's comments in *Bravery* v. *Bravery* [1954] 3 All E.R. 59.

7 See, for example, the debates in the House of Commons and the House of Lords on the Medical Termination of Pregnancy Bill (now the Abortion Act, 1967).

8 For further discussion see Gordon, *Woman's Body*; recent debates in Ireland on this subject are also illustrative; see for example *The Times* 22 February 1985.

9 A principle which permits the doing of a morally good act, e.g. saving the life of a mother, even though it inevitably involves a morally bad outcome, e.g. the destruction of a foetus.

10 Cmnd 9314/1984 (the Warnock report).

11 See Gordon, *Woman's Body*.

12 See Meyers, *The Human Body*, ch. 2.

13 Gordon, *Woman's Body*, 134.

14 Universal Declaration of Human Rights, Article 1.

15 See, for example, *Buck* v. *Bell* 274 U.S. 200 (1927); *North Carolina Association for Retarded Children et al.* v. *State of North Carolina et al.* 420 F. Supp. 451 (1976).

16 Meyers, *The Human Body*, 29.

17 *Buck* v. *Bell*, 207.

18 For example, the right to life extends to the comatose, and it is still murder to kill a very young child who will have no conscious awareness of the right to life.

19 50 Idaho 763 (1931).

20 Gordon, *Woman's Body*, 114.

21 For example, World Medical Association Declaration of Helsinki 1964, revised in 1975 (human experiments).

22 431 U.S. 678.

23 316 U.S. 535.

24 As was noted in *Poe et al.* v. *Gerstein et al.* 517 F. 2d, 787 (1975): 'Skinner . . . did not guarantee the individual a procreative opportunity; it merely safeguarded his procreative potential from state infringement.'

25 See note 15, above.

26 *Katie Relf et al.* v. *Caspar Weinberger et al.; National Welfare Rights Organisation* v. *Casper Weinberger et al.* 372 F Supp. 1196 (1974).

27 [1976] 1 All E.R. 326.

28 See, for example, S.A.M. McLean and T.D. Campbell, 'Sterilisation', in McLean, *Legal Issues*, 179 *et seq.*

29 Universal Declaration of Human Rights, Article 16(3).

30 Lord Kilbrandon, 'The Comparative Law of Genetic Counseling', in B. Hilton,

D. Callahan, M. Harris, P. Condliffe and B. Berkely (eds), *Ethical Issues in Human Genetics* (New York: Plenum, 1973), 254.

31 *Thake* v. *Maurice*, 526.
32 405 U.S. 438 (1972), 453.
33 See, for example, *Carey* v. *Population Services International*, note 22, above.
34 Gordon, *Woman's Body*, 3.
35 *Roe* v. *Wade*, 410 U.S. 113 (1973).
36 *Paton* v. *B.P.A.S.* [1979] Q.B. 276.
37 See note 35, above.
38 (1985) 2 W.L.R. 413 (C.A.).
39 381 U.S. 479. This case has been used in many others to maximize the autonomy of minors; see, for example, *Planned Parenthood of Central Missouri* v. *Danforth* 428 U.S. 52 (1976), where it was noted that: '[c]onstitutional rights do not mature and come into being magically when one attains the State-defined age of majority.'
40 See, for example, *Walker & Brown* v. *Pierce* 562 F. 2d, 609 (1977).

7

The Rights of the Mentally Ill

Tom Campbell

The rights of the mentally ill are problematic because the humanity of those who have lost the capacity to reason may be questioned. Article 1 of the Universal Declaration of Human Rights begins with the resounding assertion that '[a]ll human beings are born free and equal in dignity and rights', which could be taken to imply that, in the realm of human rights, the mentally ill have the same status as everyone else. However, the Declaration then goes on to state that '[t]hey [all human beings] arc endowed with reason and conscience and should act towards one another in a spirit of brotherhood', thereby implicitly introducing, no doubt unintentionally, an element of uncertainty about the status of those who lack the intellectual and moral capacities upon which the assertion of brotherhood is said to be founded.

Thus even the most general rhetoric of human rights, although explicitly universalistic, seems to harbour the basis for depriving the mentally ill of fundamental rights. It may not be surprising therefore that it is so often assumed in practice that those who cannot be reasoned with, those whose deranged minds render them incapable of making sensible decisions for themselves, and those whose irrational conduct, unrestrained by normal moral inhibitions, makes them menacing to others, must be controlled, segregated and removed from ordinary social interactions, if necessary against their express and vehement protests. In developed societies 'madness' is now firmly associated with exclusion from human society, with all that entails for the restrictions of liberty, self-determination and self-expression: an approach to mental illness that is licensed by the European Convention on Human Rights which states, in article 5(1)(e) that, along with criminality, an 'unsound mind' is a valid reason for the forfeiture of physical freedom.

Historically, with the physical confinement of the mentally ill went the loss of other rights, such as freedom of expression, control of personal property and political participation. Significant vestiges of such rights-restrictions remain, particularly in the limitations placed on the rights of detained patients to refuse medical treatment, a power which, except in emergency situations, renders coerced medication or surgery an illegal assault in the case of the ordinary citizen. Moreover, it can be argued that the existence of special legislation covering mentally-disordered persons is in effect discriminatory and therefore contrary to Article 14 of the European Convention on Human Rights, insofar as it permits the deprivation of liberty on grounds which do not apply to other persons. To be mentally ill is to be at risk of a level of state interference that applies to few other human groups.

Nevertheless significant progress has been made in changing the conditions under which the mentally ill are confined and contained, and some of these improvements have been the consequence of a reassertion of the equal rights of all men and the acknowledgement that madness is a 'human condition'[1] which should not of itself negate the rights of its victims. This is achieved in part by stressing the 'normality' of the mentally disordered in that many mentally-ill people can be shown to retain capacities which are not different in kind from those of the so-called normal person. But, beyond this, the language of human rights as applied to the mentally ill can be used to make the point that mental illness may be a condition with its own validity in terms of self-determination. Thus the mentally ill may be said to have a right to be mentally ill, in that they should be entitled to follow out their own perception of reality in line with their own values and beliefs, even if these are not shared by the vast majority of their fellow citizens.[2]

Further, it can be argued that mental illness gives rise to special claims within human rights rhetoric, for, according to Article 25(1) of the Universal Declaration of Human Rights, '[e]veryone has the right to a standard of living adequate for the health and well-being of himself', which explicitly includes 'medical care and necessary social services'. Thus mental illness, along with other types of ill-health, can trigger the use of human rights rhetoric to claim that there is a societal duty to provide appropriate care and treatment. The language of rights and the rhetoric of human rights is increasingly used to demand that those who are mentally ill should receive adequate health care either within or, more and more, without mental hospitals.[3] The terminology used is that of the right to treatment, which, in the USA, is taken to cover not only the right of those committed to hospital for treatment to receive such treatment (or to be released)[4] but also the right of all mentally-ill persons to be cared for, in hospital if necessary, even involuntarily in certain circumstances.[5]

The ambiguous and varied implications for the human rights of the mentally ill which follow from the full acceptance of their humanity make it difficult to assess the relevance of human rights rhetoric to the situation of the mentally ill. The same measures which appear to some to be a violation of basic human rights may be seen by others as an achievement of a rights approach to mental illness. Much depends on the extent that rational self-determination is seen as the essential ingredient which serves as the guide to the essence or core of every human right. On such a presupposition the humanity, and hence the rights, of the mentally ill have to be defended in terms of their residual rationality, the stress being laid on their relative normality. But if a modifying assumption about the basis of rights is allowed, namely that some rights depend directly on our duty to relieve grievous and avoidable forms of human suffering, then the pursuit of human rights for the mentally ill may involve giving special consideration to this group of sufferers as an element in what it means to give recognition to their equal worth as human beings. The universality of human rights may then entail placing emphasis not only on the continuity of characteristics between the mentally ill and the mentally well but also on the particular needs and special claims of persons whose condition involves a great deal of suffering combined with a significant loss of the capacity to cope with the demands of everyday life in a modern society.

Humanity and Reason

Thinking about the human rights of the mentally ill raises in an acute form the question of what it is to be 'human'.

In the context of ascribing rights and duties within society 'human' is sometimes taken as an ideal or norm indicating what it is to be a person, a condition of full humanity whose fulfilment requires certain benefits and protections. On the other hand 'human' can be given a minimalist interpretation and the idea of human rights taken to mark out what are the essential bases for a tolerable existence for members of the species *homo sapiens*, a minimum which, moreover, if not met, can be grounds for justified civil disobedience, if not revolutionary action, to rectify injustice. In fact, the model of Man traditionally associated with those who favour civil rights is of a person somewhat beyond the 'norm' in the sense of the normal: an active, rational and entrepreneurial person for whom the life which is claimed is one in which there is a degree of self-expression, self-help and self-defence: the opportunity to have and to manage property, to communicate views and pursue happiness along individually chosen lines, to share in government and freely go about day-to-day activities without the interference of officials and prohibitions of the state beyond those strictly necessary for the defence of the rights of others. The human life thus envisaged is an active, 'fully human' existence of a sort which is exemplified by the political activist and the gainfully employed.[6]

On this 'rational-activist' model human rights relate to the basic requirements of a person capable of independent living and rational choice and action, Man the doer-and-chooser, autonomous Man. Rights derive from Man's rationality, an ability to 'see reason', to make decisions on the basis of reasons and conform actions to a plan of behaviour grounded in his or her own reasoning.[7] Within this model is contained the idea that some of these reasons relate not merely to self-interest but also to moral duties, which presupposes an intellectual capacity on the part of the individual to universalize the principles of his or her actions and determine whether or not the principles on which he or she might act are such as a 'reasonable' or 'normal' person would be prepared to see exemplified in the behaviour of all persons, a moral autonomy which is at once the highest form of human living and the most exalted ground for ascribing inalienable rights to human beings.[8]

The rational-activist view of humanity enters into the very conception of rights in which the traditional human rights are usually articulated. Through the institution of rights, Man-the-chooser is given a particularly important type of choice by which he may control the actions of others in relation to himself. These choices are rights, for to possess a right is to be given the power to restrict the action of others, if one chooses to do so. To have a right is to have the moral or legal power to require others to act or refrain from acting in a certain way towards oneself. On this view, a right is an opportunity to be used as a person wills for purposes of his or her own choosing. Paradigmatically property rights entitle property owners to require others to refrain from entering into or using their property, it being also of central importance that they may, if they choose, give others permission to do both.

This analysis of what it is to be the bearer of a right is problematic in the case of the mentally ill who, by definition, are defective in the very characteristics which are highlighted by the autonomy theory. Various attempts have been made to accommodate the mentally ill to the autonomy model of human rights but none of them have been entirely successful in avoiding the conclusion that mental illness is inevitably associated with some deprivation of rights.

One such attempt takes the paternalistic line that the mentally ill are to be regarded as children and therefore have the reduced rights of this sort of incapax person. This involves comparing, for instance, those suffering from senile dementia with very young children, and by analogy all mentally-ill people are then regarded as lacking in the characteristics which give rights to adult humans. On the autonomy model the rights of children are reduced in proportion to their capacities, and similarly the mentally ill may be said to have rights only insofar as they approximate to the condition of the mentally-normal adult. Further the special rights of children, with respect to education for instance, can be accounted for by saying that these rights are necessary to enable children to develop into fully human, that is autonomous, persons. Similarly the mentally ill may be ascribed special rights insofar as intervention in their lives can help to return them to a condition in which they can resume the role of autonomous persons.

With the possible exception of the psychogeriatric, the mentally ill cannot be regarded as sufficiently like children for this analogy to serve as a guide to establishing their status as rights-bearers. Quite apart from the fact that mental illness is not a readily identifiable and objective characterization like that of age, many mentally-ill persons are manifestly not like children. For instance the loss of coherent mental functioning in paranoid schizophrenia is not equivalent to a regression to the reasoning abilities of a child. Such illness may require us to override the wishes of the sufferers but this cannot be justified on the grounds that they are like children.

Of course, the fact that the mentally ill are not like children can be used as a basis for granting them full rights, but this is really to abandon the analogy with children. It is true that in the case of those mental illnesses, such as schizophrenia, hysteria and manic

depression, which are often episodic, the temporary nature of the condition is relevant to the duration of any rights-deprivations that may be
imposed. Further the autonomy model can provide an objective for
successful treatment of mental illness, namely the re-establishment of
the capacity for rational choice. But the general thrust of this line of
thought is that mental illness is a rights-diminishing status and the
analogy with children does not provide us with a basis for ascribing
special rights to those suffering from non-episodic mental illnesses.
The autonomy theorist who wishes to defend the idea of the equal
rights of the mentally ill may, therefore, take another approach and
seek to discern at least some of the capacities for rational choice in
those categories of mentally-ill persons to whom he or she would
attribute human rights. Thus it has been objected to some forms of
institutional regime that they unnecessarily restrict patient-choices in
matters on which many mentally-ill people are perfectly capable of
making up their own minds despite their need for psychiatric
treatment. On this basis it has been argued that there is no need to
have a general restriction on patients' right to vote, or have any more
than the normal controls on letter writing and other forms of
communication.[9] This approach amounts to saying that insofar as the
mentally ill remain normal they ought to retain the rights of the
ordinary citizen, a very important point which has to some measure
been taken into account in the extension of civil rights to patients in
mental hospitals.

This line of argument gains considerable backing from the work
which has been done to break down the assumption that there is a
clear demarcation line between mental sickness and mental health.
The lack of consistency in medical diagnosis and the behavioural
nature of many of the characteristic symptoms of mental illness have
enabled powerful attacks on the whole idea of mental illness as an
objectively definable mental condition.[10] Without fully accepting
these arguments, it is noteworthy that the standard symptoms of
mental illness are extrapolations from the variations in the thoughts,
feelings and actions of ordinary human beings. This casts considerable
doubt on any attempt to deal with the mentally ill as a class apart on
the basis of the effects of their illness on the capacities in virtue of
which the autonomy model attributes human rights.

Further, despite the tendency of the autonomy model to stress the
idealized characteristics of Man as definitive of his humanity, a more
minimalist view, which still retains the idea that rationality and

choice are central to what it is to be human, can be used to enable the mentally ill to be brought within the ambit of human rights. 'Rational' may be interpreted as being opposed either to 'non-rational' or to 'irrational', that is, it may be taken to refer to the possession of the capacity to reason at all or to the capacity to reason well. It can then be argued that the attribution of human rights depends on the presence of reason in the weaker sense in which there is no requirement to reach any significant standard of normative rationality.

Such an interpretation of the 'rationality' involved in humanness is in line with the established libertarian position that persons should be free to make mistakes.[11] The right to self-determination is not in general contingent on its reasonable use but is a basic principle of liberty. There are limits of course to our freedom in that we cannot use this freedom to violate the rights of others and the mentally ill are no different here from other persons. Thus confinement of those proven to be dangerous, whether or not they are mentally ill, may not of itself be problematic for the libertarian. Even in the realm of self-protection, it has not always been the case that people have been viewed as having a right to kill themselves, although the strictly libertarian view is that people should not be interfered with purely for their own good. But this principle is clearly breached in the case of the mentally ill who are normally not only prevented from killing themselves on the grounds that they are not rational but are often treated against their wishes in many other ways. Different standards are applied routinely to the mentally ill in terms of paternalistic self-protection.

On this basis it can be argued that the 'irrational' choices of the mentally ill should be respected, making the sole cause of detention and forced medication and treatment the protection of the rights of others. The argument would be that their view of reality is their own and that this authenticates it in relationship to their own choices. On this view there is a right to be psychotic as there is a right to hold and practise a religious belief, however irrational such a belief may appear to others. Delusions, hallucinations, bizarre beliefs and practices are not in themselves grounds for rights-restrictions whether or not they are symptoms of mental illness. If Man's rationality is a broadly defined capacity which gives him rights which are not dependent on his always reasoning correctly then it may be argued that it is an unwarranted injustice to the mentally ill if their irrationalities are taken as a good reason for limiting their human rights when such standards are not applied to the mentally well.

This is perhaps the strongest type of argument that the autonomy theorist can use to defend the equal rights of the mentally ill, in that, if successful, it would secure the same rights for the mentally disordered as for the mentally normal, thus eliminating the charge of discrimination. The crucial dividing line would then be between those who are so disordered that they must be classified as non-rational rather than merely irrational, which is really a matter of mental handicap rather than mental illness, the former group having no status in terms of human rights and the latter group having full status.

Apart from its implied exclusion of the incapax the chief weakness of the autonomy approach is that it fails to take any significant account of the particular problems of the mentally ill or to found any reasons for protecting the interests of the mentally ill on the nature of mental illness. Inevitably therefore the tendency is for the autonomy theorist who seeks to extend the rights of the mentally ill to deny that there is such a thing as mental illness or to emphasize the 'normality' of the mentally ill, rather than their distinctive characteristics and difficulties. Whether or not the conditions that are called mental illness are properly classified as medical conditions does not alter the fact that many forms of mental 'illness', while they do not eliminate the individual's capacity for taking thought and making choices, so affect the coherence of their thoughts, the credibility of their beliefs and the relevance of their choices to their actual situation as to call into question the significance of their autonomy as a basis for the sort of absolute and inalienable liberties which are at the heart of the traditional human rights rhetoric. When this is coupled with the fact that in many cases these mental disorders involve a degree of misery and suffering which 'normal' people may find it hard to imagine, it can be argued that the reality of the human experiences involved in many mental disorders calls for special consideration to be given to the needs of the mentally ill. This the autonomy model is unable to do. There are, therefore, significant limits to what it has to offer this class of persons by way of its conception of human rights. By suggesting that the retention of rights depends on the vestiges of rationality or the denial of the significance of the forms of irrationality involved in mental illness, the autonomy approach does not address the important issue of whether or not the mentally ill have fundamental rights relating to their condition.[12]

To establish that mental illness gives rise to rights which are fundamental enough to be designated human rights and hence feature as reasons for creating non-defeasible obligations to protect the mentally ill it is necessary, when interpreting human rights rhetoric, to take a view of the nature of the humanness which centres on the capacity for suffering, the essential correlative obligations being to relieve the suffering of those who are in no position to help themselves. This in turn requires an analysis of rights which dispenses with the necessity for the element of choice on the part of the rights-holder in every case and regards a right as a rule-defended interest which makes obligatory certain types of action or inaction which are to the benefit of the rights-holders.[13]

This interest or benefit theory of rights is in any case more suited to the social and economic rights which are gaining acceptance as part of the corpus of human rights.[14] In addition, not all civil and political rights fit readily into the autonomy model. The inalienability of certain civil rights has often been taken to mean not only that the opportunity to make certain choices cannot be taken away from the right-holder, but also that other persons have an absolute duty to refrain from harming the right-holder in specified ways. In such cases the element of choice is said to come in by way of remedial action, in that the right-holder, if he or she chooses, may obtain redress against the right-violator. But even this secondary role of rights-related choice, where the choice is not part of the right but an ingredient in the remedy, cannot apply to all rights, and particularly it does not apply to the most basic right of all, the right to life. In the case of the right to life, not only have others an absolute duty not to kill the right-holder, whether or not he or she demands this of them, but the initiation of the remedy for the violation of the right is not and could not be in the hands of the (deceased) victim. Indeed, in all cases where violations of human rights are appropriately treated as criminal offences, the element of victim participation is usually minimal. This is no mere debating point since it brings out that the vital factor about the right to life is the protection of life itself rather than anything to do with the preservation or exercise of choice as such. Similar points may be made about such social and economic rights as the right to an education, the right to work and the right to adequate health care, none of which have to be respected only via the medium of rights-holders' choices but all of which relate to the provision of suitable and available services, whether or not they are provided only on demand.

Once the relief of the avoidable suffering of persons who are unable to help themselves is accepted as a basis for human rights, it is possible to take a direct view of the interests of the mentally ill which fall to be protected by the institution of fundamental rights and so attract priority allocation of resources. To limit the principle that suffering gives rise to rights to those sufferers who are unable to help themselves includes those distressed mentally-ill persons who, by reason of their mental condition, are unable to take the steps to alleviate their sufferings which are available to other people. This is not, however, to revert to the autonomy model, since the inability to act 'rationally' is not being taken as a reason for removing rights but is, on the contrary, an element which is operative within the attribution of certain rights.

Clearly it is not easy to say what degree of suffering combined with what degree or type of incapacity for self-help should attract such high moral significance. Moreover, to introduce suffering-based rights does not in itself negate autonomy-based rights, so that a mentally-ill person may have two conflicting rights. The diminution of the element of choice in the core of such rights as the right to receive appropriate medical treatment will mean that conflicts will arise between such a right and the liberty-rights which stem from the undeniably important value of self-determination for rational beings. Indeed, this conflict is at the heart of the problem of how to treat the mentally ill.

Such conflict may not be severe on the narrow autonomy model according to which moderately high standards of 'rationality' are used to determine who may be the bearer of rights, since the conditions which give rise to the incapacity to help oneself will largely coincide with the capacity for making rational choices. However, on a minimalist autonomy model, the conflict of rights will be more evident, since this model implies that even the self-destructive choices of irrational human beings should be given a degree of respect.

Civil Commitment

Adopting an interest theory of rights which stresses the importance of the alleviation of suffering has the merit of directing attention to the prevention of mental illness and not simply to the treatment of those who are currently suffering from it. It is significant perhaps that, in all jurisdictions, mental-health legislation is focussed much more on the latter than the former. Nevertheless this legislation is central to any study of the reality of such rights as are allocated, at present, to the mentally ill,[15] and much recent legislation can be seen as a working-out of the idea that mental illness should not be a right-less condition. This section will explore the tension between autonomy-based and suffering-based rights in relation to the civil commitment of the mentally disordered. The next section will deal with the rights of those so detained to refuse treatment. These sections will bring out the ambivalent position of the state as both the main hope for, and the principal threat to, the rights of the mentally ill.

Questions about the human rights status of the mentally ill tend to be relegated to a subsidiary place in traditional debates about mental-health legislation which, understandably enough, have concentrated on the danger of forcible intervention in the lives of those who are said to be, but are not, mentally ill. Given the potentially serious consequences for the individual who is classified as 'mad', 'lunatic', 'insane' or 'mentally disordered', the process of making such classifications has given rise to much concern, largely on account of the fear that sane persons might find themselves stripped of certain basic rights, a prospect as unacceptable to the public mind as that of convicting and punishing innocent persons. Instances of families having their eccentric and troublesome members 'put away', and the plight of 'sane persons in insane places'[16] has given rise to repeated attempts to ensure that such enormities do not happen.

Thus, in the UK and generally in the USA and in most Western countries, although applications for admission to, and detention in, a mental hospital may be, and often still are, made by relatives, they must be supported by recommendations from medical practitioners who have recently examined the 'patient' and who have no pecuniary interest in, or family connection with, him or her. Applications for compulsory admissions to hospital are either submitted to a court for approval (as in Scotland and in many US states) or are subject to review by appeal to the courts.[17] Interestingly the rights of periodic appeal to an independent tribunal on the part of those detained as 'restricted' patients following criminal proceedings have been enacted in the UK only recently following a number of cases being taken to the European Court of Human Rights.[18]

In line with the move towards equal consideration of the interests of the mentally disordered it is now accepted, at least in law, that mental illness is not in itself a sufficient reason for loss of rights. Various other requirements have to be satisfied before, for instance, a person may be detained in a psychiatric hospital, made subject to a guardianship order or accorded some other diminished legal status. For instance the Mental Health (Scotland) Act, 1984, which in this respect is substantially the same as its English & Welsh equivalent, the Mental Health Act, 1983, represents the situation in most Western jurisdictions. In essence the 1984 Act lays down that a person may be admitted to hospital and there detained if:

   a he is suffering from a mental disorder which is of a nature or degree which makes it appropriate for him to receive medical treatment in a hospital; and
   b it is necessary for the health and safety of that person or for the protection of other persons that he should receive such treatment, and
   c it cannot be provided unless he is detained in hospital.[19]

This makes it clear that mental illness alone does not make a person liable to detention. Further it is explicitly stated elsewhere in the Act that mental illness does not include sexual deviance or alcoholism *per se*, although no guidance is given as to the controversial issue of how mental illness is to be positively defined.[20] It may therefore appear that Mental Health Acts of this sort do not discriminate against the mentally ill and exemplify the recognition that the mentally ill possess full human rights. This is not, however, borne out either by a more stringent examination of the law or by observing what happens in its practical application.

The legal threat to the rights of the mentally ill is that there are special rules which apply to controlling them which do not apply to the mentally well. While mental illness is not a sufficient ground for rights-restrictions, it is a necessary condition for the application of rules which permit restrictions on liberty, either for the health and safety of the person in question or for the protection of others, of a type which do not apply to the ordinary citizen. For instance, outside emergency situations, and apart from very specific quarantine regulations for the control of infectious diseases, ordinary citizens may not be detained either for their own health and safety or for the protection of others (unless they have been charged with a criminal offence).

To follow this point further it is necessary to make a sharp distinction between the paternalistic (welfare of the patient) and the police (protection of others) grounds for detention, an obvious and important distinction which is often blurred in civil commitment rules.

It is accepted that there is no violation of human rights when a person is, after conviction in a court of law, imprisoned for a period of time which is thought to be proportional to the gravity of the offence for reasons which include the protection of others against the harmful actions that he or she might perform when at liberty. In the case of the mentally ill, however, they are liable to be detained, without conviction, on police grounds solely on the basis of a prediction of their dangerousness, and when courts make hospital orders against convicted persons who are thought to be mentally disordered these often result in open-ended periods of incarceration which usually turn out to be considerably longer than is the case with persons sent to prison.[21]

Such differential treatment of the mentally-ill dangerous person cannot be justified either by any general correlation between mental illness and dangerousness (there is none), or by the scientific accuracy of predictions of future dangerous behaviour in the case of the mentally ill as opposed to the mentally disordered (predictions of dangerousness are very unreliable for both categories).[22] Moreover, the alleged dangerousness of the mentally ill as a group, or the accuracy of the predicted dangerousness of individually mentally-ill people, is not relevant to the point that the possessor of human rights is entitled to be treated as an individual and not as a member of a group, and that it is a violation of human rights to apply a rule which disadvantages members of one group unless the same rule is applied to members of other groups. If unconvicted mentally-ill persons identified as being dangerous can be incarcerated then the same considerations should be sufficient to incarcerate the mentally well. If indeterminate sentences are applied to possibly dangerous mentally-ill persons then this should be the case for all other convicted and possibly dangerous persons. That this is not in fact the case is an example of the way in which the assumed non-rationality of mentally-ill people is still thought to be sufficient grounds to treat them as less than the sort of beings to whom ordinary human rights apply.

It might be argued that there is one crucial and relevant characteristic which marks out the mentally-ill from the non-mentally-ill dangerous person, namely that the former are treatable, whereas the latter are not, so that we may effect a cure in the case of the mentally-ill dangerous person which justifies this distinctive form of intervention, a practice which gains added support from the fact that it is in general desirable to cure illness. Again, however, the factual basis for this view is ill-founded, since drugs and behaviour therapy can affect the conduct of 'healthy' as well as 'ill' persons. Rather, it is that we are prepared to accept certain methods of altering behaviour in the case of those regarded as mentally ill which we are not prepared to see applied to ordinary, rational persons. This may be explicable, given public fears of the mentally disordered which makes it difficult to release any mentally-ill person who is thought to present any sort of threat to the community. These fears provide strong utilitarian reasons for placing special restrictions on the potentially dangerous mentally ill but they are not a factor which has overriding weight in the sphere of human rights whose express purpose is often to protect individuals against the effects of public policies which are to the advantage of majorities but inflict unjustified liabilities on individuals and minorities.

Again, while it is clear that certain mentally-ill people are dangerous on account of their mental illness (symptoms of which may include, for instance, paranoid beliefs which lead to aggressive behaviour, or, in the case of schizophrenia, hearing voices which tell the sufferer to commit specified illegal acts, while other forms of mental illness clearly affect an individual's ability to control his or her behaviour), the relevance of such matters to the proper detention of people is separable from whether or not they are symptoms of a mental illness. The erroneous beliefs of mentally-healthy persons can render them equally dangerous to the rest of society. If such factors can be shown to be causally operative in the production of harmful and illegal acts then they have an undeniable relevance to measures which may be taken to protect society, measures which need involve no violation of human rights. What is questionable from the point of view of equal rights is the application of radically different standards in the assessment of dangerousness as between the mentally ill and the mentally well, as when predictive dangerousness alone is taken to be sufficient for the detention of the mentally ill but not for other people, or when mentally-ill offenders alone are liable to indeterminate physical restriction, or are kept in confinement on a lower risk of harm to others than is the case with the mentally-well offender.

It is hard to see how such systematic discrimination against the mentally ill can be justified on the grounds of the protection of others. It is also difficult to reconcile this approach with the idea that the mentally ill are full members of humanity for the purpose of the ascription of human rights. The autonomy theorist who wishes to defend the status of the mentally ill by arguing that they partake sufficiently of rationality to be deserving of equal respect must take the view that existing laws are violations of the rights of the mentally ill. On the other hand, discriminatory laws of this type may actually be justified on such a theory of human rights by using the non-rationality of the mentally ill to classify them as non-persons for human rights purposes, for discrimination on police grounds may not be out of line with the rational-activist view of the basis of human rights.

This line of argument will be thought misconceived by those who regard the treatment of persons who are both dangerous and mentally ill in hospital as a humane alternative to their detention in prison, a view which seems in line with the avoidable-suffering model of human rights. However, while it may indeed be preferable to confine mentally-ill offenders in mental hospitals, even if these do not differ in their liberty-restricting characteristics from actual prisons (special or state 'hospitals' are in many respects rather euphemistically so called), this does not meet the point that, by the standards applied to the ordinary offender, such persons should not be detained at all. At this point in the argument it is often claimed that it is in the interests of the patient to be so confined because, in the absence of treatment, further criminal acts may be committed to the detriment not only of the victim but also of the ill person. The alternative of continued detention in hospital is therefore preferred to further appearances in court on criminal charges. Thus it is often said that to empty the hospitals is simply a way of filling the prisons. This is of course a non-sequitur in that a mentally-ill offender who is released and who reoffends can be returned to hospital rather than sent to prison, and this may be thought to be a more acceptable form of revolving door. Few would argue that the fact that a normal offender is released from prison and reoffends shows that he or she ought not to have been released from prison in the first place.

Other considerations apply, however, when we assess the use of paternalistic justifications for the confinement of the mentally ill for their own health or safety when they are suffering from a mental illness of a nature or degree that makes it appropriate for them to be treated in hospital. While this may appear to be an even more blatant violation of the principle of equal treatment than differential police rules, since ordinary citizens are never forcibly treated except in highly-restricted emergency situations, it seems more defensible to restrict liberty for the welfare of the restricted individual than it is to apply the same restrictions for the benefit of others, particularly in cases where considerable suffering can be alleviated by so doing.

Interestingly, this rationale for the civil commitment of the mentally ill is strongly at variance with the basis on which an autonomy theorist may seek to grant the mentally ill full human rights status. On the rational-activist model the central justification for the attribution of human rights is self-determination, which is precisely what is being denied to those who are forcibly detained and are forcibly treated.

We have seen that there may be no real problem here in relation to those mentally-ill people who are genuinely incapax in that they are not capable of even primitive types of self-determination due to their complete lack of comprehension of the world around them. In such cases treatment and confinement are matters of acting without the consent of the patients rather than against their wishes, for they have no relevant articulable wishes. This is more or less the case for a considerable proportion of the substantial number of elderly mentally ill suffering from senile dementia and those who combine mental illness with mental handicap. Such persons may reasonably be regarded as non-persons from the point of view of most human rights, thus lending some plausibility to the autonomy theorist's position, although it is equally plausible to attribute to them the right to be cared for in conditions of incapacity.

We have also seen that the autonomy theorist may also be able to account for the moral propriety of some cases of detention for treatment where we are dealing with highly episodic illnesses. This form of intervention may be justified, on the rational-activist model, by saying that it is a means of returning the person to a normal self-determining way of life from which the illness temporarily removes him or her, although not all autonomy theorists would accept intervention even in these cases.

However, if this were the sole good reason for paternalistic civil commitment and treatment which was allowable in terms of the rhetoric of human rights, it would not be sufficient to justify the extensive use of the paternalistic power to enforce treatment on the mentally ill. In the first place, such treatment is given to those with chronic as well as episodic illness. Second, the effects of the drugs given to alleviate psychotic symptoms are often such as to diminish capacities for the sort of autonomous rational actions which is the proposed justification for such intervention. Third, it is evident that the health which is protected by compulsory intervention is not always directly related to the ability to live a self-determined life, but is often much more directly concerned with the reduction of suffering, particularly in the case of endogenous depression. Many observers also maintain that some treatment which is actually given to detained patients has as a primary purpose making the patient more amenable to hospital routine, something which has little bearing on, and may even run counter to, the encouragement of autonomy, although it may make institutional life more supportable.[23]

Without accepting that existing practice is by any means always defensible, the suffering-based model of rights is helpful in enabling us to explore, in terms of the rights of the mentally ill, those paternalistic welfare grounds which may justify the detention of some mentally-ill persons. This enables us to distinguish clearly between detention on welfare grounds, which must be based on the rights of the mentally ill, and detention on police grounds, which can be justified only on the basis of the rights of other persons.

Major problems can arise, however, if we too readily accept the suffering-based model of human rights to justify coercive intervention in the lives of those mentally-ill persons who are clearly distressed, on the grounds that they have a right to such treatment, for the existence of this right is patently open to abuse in that it means that there is to hand a ready rationalization for the compulsory treatment of persons of high nuisance value to the rest of society. Moreover, in the assessment of what counts as 'suffering', it is easy for those with responsibility for making the relevant recommendations to assume and follow tacitly their own ideas as to what constitutes a tolerable quality of life. That is, suffering can be projected on to those who have unusual ways of life with which they themselves are not greatly dissatisfied.

Quite apart from the genuine difficulty of making interpersonal assessments of the quality of lives, it is clear that there is at the very least an apparent conflict between the state's duty to provide care and the state's duty to protect all its citizens against deprivations of liberty merely for the convenience of others or in order to control social expenditure. The ambivalent role of the *de facto* authority vested in psychiatric institutions, which may be regarded as existing both for the welfare of patients and for the good of other citizens who require to be protected against at least some of these same patients, is a prime example of the tension between seeing the state both as a guarantor of human rights (in this case welfare rights) and as a prime suspect in the violation of human rights (in this case the rights to liberty and bodily integrity).

The Right to Treatment

A similar duality in the role of the state with respect to the rights of the mentally ill can be traced in the area of consent to treatment.

Entirely new provisions have recently been introduced in the UK concerning consent to treatment by detained patients. Following lines already set out in mental health legislation in the USA, both the English and the Scottish Acts seek to define the limited circumstances in which the wishes of detained patients may be overridden with respect to treatment.[24] This has been a grey area in which, without any clear legal basis, detained patients had been routinely subjected to compulsory treatment. Moreover mental patients, along with other types of patient, had little protection in law against medical practitioners withholding information concerning the risks of the treatment to which they did give their (uninformed) consent.[25]

The Acts distinguish between three types of treatment to which different rules apply.[26]

The first type is 'any surgical operation for destroying brain tissue or for destroying the function of brain tissue' and 'other such forms of treatment as may be specified . . . by the Secretary of State' (such as hormone implants) which require both the consent of the patient and the second opinion of a psychiatrist specially appointed for the purpose to the effect that the treatment is likely to alleviate or prevent a deterioration of the patient's condition, together with the opinion of two appointed lay persons to the effect that the patient is capable of understanding the nature and purpose and likely effects of the treatment and has consented to it.

The second type of treatment covers:

the administration of medicine to a patient by any means . . . at any time during a period for which he is liable to be detained . . . if three months or more have elapsed since the first occasion in that period when medicine was administered to him by any means for his mental disorder

and 'such forms of treatment as may be specified . . . by the Secretary of State' (such as electro-convulsive therapy). These require either the consent of the patient (such consent being again verified by the specially appointed medical practitioner) or a second opinion from the same source to the effect that 'having regard to the likelihood of its alleviating or preventing deterioration of his condition, the treatment should be given'.

The third category consists of all other types of treatment, it being stated that the consent of the patient is not required for treatment which is not covered by the above provisions. It should be noted that 'urgent' treatment, which is broadly enough defined to cover reversible and non-hazardous treatment which prevents patients from behaving violently or being a danger to themselves or others, is excluded from the restrictions on treatment without consent.

The first thing to note about these rules is that, where the patient's consent is given, this is (subject to certain checks in some cases) taken as valid, so that there is no general assumption that those detained for treatment are unable to give consent. However, although the most stringent protection is given in the case of those forms of treatment which permanantly affect the patient's rational capacities, this is not a form of treatment that can readily be defended in terms of increasing the autonomy of the patient. Further it is clear that a major consideration in licensing compulsory treatment is the relief of suffering which is felt to outweigh the patient's wishes. While this may well be justifiable, it does not fit readily into the rational-activist model of human rights. Importantly, such rules allow the patient's will to be overborne in the case of electro-convulsive therapy, a treatment to which many patients have a strong aversion despite its claimed therapeutic success in relieving depression, at least in the short term.

It would therefore appear that, despite the initial assumption that detained patients can give valid consent to treatment, the general import of the rules is to permit the refusal of consent to be overruled by medical opinion, presumably on the grounds that such refusal is irrational from the point of view of the patient's health or incompatible with the reasons for which the person is detained. Further, the provision which allows for all other forms of treatment to be given to detained patients without their consent, when prior to the enactments in question this was dubiously the case in law, in effect means that the overall consequence of the legislation may be to increase the use of compulsory treatment. Thus a piece of legislation which appears to offer enhancement to the human rights of the mentally ill may in practice run exactly counter to some people's view of what the rhetoric of human rights requires when applied to the situation of the mentally ill.

However, while these points can be used to cast doubt on the alleged increase in the rights of mentally-ill persons, this is only so if human rights are assumed to be based, as the autonomy theorist holds, solely on the moral demands of the rational individual for self-determination. If we take a different view, that another relevant consideration is the relief of suffering, which may then be given potential priority over self-determination, it is possible to see the restrictions on the legal capacity of the mentally ill to refuse treatment as a way of realizing their human rights, in this case their right to health services appropriate to their needs. Thus it may be argued that it is a feature of many forms of mental illness of a psychotic type that patients do not have any real insight into the nature of their illness and consequently are unable to appreciate what can be done for the relief of their suffering. In such cases we may speak of the right to be treated against one's will, irrespective of whether or not this contributes to the present or future autonomy of the patient.

Once we have taken this step the whole matter of compulsory treatment on paternalistic grounds may seem much less at odds with the idea that all human beings, including the mentally ill, are equally the possessors of human rights. It becomes no longer necessary to indulge in intellectual convolutions to show that such compulsory treatments as we approve of can be interpreted as contributing to patient autonomy, for we can instead appeal to the more straight-forward consideration that they enable the alleviation of avoidable human suffering on the part of helpless victims. This leaves it still to be determined what weight should be given to the relief of avoidable suffering over respect for the wishes of patients, but there are advantages to presenting this issue as a balancing of rights rather than as a boundary of rights.

For instance, this presentation of the difficult choices which arise in connection with the right to refuse treatment brings out, in a way which is not the case in the Acts themselves, that there is a clear line to be drawn between compulsory treatment to relieve suffering and the same treatment when it is given to control the patient who is thought to be a danger to others. The same difficulties to which attention was drawn in connection with police grounds for the detention of mentally-disordered persons apply to compulsory treatment on police grounds for patients in hospital, particularly for patients whose detention is based on paternalistic rather than police grounds. Thus the sedation of allegedly dangerous mentally-ill persons is clearly questionable if such treatment is not also given in the case of allegedly dangerous persons who are not mentally ill.

Of course the fact that we permit such interventions even on paternalistic grounds in the case of the mentally ill but not, for instance, in the case of those physically-ill persons who are thought to be misguided in their refusal of treatment, might also be considered discriminatory, but since the interests which are in effect protected are those of the mentally ill, the discrimination is against the ordinary citizen and not against the mentally ill. Moreover there is a distinctiveness about the vulnerability and helplessness of the mentally ill which relates to their diminished capacity for making effective choices in the interests of their own welfare and which may justify the idea that mental illness, where it gives rise to genuine distress, is a basis for distinctive rights claims. To this extent rational-activist theorist are correct in asserting the relevance of the capacity for rational choice to the rights of the mentally ill, but they are mistaken as to its implications, which are to enhance, not diminish, the rights of the mentally ill. To conceptualize the matter in this way is an important protection against the use of compulsory measures for the mentally ill in a discriminatory manner for the benefit of other persons.

A final point worth noting in this context is that, despite their clear weaknesses, the new rules relating to consent to treatment do explicitly give mental patients certain rights to informed consent which are not yet secured for the mentally well.[27] If this is due to the peculiar vulnerability of the mentally ill then it is a welcome example of the idea that the rights of the mentally ill may include special protections and facilities, and are not simply a matter of the right not to be discriminated against.

Conclusion

The unease which human rights theorists may feel towards this apparently complacent view of the practice of paternalistic intervention, and its compatibility with the rhetoric of human rights, may stem in part from the fact that this view of human rights takes us in the direction of seeing rights in terms of the positive duties of states to provide for the welfare of their citizens. This is indeed the case, and the prime consequence of adopting an interest theory of the rights of the mentally disordered may be to direct attention to the removal of the causes of stress and mental illness in society. However, even those who do not want to deny the state this welfare function may not wish to articulate such governmental duties in terms of human rights because of the prior use of human rights rhetoric as a means for resisting the encroachment of the state on the life of the individual. If the language of human rights can be used to justify not only major social improvements but also such dramatic intervention by the state in the lives of the mentally ill, may it not also be used to justify similar interventions in the lives of ordinary citizens who are thought to be acting against their own interests, particularly given the shadowy boundary between mental illness and mental health? For this reason, even if the treatment given to the mentally ill is welcomed, there may be reluctance to see this as a matter of giving them their human rights.

This line of thought may depend not so much on the principle that human beings should be left with their rights intact even although this results in extreme suffering, but on the fear that to allow government action to be based on such paternalism is to invite abuse. That there is some justification for this view may be seen from the fact that one result of the consent to treatment provisions of recent legislation may be to give hospitals more, not less, control over their detained (and hence indirectly all) their patients. Hospitals may then use this to make their institutions more manageable, an understandable enough objective given that those detained in mental hospitals are often there because of their nuisance value to the rest of society, but not one which can be defended in terms of the rights of non-consenting individuals.

This possibility may incline us to adopt the autonomy model of human rights in combination with an assertion of the validity of the no doubt idiosyncratic rationality of the mentally ill. But an alternative to this theoretically shaky thesis is to tighten up the criteria for paternalistic non-voluntary treatment so that it is not permitted merely for the 'health and safety' of the patient but only for 'the relief of extreme avoidable suffering'. This then would become the core of the right to treatment.

Carrying out this proposal would require careful elucidation of the concept of suffering and the formulation of realistic criteria for what is to count as suffering for these purposes. This would not be an easy task but it is a necessary one if we are to reduce the practice of compulsory intervention in the lives of persons whose behaviour is out of the ordinary and 'irrational' in terms of the standard norms of society, but which is not a cause of serious distress to the person concerned. There is an ever-present danger that the 'health' which is pursued in the treatment of what is classified as mental illness is merely an imposition of socially conditioned standards of 'normality' rather than a condition which is thought to be undesirable by the person who is said to be ill.

If the use of human rights discourse is denied to those who seek to make general demands for adequate assistance to be given to the mentally ill, then there is a risk of perpetuating a situation in which the resources allocated to the care of the mentally ill are grossly inadequate and quite disproportionately less than the sums of money spent on other forms of human malady. Indeed, if attention is turned from the traditional human rights which relate to the liberty of the individual to those examples which encapsulate the moral demand for positive action to be taken on behalf of deprived persons, then it can be said that only very modest progress has been made towards realizing such rights for the mentally ill who remain near the bottom of the priority-ordering in all Western societies, particularly with regard to the evident need for better facilites to care for such persons in the community. The fact that the realization of the positive right to treatment in accordance with the needs of the mentally ill will place the definition of what constitutes a violation of such human rights at the mercy of political and economic considerations is a price which might have to be paid for the instrumental usefulness of being able to draw on the rhetoric of human rights to expose the unnecessary deprivations of a section of the population that is little understood and poorly placed to fight on its own behalf.

Notes

1 The phrase is taken from the influential book, Larry Gostin, *A Human Condition* (London: MIND, 1975 and 1977).

2 See Joseph Jacob, 'The Right of a Mental Patient to his Psychosis', *Modern Law Review*, 39 (1976), 17–42, and N.N. Kittrie, *The Right To Be Different* (Baltimore, Maryland: Johns Hopkins Press, 1971).

3 The UN Declaration of the Rights of Disabled Persons (1975) and The Declaration of the Rights of Mentally Retarded Persons (1971) both express a detailed concern for the rights of the mentally ill and state the right to receive adequate medical treatment and economic security in illness.

4 See *Rouse* v. *Cameron* 125 U.S. App. D.C. 366, 373, F. 2d, 451 (1966): 'The Court's duty is to test the commitment against the supposed legislative justification, the promise of treatment'; also *Wyatt* v. *Sitckney*, 344 F. Supp. 373, 380 (M.D. Ala 1972): 'To deprive any citizen of his or her liberty upon the altruistic theory that confinement is for therapeutic reasons and then to fail to provide adequate treatment violates the very fundamentals of due process.' In the UK the very broad definition of 'treatment' to cover ordinary nursing care in effect precludes such actions.

5 See J. Katz, 'The Right to Treatment: an enchanting legal fiction', *University of Chicago Law Review*, 36 (1969), 770–2.

6 See Stanley Benn, 'Freedom, Autonomy and the Concept of of a Person', *Proceedings of Aristotelian Society* 6 (1976), 109–30, esp. 113–15, and Alan Gewirth, *Reason and Morality* (Chicago: Chicago University Press, 1978), ch. 2.

7 See H.L.A. Hart, 'Bentham on Legal Rights', in A.W.B. Simpson (ed.), *Oxford Essays in Jurisprudence*, 2nd series (Oxford: Clarendon Press, 1972), 171–201.

8 For the classic statement of this moral theory see I. Kant, *Groundwork of the Metaphysic of Morals*, tr. H.J. Paton (London: Hutchinson, 1948), ch. 2.

9 See Larry Gostin, 'Contemporary Social Historical Perspectives on Mental Health Reform', *Journal of Law and Society*, 10 (1983), 47–71, esp. 63ff.

10 See R.D. Laing, *The Divided Self* (Harmondsworth: Penguin, 1965) and T. Szasz, *The Myth of Mental Illness* (New York: Paladin, 1972).

11 The classic statement of this position is J.S. Mill, *On Liberty* (1859) (London: Dent, 1910), ch. 3.

12 See Benn, 'Freedom, Autonomy', 113–15.

13 A version of this theory may be found in Tom Campbell, *The Left and Rights* (London: Routledge & Kegan Paul, 1983), ch. 5.

14 See David Watson, 'Welfare Rights and Human Rights', *Journal of Social Policy*, 10 (1977), 31–46.

15 See in particular the Mental Health Act 1983 and the Mental Health (Scotland) Act 1984; for a recent summary of mental health legislation in other jurisdictions see W.J. Curran and T.W. Harding, *The Law and Mental Health* (Geneva: World Health Organization, 1978).

16 See D.L. Rosenhan, 'On Being Sane in Insane Places', *Science*, 179 (1973), 250–8.

17 Thus, the Mental Health Act 1983, Section 3 and the Mental Health (Scotland) Act, 1984, Section 19.

18 See Larry Gostin, 'Psychiatric Detention Without Limit of Time: The Broadmoor Cases,' in Phil Scraton and Paul Gordon, *Causes for Concern: British Criminal Justice on Trial?* (Harmondsworth: Penguin, 1984), 273–87.

19 Sections 18 and 19.

20 Section 1(3).

21 For a summary of UK law in this area see J.C. Smith and B. Hogan, *Criminal Law* (4th edn) (London: Butterworth, 1978), ch. 9 and Gerald Gordon, *Criminal Law* (2nd edn) (Edinburgh: Green, 1978), ch. 10.

22 See J.J. Cocozza and H.J. Steadman, 'The Failure of Psychiatric Predictive Dangerousness: Clear and Convincing Evidence', *Rutgers Law Review*, 29 (1976), 1084.

23 See Kittrie, *The Right to be Different.*

24 See the Mental Health (Scotland) Act 1984, Part X, and the Mental Health Act 1983, Part IV, which differ only in that, in the latter, the protections relating to psychosurgery and hormone implants are extended to informal patients. For a recent US case concerning the issue of whether or not there is a constitutional right to refuse treatment with antipsychotic drugs see *Mills et al.* vs. *Rogers et al.*, 457 U.S. 291; 102 Supreme Court 2442; 73 L. Ed. 2d 16; 50 U.S.L.W. 4676 (1982); a District court in Massachusetts has upheld the constitutionally protected liberty and privacy interests in involuntary patients deciding for themselves whether to submit to drug therapy except in emergency situations.

25 A leading case regarding consent to treatment in the UK relates to a mentally-ill person who was not told of the risks associated with the administration of electro-convulsive therapy: *Bolam* v. *Friern H.M.C.* [1957] 2 All E.R. 118. The topic of consent is discussed at greater length in ch 8, below.

26 Section 98.

27 Sections 97 and 98. It must be certified in writing that the patient is 'capable of understanding the value, purpose and likely effects of the treatment in question'. This may be contrasted with *Freeman* v. *The Home Office* [1984] 1 All E.R. 1036; (1984) 2 WLR 802, where it was held that the doctrine of 'informed consent' has no place in English law and that the 'consent' of prisoners to medication is not invalidated by the fact that they are not told of the nature and purpose of the administration of the drugs in question.

8

The Right to Consent to Medical Treatment

Sheila McLean

Whilst many human rights have been created as a result of the abuse by states and their agencies of individuals, and through forces which seem inherently wrong or dangerous, the right to consent in medical treatment is in a somewhat different tradition. The language of rights is used in this area rather as a result of a combination of two forces both of which are deemed to be good in themselves: namely through the interaction of orthodox medicine and the law, as primarily represented by the judiciary. Moreover, the terminology of human rights is used both to protect freedom of choice and to impose a corresponding duty on others to facilitate that choice through disclosure of information.

Whilst there is little doubt that making choices about therapy is an aspect of the right to personal autonomy or self-determination, it merits specific consideration on a number of counts. First, that it may provide the classic example of the balancing of competing goods and may therefore be instructive of the kind of decision-making which occurs in limiting the applicability of human rights. Second, and to some extent derivatively, that health and health care are so fundamentally important to the human condition that technical interests may be given priority over the freedom of the individual to make choices based on disclosure: choices which could be technically (that is medically) irrational. Moreover, the provision of health care through therapy may be seen as enhancing autonomy. In some cases, for example the mentally ill and children, minimizing certain aspects of autonomy may actually be seen as having more importance than the immediate protection of freedom of choice, because, for example, of the existence of a right to treatment.[1] And, of course, the community attitude to orthodox medicine may reflect ambivalence about the competition between the therapeutic imperative and the rights of the individual. This aspect of autonomy is considered because it is currently very much in the limelight as an example of the possible competition between goods. Whilst not all communities have primary health care services which utilize orthodox medicine, every community has its medicine men. The rights which it is claimed patients have in the orthodox transaction are no less important in alternative forms of curing.

The practice of medicine has an ethical as well as a technical content.[2] The predominance in most cultures of high-technology orthodox medicine in no way reduces the moral content and implications of the interaction between the doctor (healer) and the patient, although it may sometimes disguise it. That is, the use of technology does not *per se* affect the essential nature of the medical transaction although it may change its form.

One feature of all medical transactions is the vulnerability of the patients who lack the technical skills on which they must rely if they are to regain, or perhaps retain, the state of health which is so precious to them. Because of this reliance, they are highly dependent on obtaining the assistance of the skilled healer. One reason why health is so important to individuals is that on it rests not only their freedom from physical and mental illness, but also their capacity to determine their current and future affairs. For these reasons, health has been equated with 'the degree of lived freedom'.[3] Further, health, and therefore treatment for ill-health, is more than a prerequisite of freedom or self-determination in life as a whole. It is also an area within which self-determination may be exercised. Indeed, given the importance of health to individuals, it is of central importance to them that they have the capacity and opportunity for choice in respect of medical intervention. This ability to make choices means that if sick people are to retain their autonomy, they must be free to seek treatment, to choose between therapies with different prognoses and even to choose illness over therapy. For where therapies carry risks which may be judged by the patient to be worse than the illness itself, or may produce side-effects of potential significance to the patient, there is no easily defined assessment of what, in these circumstances, actually amounts to 'health'. Health choices are part of life choices and cannot therefore be readily removed from the would-be autonomous individual. However, such choices may have to be made in situations where clear, long-term thought is difficult and the immediate pressures of illness and the presence of skilled persons with superior medical knowledge may not be conducive to independent decision-making by the patient.

The right to self-determination is one which communities and individuals treasure. As has been said:

> the assertion of civil rights in democratic countries has encouraged increasing interest in the rights of self-determination for every citizen and public participation in decisions which affect the general welfare. The democratic ideal has also challenged the claims of any group, professional or otherwise, to special privileges.[4]

Nowhere in the interaction between doctor and patient is Man's fundamental right to self-determination more clearly expressed, or more contentious, than in his right to provide or withhold consent to therapy or other medical intervention.

The implications of this right are fundamental to our understanding of the human state, and form a vital part of the moral and legal status of medical practice. It is not merely that the choice between accepting and rejecting therapy, or particular forms of therapy, reflected the essentially voluntary nature of the medical enterprise, but also that the provision of adequate consent by the patient can render lawful actions which would otherwise amount to an assault.[5] The skills possessed by the doctor do not in themselves give him or her the right to make alterations to the physical or mental condition of another, and the need for consent to be obtained provides a valuable protection for the autonomy of the patient.

If one of the major impacts of the provision of consent by a patient is to render the actions of the doctor in respect of that patient both moral and legal, and thereby to protect individual rights, then at first sight it is difficult to see why any problems about this aspect of medical practice should arise. It would, in these terms, seem to be in the interests of both patient and doctor that real or true consent should be obtained. In the case of patients, their right to make free and knowing choices about their physical and mental integrity is protected where they are genuinely in a position to make free and understanding choices about therapy. The doctor protects him- or herself legally in obtaining this consent, and should also find that this enhances the professional relationship with the patient.

Nonetheless, problems do arise in this area, and challenges are made. For the doctor, such challenges, especially where litigation ensues, can be both personally painful and professionally damaging. For the patient, the desire or need to act in this way against a doctor may be both anxiety-provoking and expensive. At least in theory, then, it is in the interests of both parties to any medical transaction that respect and trust are shown by each participant to the other. However, the way in which issues of consent are dealt with by courts can, if viewed from the autonomy model, seem less than protective of individual rights.

The doctor-patient relationship is based, in its best manifestations, on trust. Often, however, this trust is perceived as a one-way transaction. That is, claims that trust is essential to a good and efficient doctor-patient relationship often seems to centre on the element of trust which the patient places in the doctor. If the patient demonstrates this trust, in addition to his or her essential dependence on the skills and expertise of medicine as a discipline, then it is assumed that the medical transaction has been successfully commenced and may be satisfactorily concluded. However, trust may also – and more appropriately – be perceived as a two-way transaction. That is, the doctor might equally be expected to trust the patient to cope with potentially distressing information and also to take decisions about him- or herself and his or her integrity, bodily or mental. It is in recognition of this latter element of the trust-based relationship that the provision of real or 'informed' consent becomes so vital, and yet it is precisely this element which may lead to many of the disagreements and disputes which make the actions of a given doctor the subject of challenge or litigation, since some medical practitioners are opposed to providing a full discussion of therapies and their alternatives in every case.

Consent is, in fact, both fundamental to, and highly problematic for, the doctor-patient relationship. The implications of insufficiently or improperly obtained consent are often vital to the general well-being of the patient and thus to the medical, moral and legal aspects of medical practice. Consent is much more than a legal device or invention designed to intimidate medical practitioners. It is, of course, a concept adopted by national legal systems and by international agreements,[6] but it is primarily derivative from a more general philosophical commitment to the essential right of the individual to make choices about what can and cannot be done with one's own body and mind. In other words, the legal system's insistence on the provision of consent in medical treatment is both a reflection and an acceptance of an agreed moral principle that Man has a right to self-determination, which necessarily includes a right to physical and mental integrity.

Fundamental principles of this type may often be implicitly accepted rather than overtly stated. Nonetheless, their breach may result in general condemnation. For example, it is precisely the lack of respect for such principles which causes many people, including doctors, to condemn abuses of psychiatry wherever these occur, and the atrocities conducted in the name of medical science under the Nazi regime in Germany during the Second World War. Thus, where blatant abuses of the patient/victim occur, on grounds which are seen as malicious, political or spurious, there can be guaranteed condemnation of the perpetrators. This condemnation is much more than just a reflection of the distaste which is invariably felt when medicine, as an essentially benevolent discipline, is used in such a way as to tarnish its commitment to caring and concern. It also reflects the generalized acceptance that nothing should be done to a person without that person's actual or real consent. That is, people should have the political or human right to participate or not, and the freedom to withhold their cooperation: a freedom which is central to the right of self-determination and which is sadly lacking in the examples used above.

However, these examples are extreme, and as such tend to polarize opinion. Few have any real doubts about their reaction to the involuntary incarceration of those whose only apparent deviation from the norm is their expressed opposition to a political regime. Nor would many support the use of ethnic or religious minorities as guinea-pigs to be sacrificed on the altar of political dogma or scientific interest. The position, then, seems relatively clear. In these selected situations, Man revolts against the exploitation of fellow human beings and, in so doing, recognizes the right to self-determination within medicine. This, then, seems to reflect a level of commitment to our fellow humans which renders obsolete disputes about the manifestation of their integrity through the provision of consent to medical treatment.

The truth is, however, far from this. When situations are as clear as the alleged Soviet abuse of psychiatry, or the Nazi doctors' well-documented abuse of the Jews or the handicapped, then a powerful, vocal and fairly consistent response can safely be predicted. But the standard therapeutic medical interaction seems so far removed from these excesses that it appears at first sight to have no relationship whatever with them. Surely there is no coercion, no political overtone, in the ordinary practice of medicine?

Whilst this is an understandable question, there are those who for some time have identified just such characteristics even in the most elementary or apparently unproblematic medical action. Szasz,[7] for example, would argue that psychiatry always demonstrates just such features. Psychiatric diagnoses and treatments are, in his terms, political tools used to safeguard the community and its interests from those whose views or behaviour are unacceptable, strange or frightening. Illich,[8] further, argues that the role of medicine in the community is always, at least incidentally if not primarily, political, and he identifies several levels of political and functional deprivation which can result from iatrogenesis (medicine-induced illness) or from the aspirations and practices of medicine.

The picture, then, may be less clear than at first appears. Whilst the problems arising from the aims and functions of orthodox medicine may be overstated by Szasz and Illich, none the less, if health – physical and mental – really is vital to the human and political status of individuals, and through them to the community, then it is important that the moral principles on which the orthodox practice of medicine is based be carefully examined from the point of view of self-determination. In fact, the more subtle shades of the standard medical transaction do present examples of abuse which may be less clear-cut but which are nonetheless important, even although they may seem to have less overt political and moral import.

Of course, the subtle nature of the standard medical relationship makes the identification of abuse more difficult, and the fact that its motivation will generally be benevolent makes its exposure more painful. None the less, such abuses as do occur may be every bit as detrimental to the good practice of medicine, in both its technical and moral sense. Requirements about consent are such that they are central to the moral nature of medical practice, as well as bearing on its technical and healing capabilities. The inevitable inequality of information and technical skills between doctor and patient, plus the essential vulnerability of the patient, make this requirement at once both highly sensitive and vitally important.

How is Consent Evidenced?

For the patient to make a free and knowing decision either to consent to or refuse therapy, certain moral and legal requirements must be met. In theory at least these requirements seem to coincide. The patient should be a sane, adult person, free from duress, and the decision about therapy should be based on the provision of sufficient intelligible information for him or her to make what is often referred to as an 'informed' choice. As has been said, 'it is the prerogative of the patient, not the physician, to determine for himself the direction in which his interests seem to lie.'[9]

Before considering what is actually meant by the term 'informed' consent, it is appropriate first to consider how the patient may indicate consent to medical intervention, and as a corollary, how refusal of consent may be evidenced. It is sometimes thought that a patient evidences consent to medical treatment merely by consulting a doctor. This inference is drawn from the mere fact of voluntary consultation, but a further step must be made before this consultation bears on the question of consent. Certainly, the patient will, in the run-of-the-mill medical transaction, freely and voluntarily consult the doctor, impliedly or explicitly inviting him or her to exercise skills, make a diagnosis and perhaps prescribe therapy. And yet, can the desire for diagnosis really be equivalent to an acceptance of the subsequently recommended therapy?

Quite apart from the obvious ethical considerations which would be involved in such an assertion, common sense would dictate that the invitation to exercise the professional expertise held by the doctor and to reach a diagnosis cannot be equivalent to providing consent to whatever treatment the doctor may then regard as being appropriate to the condition. It may be that it is easier to equate the two when one considers the routine prescription of drugs whose side-effects are likely to be known and minimal. However, if consultation equals consent to therapy then the same implications would also necessarily have to apply where the therapy was more radically intrusive, for example involving chemotherapy or amputation of limbs. Clearly, if consent is to mean anything, it must involve more than the mere fact of consultation or the provision of diagnostic information. It must, in fact, be based on knowledge, and since the patient knows little or nothing in advance about the likely diagnosis and its equivalent therapy, the decision to accept or reject that therapy surely cannot be pre-empted merely because he or she took the step of consulting a doctor. Consent, in order to be meaningful, cannot be backdated to the stage at which illness is recognized and investigation of its cause and nature is sought. Further, in view of the rights which it has been claimed the patient has to make choices about whether or not to undergo treatment, it would be illogical to impute consent to therapy at a stage when the choice as to whether or not to accept it lies in the future.

Of course, the patient may come to the doctor specifically seeking a particular form of therapy, for example, anti-depressants or anti-biotics. Indeed, he or she may have already had such drugs prescribed in the past. This situation differs from that described above in that there may already be an element of knowledge. The extent to which the situations differ will, of course, depend on the extent of any prior knowledge which the patient has. Where patients seek a drug about which they have not previously been informed but request it by specific name, it may be argued that they are expressly or impliedly consenting to accept the drug, and are thereby providing real consent. However, if the nature of real consent is that it is informed, then clearly mere knowledge of a brand name cannot constitute sufficient information to provide the patient with a knowledgeable choice of therapy. Further, were such a definition of consent acceptable, it would necessarily assume that consent is demonstrated simply by the patient saying 'yes' or taking the prescription, and would beg the fundamental question as to whether or nor he or she can provide legally or morally acceptable consent in ignorance of risks and benefits.

This specific question will be considered later in more detail, but it is worth bearing in mind at this stage that doctors are consulted precisely because they have certain skills. The average patient lacks this expertise. The doctor who equates consent to treatment with the request for diagnosis or for the provision of certain drugs is placing him- or herself in a morally and professionally dubious position. Therefore, acceptance of therapy, whilst it may pragmatically seem to be the equivalent of actual consent to therapy, cannot necessarily be equated with a morally or legally acceptable or valid consent. This is an important consideration for doctors to remember since, if therapy provided on this basis causes unpleasant side-effects, they may find themselves successfully challenged on the basis that, even though diagnosis and therapy were both accurate and appropriate, the patient was not cognizant of the risks which in fact occurred. In other words, the consent which is given must be much more than the mere acceptance of the doctor's treatment plan; it should also be knowing, that is, based on information.

The second situation, involving the patient seeking the provision of a drug which he or she has been prescribed before, differs fundamentally from this example. Where the doctor has previously explained the potential risks and benefits of the drug or therapy, then recent legal opinion would suggest that no explicit subsequent reference to them is necessary.[10] However, when consent is viewed as involving discussion and disclosure of information, even previous prescription of the drug or practice of the therapy would not satisfy these requirements where no explanation was made at that time. The requirement about disclosure of information remains, even where the drug or therapy has been used before.

This is not to say, however, that non-verbally indicated consent cannot be valid. Where sufficient information has been disclosed and the patient accepts the therapy, for example the provision of a prescription, consent may be demonstrated by the taking of the prescription to the chemist, acceptance of the drugs and commencing the treatment programme. Indeed, it is probably the case that the method of indicating consent to the therapy is legally and morally irrelevant. What is vital is the basis on which that acceptance theory is made, that is, the extent, nature and sufficiency of the information on which the patient formulated his or her decision. What is fundamental to the provision of consent, then, is the protection of the freedom of the individual to make choices, and therefore what functionally makes consent valid is that aspect of it which is referred to as being 'informed'. For obvious reasons, the doctor may be better protected if the patient consents in writing, since this leaves evidence of an agreement having been reached. However, this may still be challenged if the patient claims that something other than what was consented to was actually done. Thus, in *Devi* v. *West Midlands Regional Health Authority*,[11] although a woman had signed a consent form authorizing abdominal surgery, she was awarded damages since she had not consented to the doctor carrying out a sterilization while she was under the anaesthetic. Obviously, however, the more specific the consent form, the more likely the doctor is to be protected. However, the standard medical transaction, for example patient visits to a general practitioner, does not normally involve the provision and signing of a consent form, presumably because this would be rather cumbersome.

Consent, therefore, may be demonstrated in a number of ways, ranging from simple acceptance of the therapy to a specific signing of a consent form. However, expression of a legally and morally valid consent, whichever of these devices is used, still depends on the informed nature of that consent. It is particularly important to remember this, since it is the right of the patient to choose therapy or not, but it is not the right of the doctor to treat merely because he or she can. Whilst it is easy to conceive of a doctor as having duties in respect of the patient, the doctor has no rights in this respect other than the right to practice his or her profession when asked to do so by those seeking help. This is a practical rather than a moral right, dependent on the professional requirements for entitlement to give treatment rather than on any essential moral right to exercise one's skills come what may.

'Informed' Consent

Real or informed consent is, in theory at least, a prerequisite of morally or legally valid medical practice, although English courts have recently indicated that it is not a part of English law.[12] This is not, however, to imply that they will ignore consent as an issue, nor to imply that the English doctrine has no implications about disclosure. As was said in *Hills* v. *Potter*: 'it is quite clear from the English cases . . . that on any view English law does require the surgeon to supply to the patient information to enable the plaintiff to decide whether or not to undergo the operation'.[13] As has been seen, the provision of consent is vital since it is not only a protection of the moral status of the individual patient but it also has the effect of rendering medical intervention lawful. For the patient, the former may be the more important aspect, but for the doctor perhaps the latter consideration is the more vital.

The valid provision of consent can turn what could otherwise be deemed an assault into legally protected behaviour for, whilst consent is only rarely a defence in the criminal law, it may be a defence – as in this case – in allegations of a civil (that is non-criminal) nature. The reasons for this difference are illuminating. In the criminal law, it is not possible to change the nature of a charge, say, of murder because the victim consents to it.[14] Thus even voluntary euthanasia or assault remain criminal offences.[15] This is a reflection of the fact that the behaviour involved in the act is struck at by the law on the grounds that it is in itself morally reprehensible. Of course, this effectively limits the autonomy of the individual who is not permitted to absolve his or her attacker of blame, even where he or she voluntarily submits to the assault. The only situation in which consent will be a defence in the criminal law is where the lack of consent is central to the nature and quality of the act. Thus, for example, a reasonable belief that a woman consents to intercourse (not in itself a morally reprehensible act) will provide a defence against a charge of rape.[16]

Medical practice, however, is traditionally dealt with by the civil law, in terms of which acceptance of risk and agreement to take the consequences of the risk, should it occur, is a valid defence expressed in the maxim *volenti non fit injuria*.[17] In other words, the person who freely and knowingly agrees to a course of action which involves known risks is not injured legally if one of these risks actually occurs, and therefore could sue the other party to the enterprise if he or she is damaged as a result of the occurrence of the risk. So, although medical practice may involve the doctor in undertaking a course of behaviour which, in other circumstances, would be an assault – for example surgery – the knowing and free consent of the patient will render this lawful. The voluntary and understanding acceptance by the patient will also ensure that he or she cannot successfully sue the doctor thereafter should one of the risks to which his or her attention was drawn, and which he or she indicated his or her agreement to assume, actually occur. It is therefore in the interests of both doctor and patient that valid consent (involving disclosure of risks) is provided in all forms of therapy.

It has already been pointed out that mere apparent acceptance of therapy, whether verbally or in writing, is not necessarily a sufficient demonstration that consent has been validly given. Thus even where the patient agrees to undertake the therapy, it cannot necessarily be assumed that this 'choice' was based on sufficient information to render it meaningful or sufficient to satisfy moral or legal criteria. The provision of valid consent is much more than a mechanical procedure culminating in the patient accepting therapy. More is required, implying the disclosure of information, and perhaps even the patient understanding that information. However, even this is rather vague and unhelpful; disclosure of what? Does the doctor have a duty to ensure patient understanding?

Clearly, if morally and legally valid consent is dependent on the patient being in a position to make a real choice, then there must be some information made available on which this choice can be based. Of course, even without disclosure, it could be argued that the patient has a sufficient range of choices available. Patients may choose not to consult a doctor, or they may accept or reject therapy without any information at all. Thus, if their right to self-determination is protected merely by the availability of choices, then do they not already have choices in these terms, and is their self-determination not sufficiently protected by these freedoms?

The answer to these questions will obviously depend on what we mean by 'choice'. In the medical transaction, the freedom to consult a doctor or not does, of course, bear some relation to the freedom of the individual. Equally, the patient may choose not to seek any information about diagnosis or therapy, and would be within his or her rights to do so. However, the patient who chooses the latter course of action will be rare, and the doctor should not assume that this will be the case. General rules will, therefore, be required for the average patient. Equally, the fact that patients have the freedom to consult a doctor or not, whilst it may be important, does not affect the freedoms and rights to which they may be entitled once they have chosen to enter into a professional relationship with a doctor. In recognition of this, it is seldom argued that *no* information should be disclosed to patients about their proposed therapy, although it may be the case that, for example, in the routine prescription of common drugs, such as antibiotics, little if any information actually is disclosed by the doctor about possible side-effects. This is a reflection of a number of factors, such as assumptions about a patient's understanding of the likely side-effects of such common drugs, rather than a moral statement by doctors that they are under no obligation to make disclosure.

The major dilemma in questions of disclosure, however, relates more often to its nature and extent than it does to the actual need to make it. Thus doctors may be uncertain about whether or not they are legally or morally obliged to make disclosure of risks even if a patient does not ask for information, and also about what sort of disclosure satisfies the concept of 'informed' consent.

Clearly, doctors are the possessors of both skills and information in the medical transaction. Were it otherwise, then they would not be consulted. The patients, then, are vulnerable not only because they feel themselves to be ill and therefore in need of help, but also because of the inequality of information possessed by the parties in a doctor-patient relationship. If this information is essential to the ability to make informed choices in the vitally important matter of health, then the doctor has at least a moral duty to disclose such medical information as he or she has, even where this information is unsolicited. Indeed, to make the extent of disclosure dependent on the questions asked by patients would obviously be inappropriate, since by definition they are unlikely to possess the information which would be necessary to ensure that they ask the right questions.

However, the doctor – whilst doubtless likely to accept the logic of this – is nonetheless still faced with the dilemma of what information he or she must or should disclose in order to ensure that the patient is genuinely consenting. Does the patient have to know the technicalities of drug action or of the relevant surgical procedure? Should the doctor disclose all known risks, or merely some of them? How much account should the doctor take in deciding about the level of discolosure of the chances of the therapy succeeding, even if its possible side-effects are particularly unpleasant?

One possible view, of course, is that only by making full and complete disclosure of all known risks and potential benefits can the patient's autonomy be protected. By selecting the information which is to be disclosed, the doctor is already limiting the patient's right to determine his or her own future. In so doing, the doctor makes certain assumptions about which information the patient needs or should know. The doctor's desire to be selective is easily understood, not only on the pragmatic basis that full disclosure would be unreasonably time-consuming, but also on the more general basis that the aim is to cure, or at least to alleviate, suffering, and that this is the most important aspect of the interaction of the doctor with a patient. Further, since disclosure of certain information might serve to dissuade the patient from undergoing the therapy which the doctor knows, or has reasonable grounds to believe, might ensure the improvement which the patient presumably sought when consulting the doctor, then surely the doctor has a professional duty *not* to disclose that information? In other words, if the patient voluntarily makes contact with the doctor, is it not reasonable that, where medicine can help, it should do so? Is the restoration of health not also vital to the patient's autonomy, perhaps as important as his or her right to make choices? Indeed, it may be that the restoration of individual health could also be seen as an important benefit to the community as a whole, either because of risks to the health of others, or on economic or other grounds.

Whilst this approach has certain attractions, it is based on challengeable assumptions. Most notable of these is the belief that voluntary consultation necessarily implies a commitment to cure or to undergo therapy. Further, and even more fundamentally, that the decision about whether or not to accept therapy is one which can or should be taken on the basis of purely medical considerations. It has already been claimed that mere consultation cannot amount to an indication of consent to therapy. For example, the patient may in fact only want diagnosis, and may not actually seek or accept therapy. Further, the patient may choose whether or not to undergo therapy on the basis of influences and criteria which are not medical: they may be emotional, financial and so on. Only full disclosure of known risks and likely benefits will actually allow these other considerations and factors – which are relevant to the patient – to be taken into account. The role of the doctor is to facilitate health, not to inflict it on the public. Medicine has no general right to enforce its diagnostic techniques, therapies or palliatives on an unconsenting or unwilling patient. In some situations, of course, the health of the community may be deemed more important than the individual freedom to choose therapy or not. This is often the case in preventive measures, such as mass vaccination programmes. But it is worth noting that it was precisely because the patient in these situations is persuaded or required to undergo the vaccination that the Royal Commission on Civil Liability and Compensation for Personal Injury[18] made damage resulting from vaccine a special case. Unusually in non-contract situations, compensation may be sought for vaccine damage under a strict liability scheme.

In other situations, however, there is a close link between the unknowing and the unwilling patient. Few doctors, if any, would seriously countenance deliberately inflicting therapy on a patient who has refused to participate in it, even where the therapy is likely to succeed. Such behaviour could easily be seen as immoral and unprofessional, whatever its legal implications. However, medicine does seem to countenance therapy in respect of those who are not overtly unwilling – they may even have apparently consented – but who in fact have been denied the opportunity to be unwilling by the deliberate withholding of information. This non-disclosure may be explained on the grounds that the therapy will be likely to be successful, but this may also be the case with the unwilling patient whose forced treatment the doctor would be unlikely to seek to justify. The distinction between non-voluntary and involuntary medical treatment is a fine one. Thus, even where medicine knows it can cure, an elementary commitment to the patient's right to self-determination must allow him or her the choice, and real choice is only available where disclosure is made.

Evidently, however, although full disclosure may be a morally attractive goal, it may be difficult for practical reasons. The attitude adopted by the legal system will therefore play a fundamental part in the explanation of what is valid consent, and this will be discussed below. In the meantime, however, there are further arguments beyond the purely practical one of time shortage which could be used in an attempt to justify limitation of information or even total non-disclosure.

For example, it may be argued that full disclosure of technical or specialized information is irrelevant and unnecessary because the patient cannot fully understand the information. However, the doctor may rationally be perceived as having a duty to make disclosure which – although it may ideally lead to or facilitate patient understanding – can also be seen as independent of it. That is, if the patient has a right to receive, and the doctor has a correlative right to disclose, there is no inherent implication that the received information is also understood. Whilst some writers have argued that disclosure without understanding is useless,[19] it may be that the mere act of disclosing information and inviting discussion nonetheless serves a purpose which is important.[20] Thus, although disclosure of information which is highly technical in nature and which may be unintelligible to the patient may serve little, if any, practical purpose, it may nonetheless have an important symbolic one which may prove to be vital to the creation or maintenance of trust and respect between doctor and patient, and to the enhancing of the patient's autonomy.

Further, whilst patients cannot reasonably be expected to understand the technicalities of precisely how an incision is made or why a particular drug may cause nausea, hair loss and so on, it is disingenuous to pretend that they cannot understand the fundamental point that they will be left with an abdominal scar or that they will be sick or bald. If information is presented in everyday language, then the salient points about side-effects can, of course, be grasped by most patients.

It may also be argued that disclosure of risks will cause the patient distress, and that therefore only selected (presumably non-distressing) side-effects should be disclosed. Indeed, it has been argued that disclosure of too many risks may amount to negligence if the patient is indeed distressed.[21] Buchanan,[22] amongst others, convincingly destroys this so-called 'prevention of harm' argument by pointing out its essential fallacies. First, a doctor will seldom be in a position to know precisely what will distress a patient, since that distress will inevitably be bound up with factors personal to him or her which may be totally non-medical. Second, for the doctor to act on the basis that withholding information will avoid patient distress, he must also take account of the possiblity that the withholding of information may in itself turn out to be even more distressing.

This 'prevention of harm' argument further makes the (challengeable) assumption that the patient's distress about certain types of side-effect is irrelevant in his or her calculation as to whether or not to undergo therapy, whereas it may – on personal rather than purely medical grounds – be vital to the decision, and autonomy-enhancing. It is also interesting to note the underlying paternalism of this view which, whilst it may in certain rare instances have some merit, is nonetheless a debateable basis for medical practice in general. Interestingly, the available evidence would suggest that many patients who are given full disclosure are not apparently harmed by this.[13] The implications of the approach which calls for non-disclosure seem to militate strongly in favour of the kind of one-way trust which reflects the dominance of the medical profession, and detracts from the benefits of a partnership between doctor and patient.

Whilst it is understandable that doctors may have a bias in favour of therapy, the mere fact that a likely successful therapy is available should not blind them to their patient's rights. Thus, it is unconvincing to argue against disclosure on the basis that it might prevent the patient from undergoing therapy. The patient may, as we have seen, on balance prefer the disease to the cure, for reasons which may be personally convincing but medically irrational. This apparent irrationality provides yet another argument against making full disclosure since if patients receive and understand the information what, it could be argued, is the point of taking the trouble to make disclosures if they can then ignore the import of it and act on a whim? It may seem particularly desirable to avoid irrational (in medical terms) behaviour in areas as fundamental as health and illness. However, it must be a part of the patient's autonomy that he or she can act on the basis of the information provided, or on the basis of different information. In other words, he or she may act on a mere whim or because other factors are more persuasive. It is, perhaps, only where the behaviour of the patient threatens others that we may see the justification for intervention, at least on classical utilitarian lines. The freedom to ignore professional or other advice is, of course, also a feature of other less sensitive areas of human conduct. Whilst A may freely and voluntarily consult a solicitor, who may advise A to to the best of his or her ability to pursue course X, A may none the less choose to do Y instead. As in the medical situation, A will bear the consequences of that behaviour which may seem to be professionally irrational but personally sensible.

So what then must or should a doctor disclose to a patient in order to ensure that 'informed' consent has actually been obtained? In this section, the emphasis has been on the moral and professional arguments about what constitutes reasonable or ethical consent. The final arbiter will, of course, be the legal system, since challenges which may reflect moral or professional convictions will – if redress is sought – be judged on the basis of tests set by the law. The extent of the disclosure required by the law will therefore be an important (although not necessarily satisfactory) guide to the doctor.

The Legal Position

The civil law has the function of considering and balancing competing claims and interests. In this way it distributes loss by assessing the relative merits of behaviour. Overtly, therefore, the law could reasonably be expected to adopt a disinterested view of any professional behaviour, and to offer protection of fundamental rights such as the right to autonomy or self-determination. But is the situation this straightforward where the aims of medicine compete with the interests of the individual?

The interests of the community (as represented in this case by the law) may be reflected both by the protection of the individual's freedom of choice and by the protection of medicine and the availability of therapy. Balance, therefore, may be particularly difficult to achieve in this area. Courts have, indeed, perceived this situation as one requiring special precautions in order to ensure that an appropriate compromise may be attained.[24]

A number of theoretical positions have already been identified which could be used to justify anything from full to very limited disclosure of information. Since disclosure is fundamental to the extent to which consent can be said to be 'informed' and therefore protective of individual rights, the amount of disclosure required by the law will be vital to the protection of such rights and the resolution of disputes.

The legal and the moral positions may not of course equate, even where they appear to be the same. The basic theoretical position is that consent is an essential prerequisite of lawful and morally justifiable medical intervention. Emphasis is therefore apparently placed on the rights of patients. As Pellegrino and Thomasma point out:

> The traditional stance of benevolent authoritarianism in the patient-physician encounter is increasingly under scrutiny and challenge. More patients want full disclosure of the therapeutic alternatives. Legal opinion is unanimous in requiring informed consent not only in experimental procedures but in the ordinary therapeutic encounter.[25]

Whilst British courts have claimed to be prepared to reinforce the right of the individual to make choices about therapy, the extent to which they will actually do so seems to depend on considerations which relate to the type of intervention as much as to the rights of the patient.

Thus, in some cases, the courts have been prepared to uphold the patient's claim that 'informed' consent was not given and to award damages correspondingly. Cases such as *Devi* v. *West Midland Regional Health Authority*[26] and *Wells* v. *Surrey Area Health Authority*,[27] however, where such decisions were taken, share a common characteristic which may help to explain the apparent difficulties of approach. Each of these two cases related to situations where the result of the intervention to which real consent had not been given was the sterilization of the parties concerned. In one case, sterilization was carried out during the course of another operation, as a means of avoiding the potential dangers of a subsequent pregnancy, and no mention had been made in advance that sterilization might be carried out. In the other, although sterilization had been discussed with, and agreed to by, the patient, it was decided that insufficient information had been given on which the patient could base her decision.

The common theme of these two cases may well be the fact that the implications of the surgery were so dramatic. It is claimed that there is a fundamental human right to reproduce,[28] and the courts may well have been heavily influenced by the existence of this right in reaching their decisions. They would, however, seem to be considerably less impressed by the claim that, no matter what the nature of the proposed intervention, there is a fundamental human right to self-determination in medicine which would also be worthy of legal protection, and which is best protected by requiring full disclosure of all available risks and benefits.

The law does, of course, have a role to play in the rationalization of competing interests. In cases where what is in dispute is whether or not consent has been validly given, the formal position of the law is that: 'It is clear law that in any context in which consent of the injured party is a defence to what would otherwise be a crime or a civil wrong, that consent must be real.'[29] This assertion would appear to reinforce the need for disclosure. However, although it seems to reflect an emphasis upon the rights of the patient to give real consent, such a theoretical position seems to be at variance with at least some of the cases outlined above. The perceived necessity to rationalize the interests of the patient making choices, and of medicine in curing or alleviating symptoms, seems in some cases at least to have induced the law to adopt views which can be described as pure paternalism and which can also be effectively and convincingly challenged. The sane, adult human being may, then, be vulnerable to an apparent priority awarded to therapy over the rights of the patient to make informed decisions about what is to be done about his or her body or mind. The right to choose (however 'irrationally') seems to have been subordinated to the 'right' of the doctor to make disclosure or not, and to select what information will be passed on to the patient. Moreover, this selection of information, on the basis of what are only arguably medical grounds, allows little or no scope for this kind of personalized choice which it has been claimed makes consent real, informed and valid.

British and other courts have traditionally protected the clinical freedom of the doctor on those (relatively) rare occasions when a challenge to its exercise has been made.[30] The pattern of litigation in medical cases seems to have changed in recent years, however, and courts and Defence Unions have been confronted with more regular decision-making of this type. Whilst clinical freedom has been protected in most countries, it has been claimed that the British courts have been more protective than those in other countries, perhaps as a reflection of the general prevailing attitude to medicine and its practitioners.[31] In other countries, a lesser commitment to the interest of medicine has resulted in a perhaps more genuine, but not necessarily more satisfactory, effort being made to reconcile the conflict between medicine and its patients. American courts, for example, have clearly stated that:

> A physician violates his duty to his patient and subjects himself to liability if he withholds any facts which are necessary to form the basis of an intelligent consent by the patient to the proposed treatment. Likewise the physician may not minimize the known dangers of a procedural operation in order to induce his patient's consent.[32]

This statement seems to recognize no conflict of interest between the doctor's professionalism and the patient's rights. Further, whilst not excluding an element of discretion for the doctor, the American approach nonetheless firmly restates the basic principle that the doctor's duty to disclose is based on the patient's right to receive information. However, such an interpretation still falls far short of a standard for full disclosure. In *Canterbury* v. *Spence*, it was made quite clear that there were 'formidable obstacles to acceptance of the notion that the physician's obligation to disclose is either generated or limited by medical practice'.[33] The law, therefore, as representing the community, must by implication set standards for professionals and others which reflect the status accorded to the human being, and provide redress for infringement of his or her basic rights. However, in most jurisdictions full disclosure is not required: only that which is reasonable. The reasonableness question may hinge on what the reasonable doctor would disclose or what the reasonable patient could expect but, whichever test is used, there remains an apparent assumption that not all information need be disclosed.

It is argued that all of us, including doctors, are ultimately judged by the law. Legal standards are therefore necessarily vague, since lawyers can claim no specific expertise in many of the areas on which decisions must be made. Thus architects and engineers, as well as doctors, will ultimately, in the event of challenge, find themselves governed by legal concepts and principles rather than by their fellow professionals. In this way, public accountability is said to be achieved, and the community has the benefit of continuity and consistency in decision-making. However, the law also serves a protective purpose both for the individual and for groups or professions. Thus it is not the abstract principle applied which is fundamental, but rather the way in which that principle is interpreted by the courts. Whilst both British and American courts, for example, would claim to espouse the same commitment to the individual's freedom, and the same appreciation of the difficulties of medical practice, nonetheless it can be seen that their practical approach has varied considerably, presumably because of the relative weight given to each of these factors when conflict arises. However, neither these nor other justifications make a clear-cut commitment to the rights of the patient to full disclosure leading to meaningful consent. Rather, there remains a bias in favour of therapy. This so-called disinterested decision-making, then, may ultimately lead not to an acceptable standard protecting the right of the patient to offer a meaningful consent (or to withhold consent), but rather to a reflection of the personal perceptions of judges or the interests of a particular pressure group.

The apparent legal commitment, in most jurisdictions, to seeing medical intervention as a profound good, coupled with an apparent distaste for legitimizing challenges against medical decisions, is reflected in the cases mentioned. However, there has also been a further legal move which serves to make it more difficult successfully to raise an action against a doctor where the allegation relates to apparent or real failure to obtain informed consent. This move is concerned with the methods available to the disaffected patient in seeking redress by way of compensation, and profoundly affects the capacity successfully to challenge a breach of the right to consent.

As a reflection of the rights protected by the legal process, redress is available to those who are thought to have a genuine grievance. The right of the patient to make choices about the nature and extent of medical intervention is therefore, in theory at least, legally protected, and compensation can be sought to the unauthorized invasion of what might broadly be called the privacy of the individual.

Traditionally this right of action has been based on the concept that an unauthorized intervention is a form of (non-criminal) assault on the individual, an approach which has benefits for the patient, since it involves a straightforward commitment to the protection of his or her right, and suggests that the right of action stems from a primary interest in protecting them. Simply, it depends on the patient's choices and freedoms. Patients need not have suffered measureable medical harm from the intervention but must simply have had their choice ignored, or their ability to make a choice seriously restricted by lack of information. The crucial element is that of non-disclosure, and the selection of information by the doctor could provide a sufficient basis for a successful action.

However, recent trends have indicated a tendency for this type of action not to be used. Rather the courts are demanding that – except in the most extreme cases – the appropriate form of action would be one in negligence and not on the basis of assault.[34] At first sight, this shift in the basis of the action may seem logical enough and relatively non-intrusive of the right to consent. After all, it may be said, what is essentially being considered is the behaviour of a given doctor, and such behaviour will normally be judged on the basis of what is good or normal medical practice, a type of assessment which is well suited to the negligence form of action. Indeed, in one leading decision in New Zealand, it was expressly declared that when considering matters of this sort what is being considered is not the patient's rights but the doctor's duty. In *Smith* v. *Auckland Hospital Board* it was said that:

> If the issue in the case was the maintenance of the individual's right of self-determination, the matter would quickly resolve itself. But it is not. This is a question within the duty of care concept of negligence . . . The welfare of patients would not be secured if a doctor's duty to warn about proposed treatment was to be considered in abstraction from the condition to which they were to be applied.[35]

Whilst not necessarily equating the judiciary with the state, it is clear that, in as much as judicial policy and interpretation affects the capacity of individuals to maintain human rights infringements in the courts, then they can legitimately be seen as representing the sort of decision-making which is often referred to as being 'state controlled.'

The emphasis on doctors' duties which is inherent in the negligence action could, of course, still protect individual rights if the doctor's duty is defined by law in the appropriate terms. However, courts have rather tended to emphasize the standard of care set by other medical

practitioners as being descriptive of the doctor's duty.[36] Thus, the
shift to the negligence action has, in most jurisdictions, provided less
opportunity for the individual to obtain redress for grievances of this
sort and has served to redefine the right in issue. This change in the
form of action which is deemed appropriate is more than merely
symbolic, then. As has been noted:

> How the case is pleaded in many cases is more than a matter of mere
> academic interest. It will have important bearing on such matters as
> the incidence of the onus of proof, causation, the importance of expert
> medical evidence, the significance of medical judgement, proof of
> damage and, most important, of course, the substantive basis upon
> which liability may be found.[37]

Indeed, if the purpose of providing an action in such cases is the
protection of individual rights then, whereas the duty of others will be
interesting and may be informative, to describe the right purely or
even primarily in terms of the duty owed to the person who has the
right seems to be to place the emphasis on an inappropriate aspect of
the transaction. The description of the right seems to have a logical
precedence over the description of the corresponding (and derivative)
duty. It is clear that such assessments as are made under the
negligence type of action are appropriate when the crux of the issue is
the professional behaviour of the doctor in terms of the exercise of his
or her technical skills as diagnostician and healer. However, if
requirements about consent are primarily designed to protect the
patient, then this technical behaviour is relevant only at a secondary,
rather than a primary level.

Conclusion

It has been argued in this chapter that there is a special reason for
considering the rights of patients in medical treatment. Whilst such
rights are clearly an aspect of self-determination and personal
autonomy, discussion of them demonstrates clearly how – even where
there is a public commitment to protecting self-determination –
competing 'goods' may be used insidiously to infringe on the core of
the right itself.

To some extent, this hypothesis can be further tested by considering contemporary commitments – under international law – to the notion of self-determination.[38] This concept is not neutral in respect of medical practice, and indeed the language of rights has been used to counter medical practice in some cases.[39] The international community has witnessed medical abuse in the past, resulting in mass outcry and the promulgation of codes rendering the unwarranted assumption of authority over the individual by doctors morally outlawed. The therapeutic imperative has, in international agreements at least, considerably less importance than the rights of the individual, although the translation of this moral position into the reality of individual protection is left to states whose processes and policies may not completely satisfy it.

Rights in medicine, therefore, play an important role in the general protection of the individual, and the extent to which patient's rights are protected reflects the commitment of individual states to the autonomy of individual citizens. Whilst the ascription of a special status to orthodox (or alternative) medicine is not in itself unreasonable or threatening, if national legal systems ignore or obfuscate the narrow line between unwilling and non-consensual medicine, then the rights of the individual will receive scant attention in the face of the competing interests of medicine.

Notes

1 For consideration of the issues raised by the position of the mentally ill, and an analysis of the right to treatment, see ch. 7 above.
2 For an excellent discussion of the importance of ethical considerations to the practice of medicine, see E. Pellegrino and D. Thomasma, *A Philosophical Basis of Medical Practice* (Oxford: Oxford University Press, 1981).
3 Ivan Illich, *Limits to Medicine. Medical Nemesis: The Expropriation of Health* (Harmondsworth: Penguin, 1977), 244.
4 Pellegrino and Thomasma, *A Philosophical Basis*, 159.
5 Thus the medical situation differs from that under criminal law, perhaps because 'the injuries are inflicted in such cases not for their own sake or in order to cause pain or gratify an intention to harm, but for the benefit of the patient'. G.H. Gordon, *The Criminal Law of Scotland* (2nd ed.), (Edinburgh: Green, 1978), 828.
6 See, for example, the World Medical Association, International Code of Medical Ethics (Declaration of Geneva) 1947, as amended in 1968 in Sydney, Australia.
7 See, for example, Thomas Szasz, *Law, Liberty and Psychiatry* (London: Routledge & Kegan Paul, 1963).
8 Illich, *Limits to Medicine*.
9 *Canterbury* v. *Spence* 464 F. 2d 772.
10 Cf. *Chatterton* v. *Gerson & Anor.* [1981] 1 All E.R. 257.
11 [1980] 7 *Current Law* 44.

12 *Sidaway* v. *Bethlem Royal Hospital Governors & Ors.* [1984] 1 All E.R. 1019 (C.A.), [1985] 1 All E.R. 643 (H.L.).
13 [1983] 3 All E.R. 716, 727.
14 See, for example, *H.M.A.* v. *Rutherford* 1947 J.C. 1; *Rex* v. *Donovan* [1934] 2 K.B. 498. For a full discussion of this point, see Glanville Williams, *Textbook of Criminal Law* (London: Stevens, 1978); Gordon, *The Criminal Law.*
15 As Williams, *Criminal Law*, points out at p. 531, 'if a doctor, to speed his dying patient's passing, injects poison with the patient's consent, this will be murder'.
16 See, for example, *D.P.P.* v. *Morgan* [1976] A.C. 182; *R* v. *Eatch* [1980] Crim.L.R. 651.
17 For a succint discussion of the implications of this doctrine, see Alan A. Watson and Angela M. McLean, 'Consent to Treatment – A Shield or a Sword?', *Scottish Medical Journal*, 25 (1980), 113.
18 Cmnd 7054–1/1978.
19 See, for example, the convincing arguments presented in G. Robertson, 'Informed Consent to Medical Treatment', *Law Quarterly Review*, 97 (1981), 102.
20 See *Canterbury* v. *Spence*, 'the physician discharges the duty when he makes a reasonable effort to convey sufficient information *although the patient, without fault of the physician, may not fully grasp it.*' (emphasis added).
21 M. Brazier, 'Informed Consent to Surgery', *Medicine Science and the Law*, 19 (1979), 49.
22 A. Buchanan, 'Medical Paternalism', *Philosophy and Public Affairs*, 7 (1978), 370.
23 See, for example, Pellegrino and Thomasma, *A Philosophical Basis*, 214.
24 See, for example, the judgment of Lord Denning in *Roe* v. *Ministry of Health* [1954] 2 Q.B. 66.
25 Pellegrino and Thomasma, *A Philosophical Basis*, 160.
26 See p. 156.
27 *The Times*, 29 July 1978.
28 For further discussion, see ch. 6, above.
29 *Chatterton* v. *Gerson & Anor.*, 264.
30 Indeed, Lord Denning, whose influence in medical cases cannot be under-estimated, has made it clear that this protection is vital. For discussion, see Denning, *The Discipline of Law* (London: Butterworth, 1979); S.A.M. Mclean, 'Negligence – A Dagger at the Doctor's Back?' in P. Robson and P. Watchman (eds), *Justice, Lord Denning and the Constitution* (Aldershot: Gower, 1981).
31 This is one of the assertions made in respect of prescribing practices and the attitudes of tribunals such as the Committee on Safety of Medicines in Alan Klass, *There's Gold in Them Thar Pills* (Harmondsworth: Penguin, 1975).
32 *Salgo* v. *Leland Stanford etc., Board of Trustees* 154 Cal. App. 2d 560 (1957), 578.
33 See note 9 above.
34 See, for example, *Chatterton* v. *Gerson*; *Sidaway*.
35 *Smith* v. *Auckland Hospital Board* [1964] N.Z.L.R. 241, 247.
36 *Sidaway*, *Hatcher* v. *Black*, *The Times*, 2 July 1954 (UK); *Reibl* v. *Hughes* 89 D.L.R. (3d) 112 (1978) (Canada); *Smith* v. *Auckland Hospital Board* (New Zealand); *Canterbury* v. *Spence* (USA).
37 *Kelly* v. *Hazlett* 75 D.L.R. (3d) 536 (1976) (Ontario High Court of Justice), 556.
38 Although not referring expressly to self-determination, the rights which might be encompassed by this are clearly stated in the Universal Declaration of Human Rights (1948).
39 See, for example, World Medical Association, Declaration of Helsinki (1964, revised 1975) (human experimentation).

9

The Rights of Public Assembly and Procession

Jim Murdoch

Introduction

Public protest has a long and glorious tradition in Britain, as in other Western societies. The act of joining with others in expressing dissent or disapproval has often resulted in great political and constitutional change: the activities of the barons at Runnymede in 1215, the signing of the Solemn League and Covenant in Edinburgh in 1638 and the demonstrations of the suffragettes at the beginning of the twentieth century are but three examples drawn from the past; today, protest on the streets or at an open meeting is still the most effective way of communicating passion and dissent. The level of activity is surprisingly high: community meetings, gala days, student protests, religious parades, election rallies, workers' occupations and commemorative services make up the bulk of public assemblies and processions, and pass off peacefully. Only when emotions and counter-reaction are great will the protest make news and pass into the political annals: the 1984 miners' disturbances will be seen in the future by some as equally great struggles as those marking the gradual movement towards religious toleration and univeral suffrage. That there is general agreement on the existence of a right to protest is evident in Western political thought.

However, the self-evident nature of the importance of individual's access to the means of persuading others or ventilating grievances obscures the real and practical difficulties of ensuring that legal systems accept and make provision for protest, for protest can often involve public disorder, civil disobedience, and ultimately violent insurrection. How the executive, the legislature and the judiciary attempt to distinguish between acceptable and non-acceptable protest, and where they draw these 'lines', are two of the most fascinating questions facing public lawyers. Balancing protest and public order is no mean task.

Protest, too, has to compete with other interests which may take on the cloak of rights rhetoric and thus involve even more delicate judgements: other citizens may well claim freedoms or rights to use streets for unimpeded passage, to go about their daily business without serious inconvenience, and to be protected against violent and inflammatory verbal attacks. As in other areas of civil and human rights, then, values and aspirations enshrined in notions such as freedom to protest have to compete with other conflicting collective and individual interests, demands, and legitimate legislative or executive objectives. Bartering and trade-offs inevitably take place in the political and legal arenas, but the initial bargaining strength of the freedoms associated with assembly and procession will be of importance in ensuring the ultimate recognition and survival of these values. This chapter attempts to set out the constitutional background to any discussion of human rights in Britain, and then comments upon its effect on public protest. For ease of discussion, four components of public interest have been identified as worthy of consideration: first, freedom of association with others; second, the right to static meeting; third, the right to public procession; and fourth, protection against the imposition of criminal sanctions after a meeting or march has taken place.

It might be thought that freedom of protest is simply one aspect of the more general right of freedom of speech. Restraints on protest may be applied as a form of 'pre-publication' censorship, or as 'post-publication' penalties enforced by the courts. But protest involves the *communication* of ideas, not their formulation or validity. This aspect of human rights is about the *means* of persuasion or airing of grievances, and public protest is seen as a distinct human right worthy of individual treatment in positive constitutional codes.[1]

Nor has the advent of more democratic processes rendered protest less valuable. Participation in influencing, persuading and directing decision-making is deep-rooted in Western political systems: the great gatherings of Scandinavian tribes in the *Althing* arenas may today only be mirrored in the annual town parliaments in Swiss cantons and in New England townships, but more sophisticated political devices, such as referenda and initatives, have emerged in recent years even in states in which a high degree of representative government has been achieved. Democracy requires the governors to keep in contact with the governed. Guaranteeing rights of public protest can therefore be seen as another, albeit informal, way of encouraging participation in decision-making, for it allows the governed to signal to their rulers. The existence of the ballot box does not render assembly and procession obsolete.

How, then, do the rights of protest fare in the UK? Constitutional guarantees of human rights help fulfil the task of translating rhetoric into reality: but in Britain, no such mandate for judicial or political activism exists. How do our freedoms manage without the protection of the dictates of fundamental law?

The Debate in its Constitutional Setting

One of the main themes of this book is the continuing struggle to ensure that abstract moral and political freedoms are translated into positive and enforceable rights possessing both efficacy and a general level of acceptance and definition in jurisprudence. One problem in translating rhetoric into reality centres upon the processes and procedures adopted in a state or by an international institution in formulating the precise application of a particular right at a given stage and, equally as important, in ensuring that the judicial dictat is carried out by the executive or legislature. The task is much more complicated than the jurisprudential formula *ubi ius, ibi remedium* would have it: there will be controversy and dispute over the exact scope of the protected right in question, with traditional legal reasoning involving consideration also of the rather nebulous 'public interest'. Human rights, as others have discussed, are neither absolute, nor do they exist in a political vacuum. Whether or not they are effective – that is, able to be enforced by individual citizens – depends not only upon the availability of procedures and remedies but also upon the constitutional power structures in a state. It is this last point which is often overlooked in debating the best methods of giving moral assertions real value and protection, for just as governmental organs are the main violators of human rights throughout the world, only they can ensure that power is exercised in a way which gives meaning to the concept of 'rights'.

Public lawyers may well argue that the best constitutional structure to achieve this aim is the existence of a written constitutional document containing both provisions detailing the powers and organization of the organs of government and also a code of rights or freedoms to be enjoyed by citizens, not collectively but individually (and thus by implication limitations on governmental power). How the structure is thereafter operated by governors and the governed alike may eventually be of greater importance, but the enshrinement of the notions of limited government and a charter of right may well, in itself, be the starting point for the progress from rhetoric to reality.

The point about constitutional structures is worth stressing. In European political thought from at least the middle part of the sixteenth century, concern was essentially with the allocation of political power and its control: to be sure, the Reformation stressed the importance of personal conscience and individual responsibility, but the political settlement in Central Europe contained in the Peace of Augsburg in 1555 subjected theological beliefs to state direction: *cuius regio, eius religio* (the religion of a state was to be that of its ruler). The general trend towards absolutism was checked in England in the seventeenth century only by constitutional reform (although persecution even here led many to flee to the new American colonies). Montesquieu's highly influential *L'Esprit des Lois* of 1748 identified not the claim to individual and alienable human rights as the best basis for liberty, but the separation of powers within a state.[2] The human rights movement is a later political and philosophical force, although within a short period of time both concepts were to merge into a standard model for general applicability.

Where limited government is an accepted constitutional norm, the moral and political respect accorded human rights is all the greater. Once the initial steps towards the effective policing of civil rights have been taken and asserted – judicial independence, the presumption of judicial review, and finally, judicial sovereignty[4] – the subsequent problems of converting vague and general values into specific protections via the legal process finds more ready acceptance although the courts may require continually to 'follow the ballot box' in order to retain their constitutional legitimacy.

This move towards state and international protection for human rights has often been prompted by a political rejection of and moral revulsion at wholesale violation of rights. The earliest examples of constitutional protections – the Virginian Bill of Rights of 1776, the

French Declaration of the Rights of Man and the Citizen of 1789, and the American Bill of Rights of 1791 – share much in common with the later international documents – the UN Declaration of Human Rights of 1948 and the European Convention of Human Rights of 1950 – in being born out of repression and conflict. Written declarations and guarantees of individual rights became part of the accepted constitutional package marking a new start in a country's development or in international relations.

However, British constitutional theory lacks both the notion of a written constitution and a declaration of rights, and this is a crucial factor in any discussion of civil liberties in the UK. Whereas in most other Western democracies (and certainly in other Commonwealth States with the exception of New Zealand)[5] there is acceptance of the policing of executive and legislative actions and a charter of rights by the judiciary, the UK's constitutional structures are founded upon the principle of untrammelled competence of the legislature. This Parliamentary sovereignty or supremacy was the creation of the Glorious Revolution of 1688–9. In their day the Bill of Rights of 1689 and its Scottish counterpart, the Claim of Right, were important achievements in guaranteeing the independence of the judiciary and responsible government (that is, accountable to Parliament). In the realm of what nowadays would be termed 'civil liberties', the doctrine of the rule of law provided protection. In an era when absolutist rulers reigned supreme in the European kingdoms, principalities and dukedoms, judicial pronouncements such as *Entick* v. *Carrington*[6] in 1765 emphasized the strengths of the common law.

In short, Britain's constitutional revolution came too early: more than a century before the idea of written constitutions containing fundamental rights was accepted. While the political achievements of 1688–9 made a substantial impact on the constitutional order in the kingdoms, individual liberties or fundamental rights were seen as the consequence of the new legal order, not of the revolution itself. In A.V. Dicey's words, 'With us the law of the constitution, the rules which in foreign countries naturally form part of a constitutional code, are not the source but the consequence of the rights of individuals as defined and enforced by the courts'.[7]

The result for British civil liberties is crucial, and it is much more than a problem of how to entrench a Bill of Rights. Few discussions in the political arena employ the language of human rights; seldom if ever are 'liberalism' considerations raised in the legal process.

The influence of our constitutional structure upon judicial behaviour has been described as follows:

> The role of our judges in protecting human rights is closely confined both by the subordinate position of the courts in relation to the omnipotent legislature and by a widespread public philosophy which welcomes the narrowness of the judicial mandate in this country. It is a public philosophy which doubts the democratic credentials of judges to strike down Acts of Parliament, which is sceptical about the value of paper guarantees of written constitutions, which questions the competence of judges to act as lawmakers, and which fears for their independence if judges have to decide controversial issues of policy.[8]

Not surprisingly, such ingrained attitudes are to be found widely. Lord Devlin remarked that 'the British have no more wish to be governed by judges than they have to be judged by administrators', and his own views on the proper restraint to be shown in the exercise of judicial function[9] are without doubt accepted by the great majority of his brethren. During debates in the House of Lords initiated by Lord Wade's attempt to introduce legislation incorporating the European Convention on Human Rights, several of the Law Lords expressed major reservations. Lord Morris of Borth-y-Gest declared himself opposed to legislation which would amount, in effect, to Parliament handing over 'legislative' power to judges,[10] while Lord Diplock warned that the judiciary would be involved in making 'political' decisions. 'The administration of justice in our country depends upon the respect which all people of all political views feel for the judges. And in my opinion that respect depends very much upon keeping judges out of politics.'[11] And where British judges have been compelled to interpret constitutional guarantees of rights (as members of the Judicial Committee of the Privy Council in Commonwealth appeals), their lack of self-confidence and sense of discomfort have been all too noticeable.[12]

The task in ensuring that basic human rights and freedoms in Britain are adequately protected by the legal process is thus a much more difficult one than in other states. The constitutional structures of society stress the dominant role of the legislature and the limited role of the judiciary. Judicial reluctance, though, is not merely self-imposed restraint; it is expected and required as a norm in a constitution which views as its ultimate strength the sovereignty of Parliament. But the difficulties are much further compounded: there is a general lack of awareness of and interest in even the rhetoric of human rights. Where such interest exists, it may all too readily be identified with a particular political ideology. The very language of the subject underlines the nature of individual freedom in Britain, for we talk not of 'human rights' or 'civil rights', but of 'civil liberties'. The point may appear slight, but it is of importance in any further debate; 'liberty means any occasion on which an act or omission is not a breach of a duty . . . a right exists where there is a positive law on the subject; a liberty where there is no law.'[13] Personal freedom in Britain is essentially residual in character: limits upon individual freedoms are set not by the interpretation of the content of positive, abstract rights, but by the restrictions placed upon choice or action by the state. As one writer stresses, 'the citizen may do as he likes unless he clashes with some specific restriction on his freedom. The law does not say: "You can do that", it says "you cannot do this", which means that you can do everything else except that which it says you cannot do.'[14]

The Legacy for the Right to Protest

Thus, the rights of peaceful meeting and protest attract little legal concern in terms of their social value in a democratic society; instead, attention is invariably centred upon public order aspects or the effect upon the rights of other non-protesting citizens. Lacking a constitutional mandate to uphold what in other democratic states may be generally accepted to be self-evident objectives, the judiciary has rarely attempted to provide clear protection for protesters, and in times of social unrest involving street disorders, Parliamentary and executive action invariably involves attempts to strengthen the powers available to the police. Only occasionally have judges given additional weight in their opinions to civil libertarian values. Whilst American jurisprudence contains many declarations of the values of protest and political expression such as Justice Brandeis's oft-quoted remarks that 'without free speech and assembly, discussion would be futile', and 'the path of safety lies in the opportunity to discuss freely supposed grievances and proposed remedies',[15] only exceptionally rarely are there to be found in Britain examples of similar judicial thinking. Lord Denning's dicta in a recent case stand out as a plea for additional protection:

Here we have to consider the right to demonstrate and the right to protest on matters of public concern. These are rights which it is in the public interest that individuals should possess; and, indeed that they should exercise without impediment so long as no wrongful act is done. It is often the only means by which grievances can be brought to the knowledge of those in authority – at any rate with such impact as to gain a remedy. Our history is full of warnings against suppression of those rights.[16]

At worst, the judiciary may claim a declaratory power itself to deal with attacks on public order in the absence of statutory provision (on the basis of public policy).[17] At best, claims to public protest will be disposed of by the favoured means of balancing competing interests. Thus Lord Scarman commented, 'a balance has to be struck, a compromise found that will accommodate the exercise of the right to protest within a framework of public order which enables ordinary citizens who are not protesting to go about their business and pleasures without obstruction or inconvenience'.[18]

Of course, similar line-drawing exercises are to be found in jurisdictions possessing constitutional guarantees, for no rights are absolute. Article 11 of the European Convention expressly permits derogation to the rights of peaceful assembly and association with others 'in the interests of national security or public safety, for the prevention of disorder or crime, for the protection of health and morals or for the protection of the rights and freedoms of others'. The First Amendment to the American Constitution may well unequivocally protect the 'right of the people peaceably to assemble', but the content of what has become known as the 'public forum issue' is delineated by restrictions on speech, locus and timing.[19] The continuing balancing or line-drawing in such jurisdictions involves a deliberate attempt to distinguish between legitimate exercise of the rights of protest deemed healthy by the state and abuses by individuals whose primary goal is considered not so much objectionable but harmful to society or to a section of it.

However, the terms of the debate are different in the UK. The rhetoric of fundamental rights competes at a disadvantage with more concrete and more valued considerations such as preventing violence, minimizing the cost of policing and containing disruption to the community.[20] Parliamentary involvement is often prompted by repeated instances of street violence. In 1936, as Mosley's Blackshirts paraded through English streets, the Public Order Act was hastily enacted (although it has been suggested that by the time the Act appeared, the British Order of Fascists was largely a spent force and the immediate threat to law and order had passed);[21] recent disorders have prompted a Government Green Paper, *Review of the Public Order Act and Related Legislation*,[22] and a report from the Select Committee on Home Affairs, *The Law Relating to Public Order*.[23] In both these instances, the emphasis has been on ensuring the provision of a *statutory* framework capable of enforcement by the police and in which greater weight or 'balance' is given to the 'rights' of the community (the Home Affairs Select Committee used the phrase 'the "human right" to a normal life').

There are important consequences for these rights in Britain. First there are no recognized 'rights' of meeting or of procession. Second, even where a march or static protest is being held, its organizers run the risk of prosecution for occasioning disorder, even although the disorder is the action of counter-protesters. And third, the absence of a constitutional guarantee may weaken the very rhetorical and persuasive force of the freedoms as circumstances change: the moral objectivity of the rights of protest is replaced by a somewhat subjective pragmatism. It may be argued that the emergence of means of mass communication, especially radio and now television, render assembly and procession unnecessary devices since the electronic media are now the main channel for persuasion and debate; and where conflict with other legitimate state goals arises, a gradual but discernible shift away from upholding rights of protest is permissible. Such, though, fails to recognize the lack of access to the media, and treats protest as an intellectual exercise when very often what is being sought to be communicated is not reason but intensity of feeling. Protest has long been accorded respect for its social worth in permitting the release of pent-up frustrations unrealizable through the ballot-box: a sort of safety valve for protesting students, nuclear demonstrators, striking workers or the like. Meetings and marches have rarely in themselves been efficacious: they are but limited devices in motivating public sympathy or opinion, although possessing social and democratic value.

However, paradoxically, the very existence of the media creates a rather different form of hazard for protest; while television and the press may now act as the main fora for identifying and considering political controversy, access to these means of mass communication will in many cases require protesters' actions to be newsworthy. In the absence of a sizeable audience or public-figure speakers, the use of violence or disorder is almost guaranteed to lead to air-time on national news broadcasts or to front-page coverage in newspapers. The extent to which protesters may benefit from disruptive tactics may be difficult to quantify, but arguably the use of civil disobedience will lead to a much greater degree of awareness of the existence of a social wrong or a particular political message. Suffragette activities in the early part of this century may find a parellel today in the activities of right-wing extremist groups and 'picketing' Grunwick employees or miners. This form of protest is not a device to show solidarity, persuade others, or to 'blow off steam': it is a conscious attempt to use a march or procession to achieve widespread publicity by occasioning disorder, and itself poses problems in protecting and defining the limits of the freedoms to protest.

The right to freedom of association

States, then, may attempt to place restrictions upon the component elements of protest: these restrictions may directly or indirectly strengthen the core of the rights by cutting back troublesome offshoots which may alienate public sympathy and lead to state demands for legislative intervention. It is the validity or legitimacy of the goals behind the restrictions which will determine whether or not the pruning exercise results in a weakening and eventual withering of the plant. Thus states may seek to prevent protest which degenerates into mobbing and rioting, intimidation, or stirs up hatred against minority groupings: how much further a state attempts to go (for example, in wartime or against anti-government protest) may be the best litmus-test of human rights at a particular point.

Likewise, a state may attempt to place restraints upon the types of associations which can be entered into in the pursuit of certain goals. Free association with others is the first element – a prerequisite – of effective protest. While the UK possesses no legal device which places a restriction upon individuals ('banning orders' in South Africa, for example, prohibit individuals subject to such from attending any form of public gathering – meaning a meeting of more than two people – or from having any material published),[24] sanctions may be imposed upon individuals who join with others in associations deemed to be unlawful. The objectives behind some of these restrictions may appear historical irrelevancies of no consequence in the present. For example, the establishment of quasi-military organizations designed to usurp the function of the police or military is prohibited by Section 2 of the Public Order Act, 1936. But the existence of a military tradition associated with political parties and the problems of dealing with 'defence formations' of the kind that bedevilled the fragile Weimar Republic in Germany have not arisen in practice in Great Britain in recent years.

Terrorism strikes at the heart of Western democratic society, substituting as it does the bullet for the ballot paper. It may be considered a legitimate aim of governments to restrict protest of this sort, but both the efficacy and the validity of this form of restraint have been called into question. In Britain, for example, a contentious restriction under statute is that provided by the Prevention of Terrorism (Temporary Provisions) Acts (currently, the 1984 Act) upon membership of, soliciting support for, or arranging or addressing a meeting in support of organizations specified by a Secretary of State as proscribed organizations. Only two Republican groups have been so designated on the mainland, although in Northern Ireland several 'loyalist' terrorist organizations and additional Republican associations have been proscribed. Such legislation is clearly designed to be preventive in nature: it does, however, seek to punish associations and not actions. Is it justifiable from a human rights standpoint to restrict the beliefs of those who are intent on using violence to achieve their ends? How violent does the activity have to be before proscription: murder, serious disorder, minor street skirmishes? Legislative aims may be avoided by the adherents of one proscribed organization moving to another, non-proscribed grouping; or indeed retaining membership of both a terrorist organization covertly, and a 'political' mouthpiece overtly. The difficulties in following proscription to its logical limit are apparent: freedom of belief itself will be at stake.

Greater problems exist where one or more organs of the state possess discretionary powers of both uncertain and flexible application. Particular problems have faced British jurisprudence, where another form of association subject to restriction is provided by the common law. 'A criminal conspiracy arises if two or more persons agree to render one another assistance in doing an act whether as an end in itself or as a means to an end which would be criminal if done by an individual.'[25] The crime is complete upon agreement even although no further action is taken. Its rationale is that it 'makes possible an earlier intervention by the law to prevent the commission of the substantive offence',[26] but the elasticity of the crime, its common-law basis (courts had imposed in many cases lengthy periods of imprisonment for conspiracy far in excess of maximum statutory penalties provided for the actual commission of the deeds), and the frequent use of the charge in political cases have caused much disquiet.[27] In England, statutory regulation of conspiracy was attempted by the Criminal Law Act, 1977, but certain of the more controversial features of the common law still remain.

The charge has been used against political and religious dissidents: against early trade unionists, Chartists, and Irish Nationalists in the nineteenth century, and against Communists, anti-apartheid demonstrators, students and pickets in the twentieth. English law has recently 'discovered' variants to penalize behaviour which courts have deemed immoral: conspiracy to corrupt public morals, to outrage public decency, or to effect a public mischief have been used as charges against individuals or groups in the last three decades in England. Indeed, the English courts at one stage, in a remarkable piece of judicial law-making, extended the crime to conspiracy to commit a civil wrong – civil trespass – on the basis of public interest.[28] Only this latter development was restrained by Parliamentary intervention: the others were expressly retained. The retention of this crime and its application by prosecutors and judiciary alike emphasizes the precarious state of the right to protest. As one writer comments: 'the normal facts of political activity leading to public meetings and demonstrations give wide scope for charges of conspiracy.[29]

The right to hold meetings

Judicial attitudes to questions involving static assemblies can be stated succinctly. 'English law does not recognise any special right of public meeting for political or other purposes', declared Lord Chief Justice Hewart in a 1936 case involving the conviction of a speaker for obstruction of a police officer in the execution of his duty. The court deflected attention from the right to protest: Mr Justice Humphreys regarded the issues 'as a plain case. It [had] nothing to do with the law of unlawful assembly . . . The sole question raised by the case is whether the respondent . . . was so obstructed when in the execution of his duty.'[30] Whereas the right to protest has been accorded little or no social value by the judiciary, the objective of securing the public peace is pursued with vigour and determination. Further consideration of offences which may be occasioned by protest appears below: but it is paradoxically the case that protesters who have been given or who believe they possess the right or liberty to demonstrate may end up facing public order charges involving potentially more serious consequences that those involving unlawful assembly or illegal procession.

Meetings on private premises will, however, be subject to little regulation provided always that consent of the owner or occupier is obtained. In Scotland, certain forms of trespass are criminal: the Trespass (Scotland) Act, 1865 (designed to regulate and control the activities of gypsies), penalizes the lodging in private premises and the occupation of or encampment on private land. Recently the statute has been used by prosecutors against employees staging a 'sit in'.[31] But in England, occupation of private property without consent would incur merely civil liability. The charge of conspiracy to trespass cannot now be used,[32] although certain forms of occupation (e.g. an occupation of a factory by an employee) could lead to criminal liability under a little-used statute regulating trade disputes.[33]

In one significant instance, a right to use local authority premises for meetings has been provided by Parliament. The Representation of the People Act, 1983, provides that candidates at Parliamentary and local government elections may have the use of a meeting place (usually in a school), subject to a possible charge for making the room ready and the cost of repairing any damage. The right is enforceable in the courts: for example, the National Front candidate at a bye-election in Southall obtained a remedy against the Labour-controlled council which had denied him access.[34] The validity of policy decisions of this kind by which certain political parties are denied access on the basis of their beliefs to premises owned by public authorities at times other than at a pending election is not clear; it may amount to an abuse of discretion,[35] but if the local authority were to attempt to justify its refusal on the basis of threatened public disorder, the courts would doubtless uphold the denial of access.[36] In the absence of adequate protection of the rights of assembly – especially assembly related to political discussion – at least one writer has argued for the extension of the right at election time to cover all applications by organizations whether party political or not.[37]

Meetings held outdoors in public parks and other open spaces, too, are at the discretion of public bodies. Even the 'right' to use the most hallowed shrine of public protest, Speaker's Corner in London, and the 'right' to use the most effective, Trafalgar Square, are privileges accorded either (in the case of the former) indirectly in the absence of executive action, or (in the case of the latter) upon specific permission being granted. Parliament itself has directed that no meeting be held within a mile of Westminster during its sittings.[38] Invariably, public open spaces are regulated by bye-laws which will either prohibit meetings or require the approval of the local authority. While such bye-laws can be challenged on the basis of *vires* as being unreasonable, the courts will tend to find in favour of the validity of the regulations. Indeed, in one Scottish case the High Court of Justiciary ruled that such a bye-law, requiring written consent from the authority before a meeting could be held in a public park, in fact facilitated the freedoms of speech and assembly. As Lord Justice-Clerk Alness said:

> It is a mistake to represent [the bye-law] as a withdrawal of the right of free speech. There is no interference with that right – with the right of the speaker to express any opinion which he pleases. It is also a mistake to represent it as a prohibition of public meetings. It merely requires permission to be obtained in order to hold them. It does not prevent, but it regulates the exercise of the right . . . The bye-law, in point of fact, so far from prohibiting public meetings, affords facilities for holding them.[39]

This argument appears initially attractive: the judgment at least considers the existence of the 'freedom', albeit in a rather vague and unconvincing manner. It suggests regulation is necessary to enable all who wish to 'peddle their wares' in John Stuart Mill's 'market place of political dialogue' to have an adequate opportunity of selling their message. Yet the market place is, by definition, a bustling and energetic gathering of competing claims and viewpoints between which customers are asked to choose, not a stage-managed series of one-act presentations. This judgment may well pay lip-service to the rights of assembly: it is not, as appears at first glance, a call for a regulated (as opposed to a free-enterprise or capitalist) public forum. However, the judgment ends on a more traditional note: the individual's right to protest must be balanced with the rights of others to use the park for recreation. The rights of others to be left alone and to carry on with their everyday business may be a convenient shorthand way of expressing the existence of a power to impose censorship, since ultimately the communication of an idea may be restricted by reference not to its political, social or moral content but to the nuisance of its presentation.

So, too, it is with meetings held on the public highway: 'the primary and overuling object for which streets exist is passage. The streets are public, but they are public for passage, and there is no such thing as a right in the public to hold meetings as such in the street'.[40] Obstructing the highway amounts to a criminal offence, but enforcement by the state may be sporadic and thus discriminatory. One writer has commented that 'obstruction is so loose a word that in practice everything turns on how the police interpret it in deciding whether to prosecute . . . this elasticity of the term "obstruction" provides the police with a powerful weapon to restrict freedom of public meeting, a weapon which they do not hesitate to use.'[41]

The discretion accorded the state and the absence of any positive mandate upholding protest rights are aptly illustrated by a case in the 1930s. A street had been used in the past on a number of occasions for the holding of meetings (at which police officers were in attendance to ensure the free passage of traffic), and Arrowsmith had given notice to the police of her intention to hold a meeting. It took place, and afterwards she was convicted for obstructing the highway. On appeal, the court rejected the arguments that Arrowsmith had been arbitrarily singled out for prosecution and that some element of *mens rea* was required. The law was simple: 'if anybody, by an exercise of free will, does something which causes an obstruction, then an offence is committed.'[42]

Here, even the rhetoric of rights is missing; action is justifiable against organizers since the courts can only apply Acts of Parliament and not impute any libertarian or democratic values. Judicial attempts to 'discover' some higher value for peaceful protest would be likely to be met by Lord Reid's oft-quoted dictum that 'where Parliament fears to tread it is not for the courts to rush in.' This is no mere passing of the buck by the courts to the legislature: it is the consequence of a lack of constitutional mandate for judicial activism.

On the odd occasion when the courts have urged special protection for the freedom to protest, judges have found themselves required by necessity to qualify their advocacy. Consider the difficulties in admitting a right to use a street for a meeting faced by the Scottish High Court of Justiciary:

When a man exercises a private right, he is using that which is his own; and, because the right is his own, it is exclusive of the rights of others. But when a man exercises a public right he uses that which is not his own, but belongs to the community of which he is only a constituent unit. . . . The exercise of a public right is circumscribed on every hand by the duty (which arises out of the very nature of public rights) to respect the equal rights of others to participate in them . . . I do not attempt to define the uses to which a public street, as such, is legally devoted. I have assumed in what I have said that the use for a public meeting is not wholly excluded from the catalogue of legal public uses. But, assuming that it is such a use. . . , it must be conducted under the many and serious restrictions which are imposed by the necessity of avoiding interference with other public uses.[43]

This form of reasoning may adopt the rhetoric of rights, but it does so in such a manner as to obscure the essential nature of the demand for human rights: that they exist as prescriptive values to be translated into real and meaningful applications available for use by individual citizens irrespective of state attempts at repression. Certainly, restrictions on and interpretation of the scope of each right are required. This, however, is in the nature of patrolling the boundary between the interest of citizens on the one hand and those of the state on the other. Human rights are not shared out either *with* the state (in equating this to community), or *amongst* other citizens.

The forthright rejection of the notion of the right to protest, or at best the hesitancy over its existence, or its severe limitation, is in contrast with the starting-point for discussion in countries where the right to protest is constitutionally guaranteed. This chapter's scope does not extend to consideration of the need for a Bill of Rights or equivalent, but some commentators have stressed the practical effect of reform of this nature. One result could be the provision of 'public fora': institutionalized market places for political dialogue. More often than not, what a protest is demonstrating is not the intellectual merits of a cause, but the intensity of feeling. A failure to provide unsophisticated channels for the communication of ideas, devices which are both available to all groups (when access to the media may not be) and also deemed by users to possess some efficacy (when other methods of political persuasion are not so judged) may result in peaceful protest being stifled and exploding into other forms of direct action, much less palatable to society. Identifiable open-air venues available to all would place these areas on a legal footing and make control of potential or actual disorder and traffic disruption much easier while most probably reducing the number of processions through the streets.[44]

The right to public procession

Closely linked in the language of rights to freedom of assembly is freedom of procession. Marches have, on occasion, resulted in spectacular successes: Martin Luther King's 'freedom marches' in the early 1960s through the southern states in America drew widespread attention via national and international media coverage to injustices and inequalities facing the country's blacks and were largely responsible for mobilizing the political pressure required for additional civil rights legislation. But it was the violent reaction to the marchers from Alabama's state troopers which made headline news. The problem of the 'unpopular message' and its possible or probable effect on others is the greatest difficulty facing the state in defining the right to march and the limits of justifiable interference.

To begin with, legislative and judicial attention was directed not at the use of the streets for processions, but at the criminal purposes behind the processions which often involved mobbing and rioting, serious assaults, and even treason. The basic problem facing the state then (as now) lay in maintaining public order, but processions were not seen as methods of influencing public opinion in the way that debating and canvassing at a public meeting are today. Public processions were more closely linked with public order problems than were static meetings. By their very nature, they were designed to show strength of feeling and the solidarity of those taking part. Whereas a public meeting at least offers the possibility for discussion and opposing views to be put to speakers, the only effective way to ensure dissenting opinions are heard is by counter-demonstration. Arguably, the law ought to protect processions since highways are for access and passage, and a procession is no more than a number of people collectively exercising the right of passage. Such a view has received judicial approval.[45] Protesters in a march may well be exercising a *prima facie* right recognized by law, yet concern in Britain is not with the freedom to march but with law and order. The great majority of casebooks and commentaries take 'public order' as their heading for discussion of the law in this area of civil liberties, not 'the rights of protestors'.

The practical effect on political and judicial reasoning is readily noticeable. The debate takes place with the aim of providing a legislative framework within which decision-makers (the police, and now local authorities) can operate effectively to prevent disorder. Desirable objectives are identified as the prevention of serious disorder,[46] serious disruption to the normal life of the community,[47] and marches which display sectarianism and a lack of toleration towards others.[48] Protest with democratic goals – that is, participation in democratic processes and decision-influencing – is at best quickly dismissed by a 'balancing' process taking account of competing interests which are more tangible and achievable in the short term. In denying these rights, the state may seek to don a cloak of moral responsibility by justifying its action as necessary for the protection of the 'rights' of others.

In Britain, the very existence of two separate legislative frameworks regulating processions, each with conflicting criteria, controls and procedures, underlines the overriding concerns of the state. First specific powers over public processions were provided by the Public Order Act, 1936. Section 3 allows a Chief Constable who has reasonable grounds for apprehending that a procession may occasion *serious* public disorder to impose conditions as to route, timing, and so on which appear to him to be necessary to preserve the public peace. If he feels these powers are inadequate, he may request the relevant local authority to make a prohibition order banning all processions or any class of procession over the whole of or in any part of the local authority area. Prohibition orders require the consent of the Home Secretary or Secretary of State for Scotland, and may last for up to three months.

Such powers confer discretion in no small measure upon chief officers of police. While the criterion of 'serious public disorder' is specific, the courts are unlikely to uphold a challenge against police action,[49] and the Act gives a potential power to control processions on account of political content. Conditions could be imposed, for example, on the routing of a march to take it away from the target audience, and a Chief Constable could seek a prohibition order against processions involving an unpopular cause. The Act could be used to police ideas, not public order. But, prohibition orders have been used infrequently: Chief Constables have used their powers rarely, and reluctantly. In 30 years – between 1951 and 1980 – only nine orders were made. In the month of March 1981, however, eight separate orders were made in attempts to prevent violence arising at National Front-related marches. While the police are called upon, in effect, to censor political protest (the decision to seek a banning order may only be instigated by a Chief Constable whose discretion is virtually unchallengeable, officers have been at pains to stress that prohibition orders are imposed only upon public order grounds and as a last resort. As has been indicated, recent calls have been made to review the test of 'serious public disorder' to strengthen police powers. Justification for a weakening of the right to march may come from further attempts to disguise the real values recognized by the political and legal systems:

> the law needs to balance the freedom to demonstrate with the sometimes conflicting interests of those who do not wish to do so . . . The importance of the subject justifies thorough examination from time to time, to see whether the balance struck by the law is appropriate and relevant to contemporary problems and those likely to arise in the future.[50]

No such pretexts and pretensions were discernible in the later provision of a second set of local authority controls over public processions. A number of authorities in England and Wales sought additional powers to regulate processions in the 1970s. In Scotland the revision of a series of confused and patchy local Acts and bye-laws took place by means of the Civic Government (Scotland) Act, 1982. These revised powers give Regional and Island Councils a discretion to impose conditions and even prohibit planned processions which now require seven days' notice. There is no criterion to meet before action can be taken, although earlier prohibition orders under repealed powers had been imposed by councils to prevent marches they considered 'contrary to the Highland way of life' or which threatened 'the privilege of [the community] to benefit from religious tolerance'.[51] Although there is the power to exempt certain types of processions from the requirements of notification and marches 'commonly or customarily held' are by definition exempt unless a Council decides otherwise, most Councils have chosen to override these restrictions on their powers. Only one Council has attempted to exempt as many protest organizers as possible, although admittedly on the basis of administrative convenience.[52] Licensing has come of age: the *prima facie* right to march has become a privilege, requiring prior approval and subject to interference by Councils on political and moral grounds.

Offences occasioned by assembly or procession

The rights of assembly and procession will be negated or at least weakened considerably if demonstrators may be subjected to sanctions on the basis of the effect the message has on its audience. The problem of restraining this aspect of freedom of expression is one which faces most legal systems which attempt to give some cash-value to the rights. Often, the difficulty is resolved by restricting the right of meeting or march only upon a fairly rigid test, such as the clear and present danger formula adopted by the American Supreme Court.

In Britain, this form of further restraint clearly operates upon the rights of protest: the organizers of even a lawful meeting or a march for which permission is granted are liable to criminal prosecution arising out of their activity. Once more, the crucial interests are those collective interests of 'non-protesters' (that is, the state), and the crucial value that of public order. But paradoxically, legal rules may indeed encourage the use of disruption by counter-protesters.

British law penalizes not only those who *cause* disorder, but those who *occasion* it: that is, those who cause others (i.e. counter-demonstrators) to cause disorder. Two similar cases, both concerning the Salvation Army and reported in 1882, illustrate this distinction. Early processions by the Salvation Army in the name of the Gospel provoked widespread disturbances, primarily engineered by the Skeleton Army's attempts at halting the parades. In England, the courts held in *Beatty* v. *Gilbanks*[53] that it was not the Salvation Army's officers who caused the disorder, but the 'unlawful and unjustifiable interference of the Skeleton Army'. But in the Scottish case of *Deakin* v. *Milne*[54] convictions for breach of the peace against Salvation Army officers were upheld. No matter how good the intentions of individuals are, if their actions lead to disorder they may be liable to criminal sanction.

The distinction is important. Before the development of the concept of meetings, and especially street demonstrations, as legitimate democratic devices to influence others, such assembly and processions were means to other ends usually regarded as criminal. Sedition, treason, mobbing and rioting, as well as breach of the peace were available as charges against those who used the streets or meeting-places for reasons other than protest intended to be peaceful. The effect of the *Deakin* reasoning (applied in later cases in statutory formulae such as the Public Order Act) upon democratic protest is substantial and, indeed, is an encouragement to those who disagree with a particular message to employ disruptive tactics. Fierce enough reaction will render the otherwise legal protest illegal. As the courts have indicated, a speaker must 'take his audience as he finds them'.[55] The law intervenes to punish not only the reactors but the catalysts, giving secondary concern to the content of the message sought to be communicated. The wider implications for freedom of expression are seldom realized, despite Mill's observation: 'it is not to be apprehended that the government . . . will often attempt to control the expression of opinion, except when in doing so it makes itself the organ of the general intolerance of the public.'[56]

Conclusion

British civil liberties are in a state of moral crisis. While there may be an increasing awareness of the importance of individual liberty, prompted largely by the influences of the European Commission and European Court of Human Rights, the absence of an underlying Natural Law commitment and Bill of Rights mandate make it difficult to establish a political and legal order in which certain rights are accepted either as limitations upon state intervention and activity, or as values and goals worthy of pursuit by state organs.

Constitutional structures of the state limit judicial activity and place ultimate responsibility upon the legislature. At best, human rights issues are balanced with other considerations; in the process, state interests may be identified and described as the collective interests of other individuals, although civil rights have traditionally be viewed as concerning the relationship of citizens with the state.

The effect on the rights of protest is clear. Despite occasional acceptance of the fundamental importance of association, meeting and procession, and recognition of their worth in permitting participation in democratic discussion, the value of the 'public forum' is effectively rejected. Public order considerations predominate and restrictions of freedom of expression obtain justification. In resolving the conflict between law and order and liberty (faced as a necessity by every state), often the rhetoric of rights is taken over to present the state's view of what is in the interests of the majority to the detriment of human liberty and freedom.

Notes

1 E.g. The First Amendment to the US Constitution, 1791; Sections 2(c) and (d) of the Canadian Charter of Rights and Freedoms, 1982; Article 20 of the Universal Declaration of Human Rights, 1948; Article 11 of the European Convention on Human Rights, 1950.
2 For a discussion of the doctrine's influence, see M.J.C. Vile,*Constitutionalism and the Separation of Powers* (Oxford: Clarendon Press, 1967).
3 This is discussed in J.W. Garner's *Political Science and Government* (New York: American Book Co., 1930, ch.18.
4 Each stage in the process of asserting the competence of the judiciary in this field may require to be won against competing political interests: see, for example, R.G. McCloskey, *The American Supreme Court* (Chicago: Chicago University Press, 1960), 29–30.
5 For a brief but recent review of the incorporation of human rights guarantees into the UK Constitution, see A. Lester, 'Fundamental Rights: The United Kingdom Isolated?', *Public Law* (1984), 46.
6 (1765) 19 St. Tr. 1030.
7 A.V. Dicey, *An Introduction to the Study of the Law of the Constitution* (10th edn.) (London: Macmillan, 1967), 203.
8 Lester, 'Fundamental Rights', 47.
9 *The Times*, 27 October 1976; and see Lord Devlin, *The Judge* (Oxford: Oxford University Press, 1979).
10 Parliamentary Debates (House of Lords), Vol. 396, col. 1374 [29 November 1978].
11 Ibid, col. 1367.
12 The work of the Privy Council in interpreting Commonwealth bills of rights is discussed in D.Pannick, *Judicial Review of the Death Penalty* (London: Duckworth, 1982), ch. 2.
13 Glanville Williams, 'The Concept of Legal Liberty', in R.S. Summers (ed.), *Essays in Legal Philosophy* (Oxford: Oxford University Press, 1970).
14 Harry Street, *Freedom, the Individual, and the Law* (5th edn) (Harmondsworth: Penguin, 1982), 12.
15 *Whitney* v. *California* 274 U.S. 357, 375 (1926).
16 *Hubbard* v. *Pitt* [1976] Q.B. 142.
17 See e.g. Viscount Simonds in *Shaw* v. *D.P.P.* [1962] A.C. 220, 267. 'I entertain no doubt that there remains in the courts of law a residual power to enforce the supreme and fundamental purpose of the law, to conserve not only the safety and order but also the moral welfare of the state.'
18 *Report on the Red Lion Square Disorders*. Cmnd 5919 (1975).
19 See D.G. Barnum, 'The Constitutional Status of Public Protest in Britain and the United States', *Public Law* (1977), 310.
20 These points are well made in Patricia Hewitt, *The Abuse of Power* (Oxford: Martin Robertson, 1982), 107–14.

21 Robert Berewick, *The Fascist Movement in Britain* (London: Allen Lane, 1972), ch. 6.
22 Cmnd 7891 (1980).
23 (HC 1979–80) 756 – I and II.
24 'South Africa's Legion of the Banned', *The Times*, 4 January 1980.
25 *Per* Lord Ross in *H.M.A.* v. *Stewart Ross & Others*, Glasgow High Court, June 1979 (unreported).
26 *Per* Lord Scarman in *D.P.P.* v. *Nock* [1978] A.C. 979, 997.
27 E.g. Law Commission Report No. 76: Conspiracy and Criminal Law Reform (HC 176, 1975–76) Peter Hain, *Political Trials in Britain* (London: Penguin, 1984).
28 *D.P.P.* v. *Kamara* [1974] A.C. 104.
29 Ian Brownlie, *Brownlie's Law of Public Order and National Security* (2nd edn) (London: Butterworths, 1981), 90.
30 *Duncan* v. *Jones* [1936] 1 K.B. 218, 223.
31 Twelve union members engaged in a 'walk in' were originally arrested under Section 3 of the 1865 Act: see the *Glasgow Herald*, 25 September 1982. Later, a charge under the Conspiracy and Protection of Property Act, 1875, was substituted.
32 Criminal Law Act 1977.
33 Conspiracy and Protection of Property Act 1875, Section 7(3).
34 *The Times*, 22 October 1982.
35 See S.A. de Smith, *Judicial Review of Administrative Action* (4th edn by J.M. Evans) (London: Stevens, 1980), 311 *et seq.*
36 Cf. *Loyal Orange Lodge* v. *Roxburgh District Council* 1981 S.L.T. 33.
37 Street, *Freedom*, 56.
38 Seditious Meetings Act 1817; Sessional Orders of the Lords and Commons direct the Metropolitan Police Commissioner to 'keep the passages through the streets leading to this House free and open': see Paul O'Higgins, *Cases and Materials on Civil Liberties* (London: Sweet & Maxwell, 1980), 197.
39 *Aldred* v. *Miller* 1925 J.C. 21, 27.
40 *Per* Lord President Dunedin in *McAra* v. *Magistrates of Edinburgh* 1913 S.C. 1059, 1073.
41 Street, *Freedom*, 58.
42 *Arrowsmith* v. *Jenkins* [1963] 2 Q.B. 561, 567.
43 *Per* Lord Justice-General Clyde in *Aldred* v. *Miller*, 1924 J.C. 117, 119–20.
44 This point is considered in V.T. Bevan, 'Protest and Public Order' *Public Law* (1979), 163 et 185.
45 *Lowdens* v. *Keaveney* [1903] 2 L.R. 82.
46 Public Order Act 1936, Section 3.
47 Select Committee on Home Affairs, *note 23 above*, ch. 7.
48 *Loyal Orange Lodge* v. *Roxburgh District Council* 1981 S.L.T. 33.
49 Cf *Kent.* v. *Metropolitan Police Commissioner*, *The Times*, 14 May 1981. The judiciary, at least in England, has upheld the use of police powers to prevent disorder. But *quaere*, if these preventive powers exist at common law why was the 1936 Act required? Why did it appear to restrict police discretion at a time when Mosley's British Union of Fascists were causing the very type of trouble that the Act was designed to remedy?
50 *Review of Public Order Act 1936 and Related Legislation* Cmnd 7891 (1980), Foreword by the Home Secretary and the Secretary of State for Scotland.
51 J.L. Murdoch, 'Policing Public Processions in Scotland', *Journal of the Law Society of Scotland* 28 (1983), 99.

52 J.L. Murdoch, 'The Civic Government Act and Public Processions', *Scottish Legal Action Group Bulletin* (1984), 144.
53 [1882] 9 Q.B.D. 308.
54 (1882) 10R. (J) 22.
55 *Per* C.J. Parker, in *Jordan* v. *Burgoyne* [1963] 2 Q.B. 744, 749.
56 John Stuart Mill, *On Liberty* (1859) (Harmondsworth: Penguin, 1982), 76.

10

Human Rights
and the Criminal Process

Gerry Maher

The criminal process is an obvious area for the notion of human rights
to play a central role. Human rights in their most traditional sense
have been seen as modes of protection for individuals against the
power of the state, and this negative sense of human rights has been
supplemented but not superseded by the more modern and positive
sense in which human rights discourse is a form of argument for
action by the state to protect and promote the interests of rights-
holders. In the field of criminal process it is clear that it is the state
which poses the biggest threat to human rights, since by using its
criminal process the state can deprive its citizens of their liberty and
argue for the title to punish them. It is thus no wonder that in many
legal systems, over a variety of legal cultures, it is the criminal process
which is the area of law in which human rights have found their most
long-standing and traditional application. Yet those interested in the
part played by the idea of human rights in the criminal process are
struck by a surprising fact if they confine their attention to the
criminal processes currently to be found in Great Britain, for there the
idea of human rights has little role to play in this field of law. This
chapter will attempt to argue how and why this broad (and no doubt
too general) proposition is the case and also to advance the argument
that there are advantages in conceptualizing (as British lawyers
typically do not) the criminal process in terms of rights in general and
human rights in particular. In short, if the notion of human rights
were to feature in the rhetorical armoury of British lawyers, that is in
how legal and moral arguments about the law are presented,
significant differences would result not only in how issues about the
criminal process would be presented but also more substantively in

providing reasons for better protecting the interests of those subject or potentially subject to the criminal process. Using the idea of human rights would have a significant effect on how we conceptualize and theorize about the criminal process.

As a first step in this argument, it is necessary to make clear what is meant by the criminal process, a term used here to mean the complex set of rules and practices which have as their aim the application of the rules of the substantive criminal law and of criminal responsibility, mainly by means of making the appropriate determinations of fact, so as to bring into play the rules of criminal punishment. It is important for several reasons to get clear at the outset what might seem to be a merely definitional, and indeed pedantic, point, namely that the criminal process is but one part only of the criminal justice system. The first is that it is not within the scope of the present paper to consider the relationships between human rights and aspects of the criminal justice system other than the criminal process. This is so not because there are no such relationships: on the contrary there is to be found in both the theoretical literature on human rights, and in the various conventions setting out such rights, detailed consideration of what human rights there actually are in the fields of criminal law, criminal responsibility and punishment. Examples of these human rights are rights of privacy, which lead to bars on prohibition of certain forms of sexual conduct; the rights of the mentally ill which absolve them of guilt on criminal charges; and the prohibition of cruel and unusual penal measures.[1] The point to be stressed here is rather that the criminal process is worthy of study in its own right as a possible area for the application of human rights. It might appear from the definition of the criminal process that its sole rationale is that of accuracy of fact-finding and rule-application and that any rights within the criminal process are themselves based on a similar instrumentalist form of rights of accuracy and no more. Trying to locate the criminal process in the human rights tradition will display that instrumentalism of this sort does not exhaust our understanding of the proper role of the criminal process. Yet at the same time it is important to realize that the criminal process is part of the criminal justice system, for if we consider that human rights have a part to play in regard to criminal law, responsibility and punishment, then the demands of consistency will require us to call for their equivalents in the area of criminal process. Of the various rights which are thought to exist throughout the criminal justice system, there is a need to look for and identify the core element or elements of these rights and then ask how this core is to be particularized in each part of the criminal justice system, including the criminal process.

At first blush there seems nothing strange about talking of human rights in the criminal process: indeed modern statements of human rights, such as in the European Convention on Human Rights, and older versions of declarations of human rights such as the Bill of Rights in the Constitution of the US, abound in specifications of human rights in the field of the criminal process.[2] But once we turn our attention to the situation in the British legal systems we find that the idea of rights, especially human rights, has no such similar prominent position. Paradoxically the troubles in Northern Ireland have led to more use of human rights discourse in discussions of the protections which should exist in the criminal process.[3] But because the role of human rights in non-peaceful settings is itself a problematic issue, attention will be paid to the provisions of the criminal processes only in the rest of the UK. The claim that the British criminal processes have little space for the idea of human rights should not be exaggerated, for it is not being asserted that the language of rights is totally unknown either to the legal provisions of these criminal processes or in discussions of the law. Indeed one of the fiercest debates in the British criminal justice systems in recent years was on the issue of the 'right' of silence enjoyed by suspects and accused persons, when modifications to the existing law were proposed by the Criminal Law Revision Committee in 1972.[4] One view which was put in this debate was that the right of silence was too well protected, and certainly not that the right did not exist or that it was insufficiently protected. But our present claim should not be misunderstood either, for it is to a great extent a claim about the nature of rights, especially of human rights, to the effect that neither in our present law nor in our reflection on that law do British lawyers have much place for human rights as part of their conceptual map: human rights play only a minor part in how the criminal process is understood and justified. Typically lawyers discuss the criminal process free from the idea and often free from the language of rights and human rights, and will if pressed to discuss the theoretical underpinnings of the criminal process talk in terms of the goal of efficiency of fact-finding and rule-application and the goal of restricting the power of the state necessary in an efficient criminal process. Thus in one paper, in a collection designed to compare the different approaches to human rights used in criminal processes, we find the writer stating on the subject of pre-trial procedure in England and Wales:[5]

> We need first to determine what the rights or more properly perhaps the privileges or protections of the accused are, from whence they derive, and what institutions exist to safeguard them. And here one must depart from any conventional usage of the term 'rights', as for example denoting protections bestowed by some fundamental document having constitutional significance, a pattern found in the United States or, in Europe, under the European Convention on Human Rights. It would perhaps be better to describe the protections enuring to the accused simply as such. They derive variously from statutes, some ancient such as the Habeas Corpus Act 1679, some modern, such as the Bail Act 1976, from common law, from administrative directions issued by the Home Office, and from precepts enshrined in reports which are still regarded as peculiarly authoritative or persuasive such as that of the Royal Commission on Police Powers and Procedures of 1929.

Again it must be stressed that our main point here is concerned with the ways in which discussions of the criminal process are conducted; it is not a claim about the content of British laws on criminal procedure. For the view has been put that, with some possible exceptions (such as the ways in which Scots and English law allow for pre-trial detention of suspects to allow for ease of investigation by the police), the British criminal processes do conform with the requirements of the European Convention on Human Rights, and it is certainly not part of our claim to gainsay this view. Nor is it the case that no British lawyer deploys the concept of human rights.[6] What is being claimed is that the typical approach of British lawyers to the criminal process is to eschew the notion of rights.

As our chief claim is a conceptual one, it is necessary to give some indication why the concept of human rights has had so little effect on the law of criminal processes in Britain and on discussion of that law. In general we can say that the absence of a human rights tradition in the area of British criminal processes is due to the dominance of the value systems associated with utilitarianism and legal positivism. The rise of utilitarianism as a general social philosophy during the nineteenth century occurred at about the same time as the development of the criminal process in Britain in its modern form, characterized in particular by the birth of a professionalized police force with functions of investigation and not simply peace-keeping. The underlying idea behind the differing approaches to utilitarianism is that judgements of moral goodness and badness are to be made in terms of how an act (or a more complex set of acts such as social practice) contributes to the maximization of a desired goal. What is crucial to a utilitarian judgement on an act or practice is the end-result it brings about, not the means in so doing except to the extent that some means may be more efficient (or cost-minimizing) than others. But since in utilitarian theory means are subordinate to ends, that theory has no necessary distributional implications, for questions of distribution figure only in the (always contingent) issue of efficiency in achieving a particular goal. But it is characteristic of the notion of a right that each right-holder has a claim to have his or her right respected even if this leads to disutility as measured by some particular goal.

Of course, it is possible to argue that promotion of rights should be a social goal and thus to argue that utilitarian theory does allow for the idea of rights, but it is far from clear that such a theory remains utilitarian in nature. It is also true that one can read into utilitarianism a trivial sense of rights in that someone can have a right to something whenever his or her possessing that right will result in maximizing utility. But this concept of rights is trivial, if not absolutely redundant. Thus suppose that we take the sole aim of the criminal process as accuracy of fact-finding, and we ask if suspects have a right not to be tortured (as many in the human rights camp claim).[7] The utilitarian must answer that a suspect should not be tortured, and in a loose sense has a 'right' not to be tortured, whenever but only whenever torturing would not aid overall accuracy of fact-finding. But if it were ever the case that torturing suspects would promote fact-finding and provided benefits greater than the costs involved, the utilitarian would in consistency have to accept that suspects should be tortured in such circumstances. Thus where utilitarianism does allow for 'rights', it does so only by adopting a redundant concept. There is no explanatory power in the idea of utilitarian rights which adds anything to the measure of utility.

Not all forms of utilitarianism, however, see themselves as antithetical to rights. For example, rule-utilitarianism argues that social institutions should be arranged on the basis of rules, which rules function to maximize utility at lowest cost. Rule-utilitarianism accepts that people can have rights in terms of rules and that this concept of rights is not trivial as rights of this sort can override claims that breaking rules in particular cases will maximize utility (at least in the short run). Rule-utilitarianism faces difficulties in showing how it can consistently be utilitarian without collapsing into some form of act-utilitarianism, but that problem is not one which need occupy us now. However, it is worth mentioning that this form of utilitarianism shares the same concept of rights as that of legal positivism, namely that rights exist only by virtue of rules which constitute them. Positivism (which is by far the most influential ideology among British lawyers) argues that all rights are legal or quasi-legal in nature for they all depend upon posited rules which set them out.[8] Positivism would agree with Bentham's dismissal of the idea of natural rights as 'nonsense on stilts'.[9] But the antipathy to rights without rules extends also to human rights, for the core idea of such rights is that they exist by virtue of some morally significant feature which human beings have by virtue of the fact that they are human beings. For positivists there is a one-way relationship only between rights and rules: rights are always justified by rules or similar practices but it is conceptually mistaken to argue that we should change or retain rules because to do so would be to protect or better protect rights. For positivists the whole idea of human rights, that is rights premised on humanity rather than constituted by rules, is a conceptual confusion.

Positivists of this sort face one immediate difficulty in that historically the idea of rights has been used as part of arguments against existing law and for changes in that law (as with the examples of denial of natural rights as a basis for the American revolution against British rule and more recently the gross disregard of human rights exhibited by totalitarian regimes in the 1930s as leading for calls for effective institutional protection of human rights). The positivist response to this problem is to continue to adhere to the concept of rights whereby rights exist only by virtue of constitutive rules, but to argue that rights can also be said to exist in a metaphorical or manifesto sense where they are not so connected to rules.[10] It is the metaphorical or manifesto sense of rights which is deployed when arguments are made from rights to rules or changes in rules but the positivists do seem embarrassed in admitting the idea of rights even in a non-real or metaphorical sense. Yet since the essence of human rights is precisely that they are premised not on posited rules but on morally significant aspects of human nature, it follows that for positivists human rights as such (as opposed to what are labelled rights in posited legislation or conventions) are non-real and have only this shadowy, metaphorical existence. Thus it is no surprise that for lawyers, for whom shadowy and metaphorical entities are highly suspicious, the whole concept of human rights is one which they can easily do without.

However, there are other reasons why lawyers might harbour suspicions about the whole notion of human rights, even if the idea of rights is taken in some non-trivial way as not being totally dependent upon posited rules or practices. Some of the claims often associated with human rights bear an implausibility over and above that of the basic notion of rights premised on the moral significance of human personality. Two such features of human rights are those of universality and inalienability. But these grand-sounding claims look odd to lawyers working at the level of actual criminal processes. Thus some rights which might be accorded to those involved in the criminal process, such as the right to bail or the right to trial by jury, are surely not rights available to every person, in every place, at every time. The rights in question are rather those belonging to suspects and to accused persons who have reached certain stages of the criminal process and only to such persons: there is no question of universality here.

The claim that human rights are inalienable also has a ring of the implausible about it. Thus the European Convention on Human Rights lays down a right not to be detained but immediately lists a number of instances when this right is overridden, including that where a person has been convicted by a court on a criminal charge.[11] Indeed, unless there were limitations on the application of human rights, especially on those relating to freedom of movement and property and bodily integrity, the entire penal stage of the criminal justice system could never be brought into operation.

Human rights then are often seen as rather dubious entities with attributes which are highly questionable. Why then should so many legal systems structure their provisions on the criminal process around the idea of human rights and what is deficient about the British criminal processes in that they do not use this idea? To answer this question let us consider two recent examples of legislative proposals on an area of the criminal process. In each case the proposal came from an official body set up to examine the workings of the criminal process, and in each case the proposal aroused some disquiet and controversy. Furthermore, in each case the proposal influenced legislative action in that one was embodied in legislation, whereas the other (which was that the current law should remain as it is) led to no changes in the law. This factor alone shows that there is a possible issue about the importance of human rights discourse in the criminal process, for it will be argued that had these debates been couched more directly in the language of human rights the arguments would have been different and the proposals and legislative response might also have differed.

By Section 2 of the Criminal Justice (Scotland) Act, 1980, the police were given the general power, never possessed before, of detaining a person for a period up to six hours and of questioning the detainee without resort to the arrest of that person. Such detention is authorized when a constable has reasonable grounds for suspecting that the person has committed an offence punishable by imprisonment. This provision in large part enacted one of the recommendations of the Committee on Criminal Procedure in Scotland, chaired by Lord Thomson, which reported in October 1975.[12] The proposal of the Thomson Committee was very controversial and a widely-based attack (ultimately to no avail) on its implementation was mounted during the legislative stages of the Bill. What was the reasoning underlying the Thomson proposal?

In the first place, the Thomson Committee noted that with issues such as arrest, search and interrogation of suspects there is a 'conflict between the public interest in the detection and suppression of crime on the one hand and the interest of the individual citizen in freedom from interference by the police on the other.'[13] When dealing with the problem of arrest the Committee noted the difficulties caused to the police by the rule of Scots law that when a person is arrested he or she must be 'charged', that is told the alleged offence which forms the basis of the arrest. The difficulties posed to the police by this rule were that it required an arrest only after the initial stages of investigation had been completed in sufficient detail to allow the charge to be given to the suspect, which in turn meant that the police had no legal power to detain a person while the investigation was continuing. This rule of Scots law of arrest can easily be formulated in the language of human rights by saying that everyone has the right of freedom to go as they please. Derived from this general right is the specific right not to be involuntarily detained by the police unless the police can state grounds, based on reasonable beliefs, suggesting that that person should be arrested as having committed a particular and specified crime. But the Committee also noted that whatever the legal rules, the reality was that very few people in Scotland were aware of their rights as provided by the law on arrest (which law does not of course speak in terms of rights at all), and so thinking that they had no choice in the matter the majority of suspects stayed in police custody before or without being formally arrested and charged. The Thomson Committee was explicit on why it wanted this area of the law to be clarified:[14]

> It is also necessary that it should be so framed as to allow the police to perform legally whatever functions in the investigation and prevention of crime the public regard as proper. We believe that the police at present are able to carry out their functions only because some persons whom they detain without warrant fail, through ignorance or fear of authority, to exercise their rights.

The effect of this sort of argument is that police powers in relation to investigation of crime become the focal point for discussion whether there should be a power of detention short of arrest. This issue of public interest is put in the balance with the interests of the individual and is found to have greater weight than individual interests. Note here how this reasoning shows the lack of distributional concern found in much utilitarian argument. There is no attempt to show that the persons whose rights or interests will be infringed by increased police powers will themselves gain by these powers: it is taken as sufficient that society as a whole will gain through greater police powers. Furthermore, the fact that persons have rights under existing rules which they do not know about and hence do not exercise is taken as ground for 'regularizing' a practice which shows no respect for these rights and for giving legal effect to increased police powers. But this is an argument couched in the traditional terms of utilitarian social philosophy. An outcome is posited as desired (*viz.* efficient investigation of crime), and the question then becomes one of balancing the costs and benefits of steps taken in achieving that goal (increased police powers versus individual's interests that the police do not interfere with his or her liberty). It might be thought that both the reasoning of the Thomson Committee and the result in its implementation in Section 2 of the 1980 Act are, on the whole, good. But what is fairly evident is that the whole idea of human rights is put outside this discussion. The question then becomes: if the Thomson Committee had approached this issue not by looking at the cost and benefits of increased police powers of detention as a means of achieving efficient investigation of crime but by asking what are the human rights which

all people possess against police authorities, would this have made
any difference, if not to its conclusion, then at least to its reasoning?

Before we answer this question in detail, let us briefly consider
another example of a controversial discussion on a matter of criminal
process. The Royal Commission on Criminal Procedure in England
and Wales[15] was enjoined by its terms of reference to consider the
balance between the interests of the community in bringing offenders
to justice and the rights and liberties of persons suspected or accused
of crime. What is more, the Commission saw it as necessary to devote
part of its Report to setting out how it intended to handle the
'balancing' device within its own reasoning, and in its discussion the
Commission stressed that it recognized the importance of conceptualizing problems in terms of (human) rights. For example, the
Commission discussed the debate on the right of silence which
followed the publication of the 11th Report of the Criminal Law
Revision Committee. The Commission identified a number of
different strands in that debate and characterized the views of one of
them (which it dubbed libertarian, as opposed to the views it called
utilitarian) in the following way:[16]

> The second argument was that basically an individual's rights in the
> criminal process had to be related to an understanding of what the
> individual's relationship to Government ought to be in a free,
> democratic society, and that each step in the criminal process, pre-trial
> and trial, including the right of silence, must be judged not only as a
> means to the goal of achieving a reliable verdict, but also, and equally
> important, for its coherence with a liberal understanding of how free
> persons, including suspects in the police station, at all stages ought to
> be treated.

However, this approach which uses notions familiar to human
rights theorists is not the one which the Royal Commission adopts for
its own use, either in relation to the balancing device or in regard to its
more particular proposals. Consider, for example, the Commission's
own arguments about the right of silence, that is the absence of
obligation on a suspect or accused person to answer questions posed
by the police during investigation and the absence of obligation to
present evidence in defence of a charge. In general, exercise of this
'right' cannot be used as part of the proof by the prosecution that the
case for guilt has been made out. The Royal Commission, although
not unanimous in its recommendations on this issue, disagreed with

the proposals in the Criminal Law Revision Committee and adopted the position that the present rules on the right of silence should be maintained. But what is of interest for our present purposes are the arguments used about those rules which forbid failure by the accused to give evidence or of suspects to answer questions to have evidential value for the prosecution case (i.e. the rules which constitute the 'right' of silence), for the views of the Royal Commission do not rely on any arguments about rights or human rights, not even the sort which the Royal Commission identified in the previous opposition to the proposals of the Criminal Law Revision Committee. The Royal Commission rested its support of the present rules on two factors, the nature of the accusatorial system of trial and the impossibility of ensuring truth-telling if the right of silence were taken away. Although in one passage[17] the Commission appear to recognize that the right of silence might be based on some aspect of respecting human personality as such, its own reasons for favouring the right of silence are to be found in its views about the importance of the adversary system of criminal procedure and in instrumental arguments about accuracy of fact-determination. Thus we find the Commission agreeing with the views of those wishing to retain the present rules that:[18] 'the right of silence is seen by those who take this position as an essential safeguard for the weak, the immature and the inadequate, since its removal could increase the risk of false confessions by those unable to withstand police interrogation'. Similarly the Commission disagree with a suggestion that the right of silence should be restricted to the trial stage but not made applicable to the investigative and pre-trial stages of the criminal process, on the ground that to do so would be to introduce an inquisitorial element inconsistent with adversary principles.[19]

Although the Royal Commission's proposals on the right of silence might be acceptable to some, its mode of reasoning in defence of that right might not be welcomed even by those who support the Royal Commission's conclusions. In the first place, no reasons are provided why such importance should be attached to adversary systems of procedure. This is not to say that the differences between inquisitorial and adversary systems do not reflect important moral differences in how people are treated by state authority, but rather that the Royal Commission's argument on this point is very much incomplete.[20] Also its argument on the right of silence rests on very shaky ground. What if it became know which types of people would and which would not tell lies to resist police questioning and might give false confessions, or if we devised methods of police interrogation that used proven psychological criteria for indicating that truth was likely to be told (or even if a reliable truth drug were invented)? Should then the right of silence in its present form be retained? Also in some legal systems which are broadly adversarial, such as the Scottish, there is a clearer distinction than exists in the English system between the trial and investigative stages, and there is also to be found the involvement of judges in pre-trial stages (as with the Scottish practice of judicial examination). This indicates that these features need not lead to the general introduction of inquisitorial methods in the criminal process. If this is so then the Royal Commission's argument about not restricting the right of silence to the trial stage becomes weaker. In general, then, we can conclude by saying that the Royal Commission's somewhat restricted arguments in favour of the right of silence provide little support for that right over a range of possible circumstances.

What we have identified so far are two examples of arguments about the criminal process in Britain which do not use the concept of human rights, and indeed could also be said to make little use of the more general idea of rights. These examples are, it is submitted, typical of much reasoning about the criminal process in Britain, but this is not to deny that other ways of conceptualizing the criminal process also exist, some of which might be thought to be firmly within the human rights approach. What we are claiming is that the examples we examined are typical of much public debate and academic discussion on criminal justice, which can be characterized as broadly utilitarian in nature; that is, it sets out desired end-states (for example, limitation on state power, efficiency in the application of rules of the criminal process) and balances out the costs and benefits of differing ways of achieving these goals. This is scarcely a culture of argument in which the concept of human rights can take root and flourish. But against this point it might be countered that it does not matter: good (and bad) arguments can be expressed in the language of goals or utility as much as good (and bad) arguments can be stated in the language of rights, and at the end of the day there might be no discernible difference in the outcome of our discussion. After all, the Thomson Committee proposal we noted did recognize that people have a right not to be detained but went on to argue for, and give reasons for, some qualifications to that right. Yet, as we have already seen, it is a difficult matter for any human rights theorist to claim that every human right must apply in all circumstances. If the idea of exception to human rights is admitted, then there may be nothing objectionable about the reasoning of the Thomson Committee and the Royal Commission even from the perspective of human rights theory.

However, it is argued that if the idea of rights had been taken seriously by the Thomson Committee and the Royal Commission, the arguments presented in their respective Reports would have been quite different. Of course this point is true by definition: an argument which uses the notion of human rights has a different form from one which does not. But our claim goes beyond the mere form of argument used. If the Thomson Committee and Royal Commission had used the concept of human rights as a central feature in their discussions, they would of necessity have been relying on a type of underlying moral and political theory which would have led to conclusions which would have been different, not in all cases but in many significant ones, from the conclusions of arguments which do not use rights and as such rely on different underlying moral theories.

In the first place each of the Reports makes an explicit use of the device of balancing rights or interests of the individual with the interests of the community or society. But the method of reasoning which the metaphor of the balance attempts to capture cannot properly be used in the *ad hoc* manner in which it is employed in the Thomson Committee and Royal Commission Reports.[21] For the notion of balancing to be a legitimate mode of conducting argument rather than a mere literary tool, the various interests and rights to be balanced have to be related to each other by means of a general theory which explains and justifies the area of thought concerned. But neither the Thomson Committee nor the Royal Commission attempt to set out any theory of the criminal process in this sense. It may well be that there is such a theory buried deep in the Reports, but it is not obvious that this is so nor that the committees were each consistently adopting such a theory throughout their discussions. The reason such a theory is required is that we cannot begin to do the necessary balancing until we show two features: first, that the two considerations to be balanced against each other (such as individual rights and social interests) conflict with each other. Second, it must also be demonstrated that the types of considerations to be balanced are in some way commensurable: if we are not using some common conceptual standard, it is not possible to measure the respective 'weights' of each type of consideration involved. Again, in neither the Thomson Committee nor the Royal Commission is there any attempt to show that the requirements of conflict and commensurability have been met in the balancing which they do. In what sense do the rights of individuals differ from, and in what sense are they inconsistent with, the interests of society in the field of criminal process? By what standard can we say that in some situation a particular right or interest has greater or lesser weight than some other right or interest? These questions are never properly posed, never mind answered, in the two Reports but they do present a hurdle to be cleared before any matter of 'balancing' can come into play at all.

Of course if our general theory of the criminal process is utilitarian in nature, in which the general justifying aim of the criminal process is the cost-minimizing or efficient goal of accuracy of fact-finding, then the balancing device could properly be used. But note that if that is the sort of theory of criminal process we adopt there is little need for any concept of individual rights at all: indeed, it is implicit in the nature of a utilitarian theory of criminal process that whatever protection individuals are to receive within the criminal process is merely consequential upon the process of achieving its goal of efficiency.

Thus we can conclude that the whole form of the arguments in the Thomson Committee and the Royal Commission would have differed if the idea of rights had been taken seriously, for the balancing requirement would have led the committees to ask (as at times the Royal Commission came near to doing) which other rights are to be balanced against the particular rights under scrutiny (right to be free from detention, right of silence).

If we move away from the particular device of balancing, it also becomes evident that injecting the idea of rights into discussions of the criminal process would have affected the outcomes and not just the forms of arguments used. The Thomson Committee, if it had taken seriously the values which the Scots law on arrest is meant to express (*viz.* refusal of arrest unless details of a charge, based on reasonable grounds, can be supplied), could scarcely have entertained the view that because people did not know of this right and hence did not act upon it, therefore the practice of denying the force of that right should be 'regularized' because to do so would have made the task of the police that much easier.

Consider also the reasoning of the Royal Commission that the present law on the right of silence should be retained because to do otherwise might threaten the adversary system and might also lead to inaccurate results. It was noted earlier that the point about the adversary system seems weak when it is borne in mind that the Scottish system retains its adversary nature despite characteristics which the Royal Commission saw as necessarily involved in modifying the right of silence. The further point about lack of certainty as to the accuracy of confessions does not provide firm support for the right of silence either. If inferences were to be made about a suspect or accused remaining silent and it became the case that because of this rule confessions were usually made, it would still remain the case that no confession would be of value unless the prosecution case as a whole proved the guilt of the accused beyond reasonable doubt. (This is true *a fortiori* of legal systems which insist on corroboration of prosecution evidence.)

However, if we entertained the notion that the right of silence was a human right, then we would be forced to explain the whole set of values and ideals which make it inappropriate for the state to proceed to punish a person (and thereby seek title for overriding other human rights) when it could not itself prove guilt or which relied on the accused to contribute to the proof of his or her own guilt.

What we have noted is that neither the Thomson Committee nor the Royal Commission put the notion of human rights at the centre of their arguments about the criminal process; but there is still the need to take note of one major issue, namely whether use of the idea of human rights by the Thomson Committee and the Royal Commission would have made any difference, not only to the form of their arguments but also to their substantive conclusions. In order to show that conclusions as well as the form of the arguments would have differed, it is necessary to give detail to two arguments: the first is that the notion of human rights has coherence as a method of presenting moral argument, at least as concerns its application to issues of the criminal process; the second is that there are plausible general theories of the criminal process which give a central role to the notion of human rights and that appeals to these theories have substantive implications. These issues are dealt with in the next two sections of this paper.

Any argument which wishes to deploy the concept of human rights must confront directly the view that the very concept of human rights itself is a mistake and no argument, no matter how powerful it appears, can be worth very much if it relies upon an internally inconsistent concept. What of the view that the rights within the criminal process do not share the attributes traditionally associated with human rights, such as universality and inalienability? But what we must notice in considering this criticism is that philosophers have of late been concerned with preventing misunderstanding of such features of human rights.[22] In particular the idea of universality of rights can be consistently maintained even if there are special circumstances required to trigger off the application of these rights, provided that there is nothing morally arbitrary (in the sense of inconsistent with the justification of the rights themselves) in how such triggering circumstances are defined. Thus we can say that there is a universal right to trial by jury provided all persons within the appropriate defining circumstances (for example, all who are charged with an offence punishable by imprisonment) are accorded that right. In this way we can also understand how some human rights have application only in societies with certain practices or institutions: thus the right to trial by jury might not be a right in a society which did not possess the typical institutional features of modern developed criminal processes.

Other allegedly necessary features of human rights also call for greater scrutiny than is often given to them by those who find the notion of human rights incoherent or implausible. If a right is inalienable then it cannot be overridden, but it is not a necessary feature that all human rights are inalienable in this sense. Perhaps some are: the right not to be tortured is often cited as an example of such as inalienable right. But human rights are still rights even if in certain circumstances they can be overridden. Indeed we have already noted that many of the traditional human rights such as the right to property and bodily integrity are not inalienable as they are commonly overridden once a conviction on a criminal charge has been made. But we can still plausibly and meaningfully talk of such rights as human rights provided that the conditions which justify their being overridden are in some broad way consistent with the nature of the rights concerned. Indeed one reason why so much philosophical attention has been paid to issues of criminal responsibility and punishment is that these areas of the criminal justice system do allow for the overriding of rights. Unless the conditions for punishment are morally justified, the criminal justice system can be seen as denying human rights.

What we have argued is that once we have been more exact in our descriptions of the attributes of human rights, the charge that the concept is a confused one is rebutted. But there is another and quite different point to be made in rebutting that charge. The idea of human rights would be incoherent if it rested solely on factual matters bundled together under the tag 'human nature'. Rather, a full theory of human rights has to show what it is about human nature which has moral significance and which justifies the more concrete notion of rights which belong to people by virtue of their humanity. This question cannot simply be left to rest as a matter of self-evidence, nor have any human rights theorists ever rested their case on that basis. At the core of the very idea of human rights lies a deeper and conceptually more fundamental moral theory. But it is not necessary to suppose that there is any one such justifying theory which would gain general acceptance: indeed the idea of human rights is probably an essentially contested one, different conceptions of which make appeal to different 'rock-bottom' moral theories. That (large) issue is not one to which this paper will make any contribution by way of substantive argument. But what we can offer are some comments on what follows from taking human rights as a form of giving expression to (that is, having rhetorical force as) a statement of a more fundamental moral theory. The first is that once we accept this view of the nature of human rights, it becomes possible to explain how some particular rights can still plausibly be described as human rights even though they apply only to persons in particular settings (such as the right to trial by jury applying only to those who have been charged with certain types of crime). For human rights of this sort can be seen as derivative human rights which depend upon some more basic right (for example, right to respect as a morally autonomous person, or right to treatment as a moral equal) or upon some other more basic moral concept which is not itself a right. It is here that the idea of the core of human rights has value. A fundamental moral premise (such as respect for autonomy) can lie at the base of many different rights, each of which looks quite disparate, but which are united in drawing their justification from the same core moral premise. Thus we can coherently talk of the rights of accused persons to a fair trial, of the foetus to life, and of the hungry to be fed as all embodiments of the same underlying moral premise.

The second point is that not all moral theories will generate a conception of human rights, except perhaps in some trivial sense. Utilitarian ethics are often thought to have this consequence. It is true that of late there has been some attempt to rehabilitate utilitarianism and human rights but it is equally clear that the distinctive feature of utilitarian argument, that is moral assessment in terms of the consequences of actions or the contribution of actions to some goal, is hard to square with the essentially non-consequential notion of human rights.[23]

There is a third point following on from the argument that human rights presuppose some deeper moral theory, a point which can be presented as an attack on the whole idea of human rights. If it is the case that human rights are ultimately premised on some idea (say) of respect for human dignity or moral equality, then it is these general concepts which play the crucial role in our theory, not the specific form they take as human rights.[24] Such an attack might be backed by the independent point which argues that human rights are conceptually mistaken and depend upon a questionable metaphysical basis. We noted earlier that positivist writers tended to argue that attempts to separate rights from the rules which constitute them are illegitimate for such reasons and that rights without rules, such as human rights, are strictly speaking bogus entities.

It might be thought enough to reply here that the relationship between rights and some more basic moral theory is not simply one of different modes of representing the same thing. Instead it is more a matter of a concrete expression of a general idea. Thus there is value in using the idea of rights in that it translates the more general concept (dignity, equality, respect for autonomy, say) into a form applicable in a specific sort of situation, such as the criminal process. The more general justifying principle at the core of the right will call for varying statements when an attempt is made to give the right more concrete form in particular contexts. However, although this point is true, it is not the whole truth of the matter and the point cannot be relied upon as providing a complete answer to the criticism made about the redundancy of human rights. For it is still the case that there is a need, if the point were to be pressed, to show that there is a connection between a particular human right (such as the right to freedom from interference by the state unless proof of commission of guilt is made out) and a general moral theory which justifies it.

However, note that this point of criticism can be raised also, and with greater force, against positivist theories of rights. For positivists rights are simply attributes of certain sorts of rules (for example, those which respect individual choice or which confer certain sorts of benefits), and the notion of rights is incoherent if separated from posited rules of practices. Thus positivism forces us to say that there are no human rights, for according to positivism the only rights are posited rights, and also that it is not part of proper argument that we should have or maintain a rule because to do so would be to protect a right. But the point can be made here that the concept of rights in this view is utterly redundant. The key concept on this approach is that of rules: once we state the rules concerned with any particular matter (perhaps by listing all the rules about the criminal process) we have given a complete view of the matter and there is no need to resort to the language of rights. Indeed the language of rights in this approach might be misleading for it diverts attention from positive rules and hints that rights can exist without rules. It was noted earlier that in much discussion of the criminal processes in Great Britain, issues are presented in terms of rules and practices, either actual or desirable, not in the language of rights. It may well be that for positivism to remain a coherent view it must deny the propriety of all moral discourse, apart from that used in describing particular sorts of social practice. If rights are not 'real' because they are not reflected in actual social practices, it is hard to see that any moral concepts have reality.

It is thought, though, that the poverty of positivism lies especially in the way it fails to give any special place to the concept of rights, as rights are merely a sub-category of the more conceptually significant idea of rules. The reason it does so is because positivism refuses to accept that some concepts, and this includes the concept of rights, have a function to play especially in argument rather than in description. It is one of the central themes of this present book that the notion of human rights has its special application in the realm of argument known as rhetoric. It is when we are concerned with the special modes of reasoning involved in argument that we can see the special significance of rights, and particularly of human rights. Once we accept that rhetoric provides a special role for the idea of rights and human rights, many of the puzzles about the notion of human rights begin to disappear. For example, we can appreciate the importance of using the language of human rights, even though we are making use of a moral theory which also calls for argument. We can also now avoid the narrowness and triviality of positivist approaches to rights, for the concept of human rights is particularly appropriate as a source of assessing actual rules as much as, if not more than, describing them. Indeed part of the significance of human rights is that they provide reasons (and have rhetorical force in so doing) for changing rules so that posited rules can better protect actual rights. Far from this aspect of rights being fictitious or 'manifesto' in nature, it is central to the idea of rights. The language of human rights, then, is to be understood as a contribution to translating existing human rights from rhetoric to reality.

If rights have a role as rhetoric, how is this role performed in the field of criminal process? What is the more fundamental theory of the criminal process which criminal process rights express? It should not come as too much of a surprise to discover that in the UK (again unlike the USA) there has been relatively little attention paid to normative problems of the criminal process, certainly when contrasted with other parts of the criminal justice system. Indeed it is probably this lack of explicit theorizing on the criminal process which accounts for the frequent use made of the balancing of the various interests involved in the criminal process. It is beyond the scope of this chapter to present a developed theory of the criminal process but what we can show is that arguments about the criminal process which use human rights fall back on a general theory of criminal process which will give rise to noticeably different conclusions from arguments about the criminal process which have no place for human rights.

Consider for instance an approach to criminal process which we can call instrumentalism and which can be found in fairly explicit statement in Bentham's many writings on adjectival law.[25] According to instrumentalism, the criminal process functions solely as a mode of fact-finding, that is, it gives effect to the criminal justice system by supplying the facts which bring the other parts of the criminal justice system into operation. Although instrumentalism takes fact-finding as the sole rationale of the criminal process, it accepts that the accuracy of fact-finding procedures may be compromised if their cost is too prohibitive. Bentham himself argued that these collateral costs, such as the use of the time of the various participants (for example, judges or the police), or the pains associated with the criminal process, such as the detention of suspects prior to trial, had always to be balanced against the advantages gained from the methods used in arriving at fact-finding. (His own theory does not provide a clear criterion or set of criteria as to how this balancing is to be carried out in each case.)

This instrumentalist view of the criminal process is certainly not without some value as a way of understanding our existing criminal process. Instrumentalist theory led Bentham to an antinomianism on issues of legal processes.[26] For him fact-finding was a matter of fact and legal rules of evidence and procedure undermined, or at any rate did not promote, efficiency in fact-finding. And instrumentalism is not lacking as a source of argument in relation to modern criminal processes. Certainly the trend has been to move away from technical rules of evidence towards methods of 'free' proof.[27] But at the same time it is evident that instrumentalism is not completely successful as a descriptive theory of the criminal process. For example, there are many rules, including some of the more distinctive rules of the criminal process, which have no obvious instrumentalist justification, such as rules which exclude (factually reliable) evidence because of the means used to obtain it, or rules which forbid a trial taking place because the accused has been held in pre-trial custody for a certain length of time, or rules which place the burden of proof on the prosecution. Of course these rules may seem anomalous and in that case instrumentalism may well provide us with a coherent theory for removing them from our legal system, but it must be made clear what would be involved in getting rid of such rules. It is here that putting the question in terms of rights brings out the issues clearly.

It is evident, for instance, that instrumentalist theories of the criminal process have no place for the notion of rights. If some procedure has value in leading to the discovery of relevant facts, it has value precisely because of that feature: the means used in discovery of facts are only secondary to the end of fact-finding. It is also the case that instrumentalism cannot even support a right to accurate fact-finding. Consider a case suggested by Ronald Dworkin.[28] He instances the case that a jury of 25 people might be more likely to arrive the truth than a jury of 12. Can instrumentalism justify the right of an accused to a larger jury because of its greater potential in fact-finding? The answer is that it cannot, because the extra cost in the increase of the jury size is a collateral cost which must be calculated and may outweigh the value of the increase in accuracy of fact-finding. As the solution to this calculation is always a contingent matter of measurement in each case, the accused has no right to the larger jury.

Note that this point can be generalized to cover all possible candidates for 'rights' in the instrumentalist theory of criminal process. Thus if we argue that the justification of the criminal process is fact-finding but that individuals have rights, for example, not to have their house entered or not to be detained prior to trial, it is not clear that these rights are rights (except in some trivial sense), as the social benefits in terms of fact-finding of entry by the police or pre-trial detention can be held to override the undoubted evils caused to the individuals whose premises have been entered or who have been detained.

A theory which uses the notion of human rights has the effect of blocking arguments which allow or require the interests of individuals in the criminal process to be overridden because of the social value in increased fact-finding. Can it be shown that the notion of rights and human rights in the criminal process can be located as an expression of a coherent theory of the criminal process? It is probably the case that many different moral values can generate rights discourse. Each will use the idea of rights to state the particular value in question (such as dignity, autonomy, equal respect), but what all these share is opposition to instrumentalist arguments and particularly a refusal to let fact-finding act as the sole justification of the rules and practices of the criminal process.

Imagine, for instance, that we wished to build a theory of criminal process on the principle of respect for the autonomy of persons. The notion of human rights would be a highly congenial one in which to express such a theory. Consider in this context debates in this country about the extent to which legal aid should be provided to defendants in the criminal process. The idea of a right to counsel is one specified in the Sixth Amendment to the US Constitution and in Article 6(3) of the European Convention on Human Rights. But if debates on legal aid in Great Britain were conducted in the language of rights, then mere consideration of costs and of accuracy of fact-finding and the balancing of these two elements would have no exclusive or necessarily direct role in the arguments to be used. Instead we would have to show what there was about legal aid and the assistance of counsel which was required by the principle of respect for persons. Certainly there is an instrumentalist form of support for the right to counsel. In *Gideon* v. *Wainright*, the US Supreme Court pointed out that given the adversary system of trials, the accused who lacked legal advice might not present his or her case in the strongest form and thus the trial might have the wrong outcome.[29] But this ground of support for legal aid provides no basis for a right to counsel over and above the contribution which legal aid can make to accuracy of fact-finding and is open to the argument that there may be cheaper ways of ensuring accurate fact-finding (for example, adoption of non-adversary methods of trial or pre-trial procedure).

If we argue, however, that our criminal process must display respect for the autonomy of the person on trial, a different justification for legal aid emerges. By treating the accused as an autonomous agent, we must communicate reasons to him or her why it is that proof of guilt against him or her is being carried out. On such a view a trial is a process of communication with the accused and it is a mode of providing reasons why that person is being singled out for the unpleasant treatment both in the very fact that he or she is facing a criminal charge and also for his or her liability of punishment at the penal stage of the criminal justice system.[30] To the extent that the accused cannot fully understand or participate in a trial without legal aid, then respecting that person's autonomy calls for provision of legal aid. Legal aid is not on this view simply a means to an end (such as fact-finding) but is something due to an accused as of right, such a right deriving from the need to respect someone's moral autonomy.

Of course this sort of argument could have proceeded direct from the requirements of respecting human autonomy to the issue of legal aid. But the significance of stating the issue in the language of rights is that by using rights in our arguments on the criminal process, we restrict the range of background theories of the criminal process to those which allow for the notion of rights in the criminal process in a non-trivial sense and specifically do not permit instrumentalist approaches to criminal process theory. Human rights as rhetoric are important because they are powerful statements of certain sorts of moral position, and human rights in the criminal process are similarly important because they make an appeal to certain sorts of fundamental theory of the criminal process. The criminal process is by its very nature of moral importance, for it involves the actual application of the rules of the criminal justice system (in the way that other parts of the criminal justice system do not) and thus involves also the use of the power of the state against individuals. Many legal systems indicate this feature by providing institutional safeguards for a list of detailed rights, such as rights of freedom from detention and right to a fair trial. In such legal cultures legislation and court decisions can be assessed, approved and criticized by appealing to such rights and to the more abstract moral theory upon which they depend. Thus the idea of human rights functions as part of the critical reflection on the criminal process, and human rights discourse makes an appeal to specific sorts of theory of criminal process. In Great Britain, however, the traditional theories of utilitarianism and positivism lead to the view that the very idea of rights is regarded as dubious and the notion of human rights as incoherent, and have often also led to an implicit acceptance of an instrumentalist theory of the criminal process. The dominance of these theories in contemporary legal and moral debate in Britain means that the function of rights as rhetoric is denied a genuine place in discussion of the criminal process, even in critical discussion. But in our examination of the Thomson Committee and the Royal Commission and in the example of legal aid in the criminal process, we saw that the present law can be represented in the language of human rights and that doing so did affect our approach to changes in the law. British criminal lawyers are put to the election either of adhering fully to utilitarian and positivist theories and dropping the idea of human rights from their conceptual map, or embracing the idea of human rights as crucial to discussion of the criminal process and rejecting the sterile theories of utilitarianism and positivism which deny human rights their basic role.

Notes

1 Fuller discussion of such rights can be found in Richard Card, 'Human Rights and Substantive Criminal Law', in J.A. Andrews (ed.), *Human Rights in Criminal Procedure. A Comparative Study* (The Hague: Martinus Nijhoff, 1982), 349–74; Graham Zellick, 'Human Rights and the Treatment of Offenders', Ibid., 375–416.

2 For example the Fourth Amendment to the US Constitution provides for protection against unlawful search and seizure. The Fifth Amendment provides for the right of protection against double jeopardy, and the right not to incriminate oneself; and the Sixth Amendment provides for the right to a speedy and public trial, to trial by jury, the right to confront witnesses and the right to counsel. Various provisions of the European Convention on Human Rights also provide for criminal process rights. Article 5 prohibits deprivation of liberty except in certain defined circumstances, and Article 6 provides a detailed list of rights relating to the permissible methods of determining a criminal charge (such as the right to a fair and public hearing, the right to prepare one's defence, the right to legal assistance, and the right to have guilt proved rather than being assumed).

3 Standing Advisory Committee on Human Rights, *The Protection of Human Rights by Law in Northern Ireland*, Cmnd 7009/1977; Kevin Boyle, 'Human Rights and the Northern Ireland Emergency', in Andrews, *Human Rights*, 144–64.

4   Criminal Law Revision Committee, 11th Report, Evidence (General), Cmnd 4991/1972.
5   Leonard H. Leigh, 'The Protection of the Rights of the Accused in Pretrial Procedure: England and Wales', in Andrews, *Human Rights*, 31.
6   See, for example, Andrew Ashworth's paper on the rules which exclude evidence directly or which give judges discretion to exclude evidence because of the way in which the evidence was obtained: 'Excluding Evidence as Protecting Rights', *Criminal Law Review* (1977), 723–35. Ashworth argues that discussion of these rules as they exist in English law usually falls into one of two approaches. The first finds the rationale of exclusionary rules or discretion to exclude evidence solely in the accuracy of the evidence in question. If the accuracy of the evidence is not affected by the means used to obtain it (e.g seizure of real evidence without a warrant) the evidence should not be excluded. The second approach relies on the disciplinary principle, that is, courts should exclude improperly obtained evidence, no matter its reliability, since courts should seek to discourage improper practices being used by law enforcement officers. Instead Ashworth favours a different argument which is based on what he calls the protective principle. According to the protective principle, the purpose of excluding evidence is that to permit evidence of certain types to be admissible would place accused persons at a disadvantage by denying their rights, and Ashworth offers a detailed argument that the protective principle provides a plausible explanation of the existing English law and also a stronger justification for exclusion of improperly obtained evidence than is provided by the reliability and disciplinary principles.
7   For an instructive account of Bentham's own views on the circumstances in which torture should be permitted in the judicial process, see W.L. and P.E. Twining, 'Bentham on Torture', *Northern Ireland Legal Quarterly*, 24 (1973), 305–56.
8   A spirited defence of the positivist approach to rights is given by Tom Campbell, *The Left and Rights* (London: Routledge & Kegan Paul, 1983), especially ch. 2.
9   J. Bentham, *Anarchical Fallacies* (*Works of Jeremy Bentham*) (ed. by J. Bowring), vol. II (Edinburgh: William Tait, 1838–43), 501. For a full discussion of Bentham's critique of natural rights, see H.L.A. Hart, *Essay on Bentham* (Oxford: Clarendon Press, 1982), ch. 4.
10 See e.g. Joel Feinberg, 'The Nature and Value of Rights', *Journal of Value Inquiry*, 4 (1970), 243–57.
11 European Convention on Human Rights, Article 5.
12 (Thomson) Committee on Criminal Procedure in Scotland, 2nd Report, Cmnd 6218/1975.
13 Ibid., para. 2.01.
14 Ibid., para. 3.11.
15 Cmnd 8092/1981.
16 Ibid., para. 1.27.
17 Ibid., para. 4.36.
18 Ibid., para. 4.41.
19 Ibid., para. 4.52.
20 The Royal Commission's support for the adversary system probably rests on the fact that that is the system we have got. At para. 1.35. of its Report, the Commission stated that it intended to use the traditionalist argument that it would support existing institutions unless it could be shown that these had defects capable of adequate remedy.
21 G. Maher, 'Balancing Rights and Interests in the Criminal Process', in Antony

Duff and Nigel Simmonds (eds), *Philosophy and the Criminal Law* (ARSP Beiheft No. 19; Wiesbaden: Franz Steiner, 1984), 99–108; John Cottingham, 'The Balancing Act: Weighing Rights and Interests in the Criminal Process', ibid., 109–15. It should be stated that the criticism of the *ad hoc* use of the device of balancing has less force against the Royal Commission than against the Thomson Committee.

22 See e.g. J.W. Nickel, 'Are Human Rights Utopian?' *Philosophy and Public Affairs*, 12 (1982), 246–64.

23 Allan Gibbard, 'Utilitarianism and Human Rights', *Social Philosophy and Policy*, 1 (1984), 92; James Fishkin, 'Utilitarianism Versus Human Rights', ibid., 103; John Gray, 'Indirect Utility and Fundamental Rights', ibid., 73. See also the essays by David Lyons, Kent Greenawalt, R.M. Hare, Alan Gewirth, Richard E. Flathman and George P. Fletcher, in J. Roland Pennock and John W. Chapman (eds), *Ethics, Economics, and the Law – Nomos XXIV* (New York: New York University Press, 1982), 107–215.

24 This general approach is adopted by R.G. Frey, *Interests and Rights* (Oxford: Clarendon Press, 1980), ch. 1.

25 For a useful introduction to this aspect of Bentham's thought, see Eric Halevy, *The Growth of Philosophic Radicalism* (London: Faber & Faber, 1982), 373–403; G.J. Postema, 'The Principle of Utility and the Law of Procedure: Bentham's Theory of Adjudication', *Georgia Law Review*, 11 (1977), 1393–424.

26 W. Twining, 'Rule-Scepticism and Fact-Scepticism in Bentham's Theory of Evidence', in W. Twining (ed.), *Facts in Law* (ARSP Beiheft No. 16; Wiesbaden: Franz Steiner, 1983), 65–84.

27 In its 11th Report the Criminal Law Revision Committee made the point: 'Since the object of a criminal trial should be to find out if the accused is guilty, it follows that ideally all evidence should be admissible which is relevant in the sense that it tends to render probable the existence or non-existence of any fact on which the question of guilt or innocence depends.' See Cmnd 4991/1972, para. 14.

28 Ronald Dworkin, 'Principle, Policy, Procedure', in C.F.H. Tapper (ed.), *Crime, Proof and Punishment: Essays in Memory of Sir Rupert Cross* (London: Butterworths, 1981), 193–225.

29 372 U.S. 335, 344–5 (1963).

30 See further R.A. Duff, *Trials and Punishments* (Cambridge: Cambridge University Press, forthcoming), ch. 4. Duff's book is an excellent illustration of a consistent approach to theorizing on different aspects of the criminal justice system.

11

The Right to be a Member of a Trade Union

Elspeth Attwooll

If anything is clear about rights, it is that people mean different things when they talk about them. For some, rights are creatures only of the positive legal rules in force within a given state.[1] In certain cases, too, it may be accepted that rights can be established by forms of procedure recognized as 'legislative' at the international level. For others, however, rights are not confined by the bounds of man-made laws. Instead, they may owe the whole or part of their existence to some rule of positive political morality, be it particular or universal,[2] or to some rule of natural law, held to persist independent of human acceptance or adherence.

In modern times, the rhetoric of human rights is, for the most part, that of positive political morality: neither particular nor fully universal, but at least sufficiently pervasive throughout the world to be recognized as dominant. The right to be a member of a trade union clearly qualifies as a right so understood but, more than this, it has achieved the status of a right at positive international law by means of various Conventions adopted under the aegis of the ILO.[3] Despite the effectiveness of the ILO in policing the application of these Conventions, attitudes expressed from within particular positive political moralities – by comparison with the views taken by the ILO's own bodies – as to what amounts to a proper implementation of the right indicate continuing disagreement as to the nature of the core.

Part of the problem arises out of certain conceptual divergences as to the nature of rights, irrespective of their source. One aspect of such divergence may be illustrated at municipal level in comparing the common-law and civilian traditions. Any democratic legal system considers itself concerned, at least in part, with establishing the conditions under which liberties may be exercised. According to the common-law tradition, the positive law is created in a piecemeal fashion, whether by courts or legislature, to meet situations as and when they arise. The method is that of imposing certain duties, usually general in their application and broad in their scope, with the intended effect of achieving 'not the absolute liberty of one but the qualified liberty of all'.[4] Insofar as the law contains no specific prohibitions concerning a particular activity, the citizen is regarded as free to act as he or she pleases, within the limits of his or her own physical and mental powers.[5]

In the civilian tradition, however, the emphasis is a different one. The basic conception is of a law that is all-embracing, offering guidance to citizens in every aspect of their conduct. Liberties are, accordingly, conferred and, with a greater or lesser degree of precision, defined by law. It is thus encapsulated by the view that Man, on entering political society, acquires civil liberty in place of natural liberty. Accordingly, 'Les libertés publiques . . . sont relatives dans la mesure . . . où le législatif individualise chacune d'elles et lui donne une physionomie particulière.'[6]

It may be argued, though, that a liberty remains only a liberty where it is merely protected by a 'penumbra' of duties or simply delimited by legal rules. In some cases, however, the law may impose a specific duty on others not to interfere with, or even to cooperate in, its exercise. Where this occurs, it may be claimed that it is no longer a pure liberty that is under consideration but that there has been a transformation into a liberty-right.[7]

The Core of the Positive Right

The right to be a member of a trade union would appear, predominantly at least, to take the form of a liberty-right. Accordingly, at its minimal level, it implies that the worker must be afforded the opportunity to join and to continue to belong to a trade union without interference from others. Those from whom relevant interference is likely to flow include employers, the public authorities and the trade unions themselves. Further, it may be argued that a full liberty-right has a double aspect, in the sense that it must sustain a liberty *not* to do X, as well as a liberty to do X. In this context the liberty-right must be understood as a freedom from compulsion to join. Such compulsion may equally flow from employers, from the public authorities and from the trade unions themselves. While the present chapter is centrally concerned with the right to be a member of a trade union, the issues raised in relation to the existence of any right not to be so cannot be ignored.

The right to be a member of a trade union is, obviously, logically dependent on the right of trade unions as such to exist. In this context, the right must be regarded as a specialized aspect of the right to freedom of association. It is a basic premise of the present argument that the right to freedom of association, in the positive sense, is so fundamental a human right that restrictions upon it can only be justified in the most exceptional of circumstances, such as isolation of those whose presence constitutes actual physical danger to others. This is not, however, to suggest that limits may not be placed on what may be done by persons acting in association, just as limits may be placed on an individual acting alone.

Where trade unions are concerned, the purpose of such association is seen as furthering and defending the interests of workers. Such interests are dominantly, although not exclusively, economic interests, whether they be perceived as rights to be defended or goals to be achieved. The latter are frequently expressed as demands for the incorporation into positive law of certain perceived human rights. Given the largely economic nature of the ends of such associations of workers, it is clear that the interests they promote are liable to conflict with other economic interests, whether those of employers or the public authorities. Less apparent, but none the less real, is the possibility of conflict with the, at least immediate, economic interest of the individual worker.

In the light of such potential for conflict of interest and of the ways in which economic interests perceived as adverse to those of the workers may be promoted by the exercise of political and economic power, the desired end cannot be achieved by dint of a simple liberty, whether pure or conferred, that is by the mere fact that combinations of workers are allowed to exist. Rather, protection must be afforded against interference not only with their existence as such but also with the forms that such combinations may take. Unless both these conditions are fulfilled the freedom to associate is a restricted one. Accordingly, the core of the right may be expressed as that 'to establish combinations of any type in support of common economic interests'. The right so expressed cannot, of course, be regarded as one exclusive to trade unions: it belongs equally to employers' associations and to other groups both within and outside the industrial and commercial contexts. It is distinct in relation to trade unions, however, in the sense that it takes the form of a right exercised by workers as workers. Consequently, the right may be redefined as that 'to establish combinations of any type in support of economic interests held in common by workers'. Further, certain specific implications follow from the core in relation to trade unions given that, *qua* a right, interference in its exercise is precluded. Thus the public authorities must be debarred not only from banning trade unions but also from regulating their internal organization and their relationships with one another: other, at least, than in purely formal terms. The same restrictions must apply, *pari passu*, to employers.[8]

In respect of individual membership, the core of the right may be expressed as that 'of joining and continuing to belong to any combination of any type in support of economic interests held in common with other workers'. It follows that the public authorities must be precluded from debarring an individual from joining a trade union or any particular type of trade union. In this context the removal of trade union membership from workers at Government Communications Headquarters (GCHQ)[9] is to be seen as a direct attack on the core of the right. Similarly, employers must be taken to be debarred from refusing to employ, from dismissing or otherwise discriminating against an individual on the grounds of union membership. In addition, a right to join and to continue to belong to a trade union suggests that the trade unions themselves are not entitled to refuse to admit individuals or to expel them from membership.

This last conclusion, however, is incompatible with there being an unfettered right to establish combinations 'of any type', in that such a phrase allows for the possibility of exclusivity. The implication is that even fundamental rights cannot be absolute: where they are in direct conflict with each other one must be made to yield, whether by reference to some overarching right or to some broader theory in terms of which the system of rights is justified. It must be added, however, that, where rights are in conflict, the modification of the one in favour of the other must be kept to the minimum necessary to avoid the conflict. To give greater preference than this is to establish an abuse of right.

Thus far, the core of the right to establish trade unions has been stated in relatively narrow terms as a specialized aspect of the right to freedom of association related to the support of common economic interests and specific to workers as such. It may, however, be contended that the core has been too narrowly stated and that the right is not exhausted by affording protection from interference with the establishment of trade unions, with the form in which they are established and with individual membership. That core was established by reference to the need to offer safeguards from the exercise of antithetical political and economic power by both public authorities and employers. Yet the right to combine in support of common economic interests may be taken to imply the right to exercise the countervailing political and economic power established by these means. Mere liberties in this regard are insufficient. Freedom to withdraw one's labour is worthless if the consequence is dismissal or an action for breach of contract. It is clear, too, that in many circumstances it is not enough for the protection to be afforded to the union alone: it must extend to the individual member also. In consequence, if the right to combine is to be anything other than nugatory it must include a number of concomitant rights, such as the right to withdraw labour and the right to engage in political activity – at least insofar as these may be traced to the support of common economic interests. As rights, interference with their exercise becomes precluded, this clearly having the effect of restricting the scope for exercise of power by public authorities and employers alike.

It was suggested earlier that to assert an effectively unlimited right to freedom of association was not to assert an unlimited right to freedom of acting in association. The problem then arises of identifying the criteria by reference to which the freedom of acting may appropriately be limited and, thus, the core of each concomitant right delineated. It is contended here that the only admissible criterion is the presence of conflicting human rights, wherever in society these may be vested. In this context justification for certain limitations on the right to strike may be offered in terms of the right 'to life' or 'to security of person'. Difficulties become apparent, however, in that the exercise of political and economic power, by employers and public authorities alike, is frequently accounted for in the language of rights: as, for example, the 'right to manage' recently asserted by the National Coal Board in the UK in respect of the closure of pits designated by them as uneconomic. The question of whether such 'claims of right' have any kind of basis and, indeed, proper exploration of the range of rights that may be opposed to that of freedom of acting in association are beyond the scope of the present chapter.

Directly germane, however, is the common practice of professing respect for a right while engaging in persuasive redefinition of its core. Thus common economic interests, at their broadest, may be taken to be those common to workers wherever in the world they may be. At the next level this becomes those common to the workers in the one state, then those common to workers in the one industry or occupation, and ultimately those common to workers in the one enterprise. Further, this may be cross-referenced to existing forms of organization, so that common economic interests are taken to be those common to workers within the same trade union. Accordingly, the claim may be advanced that all that is required, in terms of the core of the right, is that protection is afforded to the wielding of the political and economic power at the disposal of the members of the one union in the one enterprise.

Clearly, though, if the core of the right – that 'to establish combinations of any type in support of the economic interests held in common by workers' together with the right 'to exercise the countervailing political and economic power established by these means' – has been correctly specified, then the formal categories into which workers have organized themselves must be treated as irrelevant. What is at issue, rather, are what may properly be termed common economic interests. Since it is combinations of workers that are under consideration, no erosion of the right appears to be involved in specifying that such must be ones shared by the workers as workers. Thus however laudable the wielding of political and economic power in favour of other sectors of the population perceived to be disadvantaged may be, protection for this does not seem to be demanded by reference to the core. This much granted, though, it is contended that the scope of the common economic interests of workers as workers cannot be confined to those shared by particular groups or categories of workers, for to impose limits on the interests that may be regarded as common is to restrict the right to freedom of association. It follows that to afford protection to the exercise of countervailing political and economic power only to the extent that the interests are direct and immediate to the group or category is also restrictive of the right to freedom of association. It is argued, accordingly, that placing limitations on rights under positive law, in terms that involve an implicit redefinition of the human right that is at the core, is no more than a sleight of hand disguising the fact that the abrogation flows from policy considerations. As already stated, however, this is not to assert that there can never be any reassessment of the nature and scope of the core of a given right: it is rather to reinforce the point that this is legitimate only in the context of conflict with the cores of other rights.

Before turning to an illustration of the ways in which the establishment of rights under positive law is affected by attitudes concerning the proper distribution of political and economic power which, though sometimes couched in the rhetoric of rights, are rarely genuinely informed by them, one further aspect of the right to combine in support of common economic interests requires consideration. Thus far, the treatment has been confined to its establishment by means of protecting the exercise of certain liberties from interference. It was suggested earlier, however, that a liberty-right may demand actual cooperation by other parties. This must occur where cooperation is regarded as so necessary to the exercise of the liberty that this is, at worst, impossible or, at best, seriously hampered by lack of it. In these instances it may be regarded as essential to the realization of the right. Where trade unions are concerned, such cooperation may be called for in a wide range of cases: for the individual member, particularly the official, in allowing time for his or her conduct of union business; for the trade union, from affording facilities for its operations through to ensuring recognition by the public authorities of its legal personality. Again, there is an issue as to the nature and extent of the cooperation required for the realization of the right, as to what is demanded by the core.

The Development of the Positive Right within the UK

The provision of assistance to trade unions by means of requiring cooperation in their activities is, by and large, a recent development. The main focus of efforts to sustain the right to combine has been directed towards getting it established at all. For example, within the UK, the initial reaction to combinations of workers seeking improvements in wages and conditions was that these amounted, at common law, to criminal conspiracies in restraint of trade. The attitude of the common law was reinforced by statute and even though combinations to agree hours and wages became permitted with time[10] it was not until 1875, with the Conspiracy and Protection of Property Act, that agreements or combinations concerning acts in furtherance of a trade dispute were removed with any certainty from the realm of criminal conspiracy. Accordingly, workers acquired first the liberty to combine for relevant purposes and then the liberty to act in combination in ways that would not be criminal for one person acting alone.

At the outset, any combination could be regarded as a union no matter its size and whether intended to be temporary or permanent. The first formal recognition of trade unions as a form of organization to be accommodated within the legal system came with the Trade Union Act of 1871. Together with subsequent legislation,[11] it had the effect of defining a union as a combination with the objects of regulating the relations between workmen and masters, workmen and workmen or masters and masters,[12] of imposing restrictive conditions on the conduct of trade or business and, in addition to the former, the provision of benefits.[13]

The 1871 Act allowed unions to register, on a voluntary basis, if they complied with certain rules as to their constitutions, submitted annual accounts and so forth. Despite little practical advantage in registering, the majority of unions did so. The effects of this new recognition on the status of unions remained obscure, however, for some considerable time. Initially it appeared that they were to be regarded as no different from any other voluntary association. A clear difference from other voluntary associations did, however, emerge with the cases of *Taff Vale Railway Company* v. *Amalgamated Society of Railway Servants*[14] and *Quinn* v. *Leathem*,[15] establishing respectively that a trade union might be sued in its own name for injuries done by its authority and procurement and that a combination to do damage might be actionable even where the acting of an individual was not.

This was, clearly, more than mere erosion by positive law of the right to freedom of action in association: it amounted to its almost complete abrogation. The solution adopted was by means of conferring a statutory immunity. Although it remained the case that trade unions could sue and be sued in their own name, the Liberal Government of the day introduced the Trade Disputes Act 1906, Section 4(1) of which read:

> An action against a trade union, whether of workmen or masters, or against any members or officials thereof on behalf of themselves and all other members of the trade union, in respect of any tortious act alleged

to have been committed by or on behalf of a trade union, shall not be entertained by any Court.

The Trade Disputes Act thus accorded an immunity to trade unions, both directly and through their membership, further specifying in respect of the latter[16] that acts done in contemplation or furtherance of a trade dispute would not be actionable, whether performed by an individual or a combination of individuals, merely because they induced breach of a contract of employment or interfered with trade or business. It may be claimed that, by means of this immunity, the legislation conferred on trade unions, beyond recognition of their liberty to exist, a substantive, and substantial, liberty-right to act.

This immunity apart, however, the precise legal status of trade unions remained uncertain. The preferred judicial view appeared to be that while for certain purposes they might be treated as if they were legal entities, ultimately they were to be regarded as simply collections of individuals.[17] Judicial decisions, too, had progressively narrowed the extent to which individual action was afforded protection by the 1906 Act, leading to legislative action to restore that protection in the form of the Trade Disputes Act, 1965. Nevertheless, opinion that the role of trade unions should be re-examined, sustained by increasing anxiety at the number of working days being lost through strikes, led to the establishment in the same year of the Royal Commission on Trade Unions and Employers' Associations,[18] better known as the Donovan Commission. It reported in 1968 and gave rise to the Labour Government's *In Place of Strife*, a White Paper embodying a number of proposals for legislation, including a 'cooling-off period' before a strike could be called.[19]

Trade union pressure was such that the proposals were never implemented. With the return, however, of a Conservative Government came the Industrial Relations Act, 1971. This introduced the concept of 'a registered trade union', along with a number of specific provisions governing the conduct of such unions. Non-registered trade unions retained the degree of legal personality that enabled them to sue and be sued in their own name and to have judgment enforced against their property. They and their officials, though, became responsible for industrial practices that, had they been committed by a registered union, would not have been regarded as unfair. In addition they were subjected to a number of disabilities, relating mainly to collective bargaining, while still expected to conform to the conditions of conduct applicable to registered trade unions.

The 1971 Act did not find favour with the trade union movement. As Rideout puts it: 'Trade unions, which had usually registered when there was a voluntary choice conferring few advantages, objected strongly to registration as the price to be paid, as they saw it, to carry out their legitimate functions.'[20]

It was not merely the requirement to register, though, that gave rise to these objections but the fact that registration conditions would have necessitated changes in the rule books of most unions. Further, the Act imposed corporate status on registered unions; made written collective agreements legally binding; specified provisions for sole agency bargaining agreements that appeared to give employers an opportunity to establish 'dummy' unions; and set out an exhaustive, and to the unions unrealistic, list of unfair industrial practices, which were made statutory wrongs subject to the jurisdiction of the newly-created National Industrial Relations Court. This list, taken together with the removal of the 1906 Act immunity from suit in tort, made large inroads upon the scope of industrial action afforded protection. The legislation, accordingly, encroached considerably upon both the notion of a right to establish combinations of any type and that of a right for such combinations to act 'to further and defend the interests of their members'.[21]

The considered reaction of the trade union movement was that of mass refusal to register, thus rendering the legislation to most intents and purposes ineffective. The return of a Labour Government in February 1974, after the 'three-day week',[22] brought a rapid repeal, with the Trade Union and Labour Relations Act, 1974, being on the statute books by July. Despite its repeal, certain provisions of the 1971 Act were reinstated; amongst these that the term 'trade union' should be reserved for organizations of workers, those of employers being referred to as associations. Registration again became a formality and was soon changed to certification,[23] the main concern shifting to whether or not the trade union could be certified an independent one: that is one neither under the domination of employers nor open to interference from them arising, for example, out of financial or material support.[24]

The 1974 Act also reinstated the immunity of trade unions from being sued in tort in relation to actions in contemplation or furtherance of a trade dispute,[25] specifying that the latter covered disputes between employers and workers and workers and workers.[26] At the same time, under Opposition pressure, it narrowed specific individual protection to actions inducing breaches of contract of employment.[27] This was later extended by the Trade Union and Labour Relations (Amendment) Act, 1976, to actions inducing breach of any contract.[28] In contrast, therefore, with the restrictive provisions of the 1971 Act, the 1974 Act switched the emphasis from the narrowing of a set of liberties and the qualification of existing liberty-rights (with those that remained being accorded mainly to registered trade unions under specified conditions) to the provision of an enhanced set of liberty-rights.

All did not, however, remain quiet on the industrial front. Various factors – such as cases of large-scale picketing, well-publicized instances of workers being dismissed following refusal to join the union where a closed shop was in operation, firms being adversely affected by disputes in which they were not directly involved and fears of intimidation in strike decisions – led the Conservative Party to a pledge to curb union power. The return of Conservative Governments after the General Elections of both 1979 and 1983 was followed by legislation to this end in 1980, 1982 and 1984. The effect of this legislation has been: the imposition of very stringent conditions for the establishing of union membership agreements (closed shops);[29] the removal again of union immunity to suit in tort;[30] narrowing of the definition of a trade dispute to one between 'workers and their employer' and of a listed type;[31] revived liability for inducement of breach of contract in cases of secondary action[32] and for acts to compel union membership[33] or union recognition requirements in contracts,[34] such liability extending to the trade union where the action was officially endorsed;[35] and the enjoining of secret ballots prior to the calling of strikes, on pain of liability in tort; for the election of trade union leaders; and for the maintenance of political funds.[36]

It is noteworthy that most of these provisions place the onus of curbing industrial action on the employers involved. That is to say, the activities concerned have not been made the subject of direct prohibition by the criminal law, although in certain cases – particularly that of picketing – they may have implications for it. Rather, employers have been granted certain remedies, including that of obtaining an injunction, under the civil law. The effect has been a transference of liberty-rights from workers to employers, with the legal immunities of the former being replaced by legal liabilities. This offers a clear illustration of the vulnerability of liberty-rights in cases where they remain unsecured. While there has been no direct attack on the existence of trade unions, curbs have been placed upon their liberty-rights to act and thus to be effective in defending and furthering the interests of their members. Further, the pattern followed by the legislative changes shows clearly the ways in which the incorporation of the right into positive law may be affected by the view taken by the public authorities as to the proper distribution of political and economic power.

Parallel considerations apply in relation to the right to be a member of a trade union. Such a liberty-right in the fullest sense requires both a duty on the trade union to admit and a duty on the employer not to dismiss or discriminate on the basis of membership. At common law it at first appeared to be clearly established that there was no duty on the part of a trade union to admit: such was a matter for the exercise of discretion on the part of the union in terms of its own rule book. In *Tierney* v. *Amalgamated Society of Woodworkers*,[37] for example, it was indicated that, even if a generalized right to work had been established under the Constitution of Eire, this did not in turn imply the right to work in a particular way as the member of a particular body.

The common law did, however, show a movement toward the view that the discretion of the union might be subject to limitation. In *Nagle* v. *Feilden*,[38] for instance, where the refusal by the Jockey Club to grant a trainer's licence appears to have turned not on the qualifications but on the sex of the applicant, Lord Denning, in concert with other members of the Court of Appeal, made a characteristic attempt to establish a limited right to admission by agreeing that there was a cause of action where the rules of the organization, or its interpretations of them, were arbitrary or unreasonable.

The 1971 Act[39] followed a similar line in stating that 'a qualified worker shall not by way of arbitrary or unreasonable discrimination be excluded' and this approach survived in the 1974 Act which referred to exclusion or expulsion by way of arbitrary or unreasonable discrimination.[40] This was repealed by the Trade Union and Labour Relations (Amendment) Act, 1976, along with the requirement on the union to have certain specified rules concerning admission. The right reappears, however, in qualified form in the Employment Act, 1980, Section 4, as one 'not to have an application for membership of a specified trade union unreasonably refused' and 'not to be unreasonably expelled from a specified trade union'. The qualification is that the right only applies where there is a union membership agreement (a closed shop) in operation.

This apart, the situation now appears to have reverted to that obtaining at common law. As far as expulsion is concerned, the tendency has been to treat union membership as a contract between the member and the union and to construe the rule book to see whether expulsion amounted to breach of contract. At the same time, the proceedings involved appear to have been treated as disciplinary ones with the courts concentrating on issues of natural justice: an attitude reinforced by the requirement under the 1974 Act that trade union rules should not conflict with this.[41]

The history of the law in relation to discrimination or dismissal by an employer has also been a somewhat chequered one. The first step was the Fair Wages Resolution of the House of Commons in 1946, involving steps to deny public contracts to any employers discriminating against trade unions. Then, in 1971, protection was afforded for membership of workers' organizations and for trade union activities, although the latter appeared only to extend to registered unions.[42] While this qualification disappeared in the 1974 Act, a new limitation of the protection – to dismissal for membership of, and activities in, independent trade unions – was introduced, similar protection also being afforded to the obverse case, that of refusal to join or remain a member of a non-independent trade union.[43] Later employment protection legislation extended cover to action short of dismissal in these respects, activities as such being limited to 'an appropriate time' (defined as outside working hours or within them by agreement with, or with the consent of, the employer).[44]

Further changes to the law in respect of compulsion by an employer to join have been effected by the Employment Acts, 1980 and 1982. The 1980 Act, where action short of dismissal was concerned, altered the whole emphasis of the provision by excising the reference to non-independence on the part of the trade union.[45] This was reinforced in relation to actual dismissal by the 1982 Act, which refers to dismissal of an employee because he 'was not a member of any trade union or of a particular trade union, or one of a number of particular trade unions or had refused or proposed to refuse to become a member'.[46] The 1982 Act also classified as action short of dismissal attempts by an employer to impose membership by deducting payments in such cases. Thus what had originally been designed to provide a safeguard against 'dummy' unions was converted into part of a whole new battery of provisions restricting the union membership agreement or 'closed shop'.

The Negative Right

While this chapter is principally concerned with the right to be a member of a trade union, it may be argued that any fully blown liberty involves 'liberty not to' as well as 'liberty to'. And liberty-right not to be a member of a trade union must include the right to cease being one and the right not to become one at all. The right to resign was accepted at common law, subject to express provisions limiting or removing it in the rules of a particular trade union. The 1971 Act cancelled this power of limitation, allowing resignation where the member had given reasonable notice and had complied with any reasonable conditions. A similar provision in the 1974 Act proved defective as unenforceable. It was replaced in the 1976 Act by one making the right to resign under these conditions an implied term of the individual's contract with the union.

As far as not joining at all is concerned, this remains, as against the unions themselves, a largely unprotected liberty. To the extent that a right of any kind may be said to exist, it is constituted by placing restrictions on the right of the employer to dismiss an employee for failure to join. The scope of such restrictions has, typically, been subject to a considerable amount of variation. The 1971 Act operated on the premise that dismissal for failure to join a trade union was unfair but allowed it to be fair in one of two sets of circumstances. First, such dismissal, as also discrimination by an employer, was fair where an agency shop agreement was in operation and the employee either was not a member of the union or did not make contributions to the union in lieu of membership or make conscientious contributions to charity.[47] Second, under the strictly controlled conditions under which post-entry union membership agreements could be in force, the dismissal became fair where the employee refused to join the union, unless this was on the grounds of conscience.[48]

The first of these provisions disappeared with the repeal of the 1971 Act. The second was altered so that the exception became objection on the grounds of religious belief to joining any trade union, together with objection on any reasonable grounds to becoming a member of a particular trade union.[49] The latter part was repealed by the 1976 Act[50] and the 1978 Act rephrased the exception as 'genuinely objects on the grounds of religious belief'.[51] Another change was effected by the 1980 Act, the provision reading 'genuinely objects on the grounds of conscience or other deeply held personal conviction to being a member of any trade union whatsoever or of a particular trade union',[52] a formula repeated in the 1982 Act.

In sum then, there is a right against the employer not to be dismissed for failure to be a member of a trade union unless there is a closed shop in operation, in which case the right is limited to those whose failure to join has its basis in conviction. In the case of a government sympathetic to the closed shop the type of conviction affording that right is very narrowly defined; in the case of one unsympathetic it is broadened considerably. There is no doubt that the closed shop raises complex questions where freedom of association is concerned. Although many states reserved their positions in relation to it where the European Convention on Human Rights was concerned, it appears that the court may, under certain circumstances, regard the closed shop as in contravention of the provisions of the Convention.

In *Young, James and Webster* v. *The U.K.*,[53] three British Rail employees were dismissed for refusal to join any of three trade unions after a closed shop agreement had been concluded. At the time the provisions of the 1974 Act were in force, so that the sole exception was for those objecting on religious grounds. All three applicants, however, maintained only that union membership should be a matter of personal choice, while two of them objected also to the policies and political activities of the unions concerned. The European Court decided, by 18 votes to 3, that the compulsion to join was in violation of Article 11 of the Convention, guaranteeing freedom of association, both viewed on its own and in the light of Articles 9 and 10 which protect freedom of thought and expression. It was further held that the compulsion could not be justified by reference to paragraph 2 of Article 11 which allowed interference with freedom of association where prescribed by law for the purposes of protecting the rights and freedoms of others. In a democratic society the interference had to be limited to what was necessary in pursuit of a legitimate aim and a balance had to be maintained between the interests of the majority and the fair and proper treatment of even a small minority. In this case it was difficult to see how the interests of the unions would have suffered if the few existing non-union employees had not been compelled to join.

The main disagreement within the Court centred on the relationship between the positive and negative aspects of freedom of association. Six of the judges asserted that these were complementary and inseparable, while the three dissenting ones argued that they were quite separate. The six also held that even to require reasons for refusal to join amounted to a violation of the Convention. The mere fact that the positive and negative aspects can be regarded as complementary, however, suggests that they are at least separable. That this is the case analytically is demonstrated by their capacity for separate protection, illustrated by the fact that under the 1974 Act in the UK protection from unfair dismissal was afforded individually for: (a) membership of an independent trade union; (b) taking part in the activities of an independent trade union; and (c) for refusal to belong to a non-independent trade union.

Accordingly, the real issue at stake is whether there is a fundamental human right *not* to associate: to separate oneself from others. Even if there is such, most people do live in some form of association with others. It is generally accepted that we cannot both approbate and reprobate: by remaining within society we acquire its burdens as well as its benefits. As a member of a work force one is a participant in a particular form of society. One argument frequently advanced in favour of the closed shop is that those who do not join a union negotiating on their behalf are, in most instances at least, taking the benefits without assuming the burdens. Nonetheless, in the context of human rights, this cannot be enough to establish that no right is invaded by compulsion to join or that, if such a right is invaded, the invasion is warranted by the requirement to sustain other rights. Clearly, it cannot be argued that waiver, by actual participation in society, of any right not to associate amounts to its complete alienation, for to suggest that participation in certain forms of association permits of compulsion to join all associations is to deny the existence of such a right in the social context. Rather, it has to be considered whether, given the existence of one form of association, that of working together, it is or is not legitimate to impose another at the same or similar level.

Since the positive right to associate was framed as that to form combinations *of any type* it would appear not to be so, in that associations of union members and non-union members are denied existence. It may be argued, however, that such associations are not in support of but are rather antithetical to common economic interests. Accordingly, any right for an individual not to join must be seen as an interference with the right to freedom of action in association in support of common economic interests; equally, any compulsion to join must be seen as an interference with an individual's right to freedom of action in isolation in support of individual economic and other interests.

One method of resolving apparent conflicts of rights is to subsume both under some overarching right. It would seem that both positive and negative rights to freedom of association and to freedom of action, whether in association or isolation, can be accommodated within a more general type of right, as articulated by John Stuart Mill: the right to individual self-development, to frame one's own plan of life. In this setting the contention of one judge in *Young, James and Webster* v. *The U.K.*, that trade union freedom is a collective right, falls;[54] it is clear that the opposition is between one individual's right to pursue his or her own individual self-development in isolation and other individuals' rights to pursue their own self-development in association. Given that there is a straight conflict of rights, these may be modified in relation to each other, but only to the minimum extent necessary to avoid the conflict.

It is, however, by no means clear that positive political morality does perceive an unqualified right to negative freedom of association. In many cases, such as those of the Law Societies in Britain or the British Medical Association, membership of a specific organization is regarded as a prerequisite to the exercise of a profession. In such cases the attainment of a certain training standard is a requirement for admission. Further, conformity with established standards of conduct is a condition of continuing membership. It is clear that both of these limit individuals in framing their own plans of life, yet such limitation is regularly justified by reference both to rights residing in the consumers of the service and to the interests of the profession as such. The restriction of the positive right to freedom of association, to the extent that the right to join a particular organization may be limited by its rules, is thus regarded as acceptable, and the individual's general right as adequately protected by provision that the exclusion should not be arbitrary or unreasonable.

Nonetheless the fact that following a certain type of life plan is made conditional on membership of some particular organization does suggest that freedom not to associate may be an instrumental and not a substantive right. Even, however, if it is regarded as a substantive right, the question remains as to how far it may be modified by reference to conflicting rights. As with the positive right to freedom of association, any negative right will have concomitant rights. The consequences that flow from union membership can include contribution to its funds, participation in its decision-making process and conformity with the rules and decisions so established. The second of these is not mandatory, so that only the financial penalty and the conformity are directly limiting on the individual's capacity to frame his or her own plan of life. On the other side, a person is limited in that capacity also by the attendant threat of dismissal should he or she refuse to accept these requirements. Thus the right to work is rendered a conditional one.

It is, however, not the individual's right to work as such that is in question but rather the right to work in a particular job. It is thus conditional in the same manner as that regarded as acceptable in relation to the professions. In respect of the concomitant rights, the question then becomes whether the individual ought to have a right to work without requirement of payment to and conformity with the decisions of some particular body. Clearly, limitations on the extent of any such right are already to be found in that payments to the public authorities may be deducted and adherence to the employer's instructions is expected. It follows that the individual's ability to frame his or her own plan of life is already considerably confined in these directions.

In the context of trade unions, the issue becomes whether the individual should have the right to work in a particular job without formally entering in, making payments to and abiding by the decisions of an association of fellow workers. Further, it must be determined whether any such right is absolute or only conditional upon a certain level of conviction. In counterpoise is the freedom of the other workers to associate and to act in association to further and defend their common economic interests. As rights, these are defended in varying degree from interference by both public authorities and employers. The issue of the closed shop resolves itself into the question of whether the same should apply in respect of interference by fellow workers and to what extent.

The International Dimensions

It is noteworthy, in this context, that ILO Convention No. 87, The Freedom of Association and Protection of the Right to Organise Convention, 1948,[55] which confers a right on workers to join organizations of their choosing, has been interpreted in a manner so as to concentrate only on the positive aspects of freedom of association, leaving the interrelationship of the positive and negative aspects to the discretion of municipal systems. In the former respect, however, the ILO Conventions provide interest both in terms of the form in which and the degree of flexibility with which trade union rights are constituted. The terms of Convention No. 87, which is generally regarded as the most important, are applicable to workers and employers alike and to both of these without any distinction as to category of worker or employer.[56] An unqualified right is established for them to establish trade unions of their own choosing without previous authorization. The right to join such trade unions is set out in similar terms, with the additional specification that this right may be limited by, but only by, the rules of the organization concerned.[57] Such provisions extend also to the organizations themselves in relation to their rights to join federations and confederations.[58]

In order to meet the point that such organizations, to exist in any real sense of the term, must be able to be effective in defending and furthering the interests of their members, it is specified that they 'shall have the right to draw up their constitutions and rules, to elect their representatives in full freedom, to organise their administration and activities and to formulate their programmes'.[59] The same right is extended to federations and confederations.[60] The means by which these rights are secured is by placing a duty on the public authorities not to abrogate them either by law or practice. Accordingly it is specified generally that: '[the] law of the land shall not be such as to impair, nor shall it be applied so as to impair, the guarantees provided in this convention.'[61] More specifically, the public authorities are required to refrain from interfering with the organization's autonomy of action,[62] from dissolving them by administrative authority[63] and from making the acquisition of legal personality the subject of conditions that would restrict the scope of the protection afforded by the Convention.[64] The Convention may, accordingly, be regarded as an articulation of the nature of the human rights of freedom of association and of freedom of action in association as perceived by international positive political morality and as an attempt to secure such human rights in municipal law.

Over and above the duty not to abrogate or interfere with the exercise of these rights, there is a positive duty placed on member states for whom the Convention is in force 'to take all necessary and appropriate measures to ensure that workers and employers may freely exercise the right to organise'.[65] By requiring regular reports, as a matter of routine, from states that have ratified the Convention,[66] and by procedures allowing the governments of member states to be the subject of complaint by both national and international workers' and employers' organizations, irrespective of ratification,[67] the ILO effects a close monitoring of the extent to which there is conformity with the Convention.

In consequence of the relatively general terms in which the Convention is framed, the monitoring exercise has involved both the Committee of Experts on the Application of Standards and Recommendations and the Committee on Freedom of Association in a considerable amount of interpretation, refining the rights articulated in the Convention so as to sustain their core. Some of this has amounted to no more than a literal application of the wording. Thus the right to establish and join organizations is established for workers and employers 'without distinction whatsoever'. Accordingly, all instances where the public authorities have either excepted categories of workers from the provisions of legislation conferring basic trade union rights or protecting their liberties, or else have omitted such categories from its scope have been deemed, respectively, in contravention of the Convention or in sufficient conformity with it. Examples of these include agricultural workers, forestry workers, home workers, casual workers, domestic workers, seafarers, prison officers, firefighters, hospital workers and variable categories of workers involved in the public service. In the latter context, it may be remarked that the Committee on Freedom of Association entertained no doubt that the removal of trade union rights from workers at GCHQ was in contravention of the Convention.[68]

On the other hand, in relation to provisions for organizational autonomy, the ILO's bodies appear to have taken the view that a certain degree of oversight of internal conduct is permissible, in any event for the purposes of legal recognition, provided that this is purely formal in its scope: that is to say, as long as it is confined to specifying the matters that are to be covered by union rules and does not purport to prescribe their content. Any closer control – such as insistence on a minimum membership, stating occupational requirements for trade union office, prohibitions on the re-election of officials, setting of minimum dues or pre-determined allocation of dues, right of access by the public authorities to books and records – is deemed in contravention of the Convention.

Where the right to organize activities is concerned, the situation is a little more complex. The need for permission to hold meetings or oversight of them by representatives of the public authorities are regarded as clear examples of the type of interference precluded by the Convention. So also is any blanket ban on participation in politics, including electoral or party politics. Such, it is maintained, could be justified only in matters having no relation to the interests of trade union members. On the other hand, as far as strikes are concerned, the ILO bodies have countenanced, with reluctance, emergency bans on all strikes over strictly limited time periods and permanent bans on strikes in equally strictly defined sectors. The latter are confined to public and essential services, that is to services the interruption of which would endanger the life, personal safety or health of all or part of the population, and are subject to the existence of appropriate, impartial and rapid procedures for conciliation and arbitration. Legislation precluding the right to strike in wider sectors or attempting to pre-empt it by imposing compulsory arbitration is, however, treated as in contravention of the Convention. So, too, is the imposition of secret ballots prior to strikes where the procedure is sufficiently cumbersome or the required quota in favour so high as to have the effect of hindering the exercise of the right. Further, in those cases where it is accepted that strikes may be made illegal, use of the sanction of imprisonment is disapproved.[69]

The above examples are merely indicative of the many issues concerning which judgement has had to be exercised by the ILO's bodies in their interpretation of the Convention. In a significant number of cases the mixture of advice, persuasion and pressure of opinion afforded by technical assistance, direct contacts missions, reports of the Committee of Experts, investigation of complaints by the Committee on Freedom of Association and review by the Conference in annual session has been effective in bringing the law of individual states into, or back into, conformity with the Convention.[70]

Nonetheless, a number of major problems remain and not all of these relate to direct attempts to suppress or restrict the trade union movement in the ways illustrated above. The member states of the ILO[71] are characterized by a considerable variety of social, economic and political systems. The Conventions in some measure take account of this fact by the very terms in which they are expressed. Thus Convention No. 98 (The Right to Organise and Collective Bargaining Convention, 1949), in seeking to secure adequate protection against both anti-union discrimination and interference by employers, requires the establishment of machinery 'appropriate to national conditions'.[72] The same terms are applied to the implementation of the duty to promote the utilization and development of voluntary procedures for collective bargaining.[73] Similarly, Convention No. 135 (The Protection and Facilities to be afforded to Workers' Representatives in the Undertaking Convention, 1971), which reinforces the protection of workers' representatives and enjoins the provision of appropriate facilities for them, specifies in the latter respect that 'account shall be taken of the characteristics of the industrial relations system of the country and of the needs, size and capability of the undertaking concerned'.[74] Added to this is the fact that closer specification of the type of protection and facilities to be afforded is to be found in a parallel – non-binding – Recommendation.[75]

The problem of accommodating the differences between systems remains, however, a significant one. This is clearly illustrated by the provision in Convention No. 87 that workers and employers shall have the right to establish and join 'organisations of their own choosing'. This has been taken by the majority of the Committee of Experts to preclude the establishment of a unitary trade union movement. In consequence a number of states of Marxist persuasion are considered to be failing to conform with the provisions of the Convention. In recent years members of the Committee of Experts representative of such states have been expressing their reservations as to its Report. Their argument is to the effect that universal international Conventions may engender in their implementation norms that are either socialist or capitalist. In consequence the social realities faced by the Conventions or produced by their implementation may be different, yet in both instances still in conformity with them. There is, however, a tendency to assume that the methods and results of the implementation of such Conventions in the capitalist countries are the only ones that are in conformity with them. Such an approach 'was incompatible with the very foundation of international law, which was peaceful coexistence. In this particular case it resulted in an erroneous evaluation of the USSR legislation.'[76]

This approach has been adopted by various of the other member states in their reports on the application of Convention No. 87. Thus it has been claimed by one state that trade union rights there are in advance of those laid down by the Convention, 'a Convention adopted in a context that has been rendered out of date by the coming into existence of a very large number of socialist countries or countries with socialist tendencies.'[77] Similarly, the preclusion of the existence of a unitary trade union movement has been described as an 'anachronism'. The Committee of Experts, however, reiterates its position to the effect that it has never ignored the fact that different social and political realities exist and that these, while differing from one another, may be in conformity with particular ILO Conventions. It states that its task is to examine, from a strictly legal point of view, the extent to which countries that have ratified the Convention give effect in their legislation and practice to the obligations deriving from it. Further, 'The Committee's observations are the conclusions drawn by it from a uniform application of this objective approach.'[78]

The core of the positive workers' right to freedom of association and the ambit of that to freedom of action in association was delineated earlier in this text as that to 'establish combinations of any type in support of economic interests held in common by workers as workers'. In this context it was argued that the freedom required protection against the exercise of countervailing political and economic power by public authorities and employers alike. For a state of Marxist persuasion, however, the latter notion is an incoherent one. There is, first, no dividing line between public authority and employer. More important the state, in both these capacities, and the workers are regarded as united in a common economic interest and as mobilized toward a common political end. To envisage even the possibility of divergence is to deny the whole ideological base. It is not just that the establishment of combinations of workers outside those provided by the state is not, and cannot be, needed. It is that they, too, would constitute a denial of the ideological base.

Nonetheless, it remains the case that the right constituted by the Convention is that for 'workers and employers', 'without distinction whatever', 'to establish . . . organisations' 'of their own choosing', 'without previous authorisation'. The view of the majority of the Committee of Experts is that municipal law must protect this freedom irrespective of the ethos of the system as a whole and of the degree of desire of those within the system to avail themselves of it. This is taken to be the clear implication of the right as expressed in international positive law as established by international positive political morality and as endorsed by states ratifying the Convention. Even so, it is not unthinking heresy to suggest that international positive political morality, as expressed in 1948 and as directed to this one issue, may not have told the whole story.

Trade union rights are but tiny pieces in a very large jigsaw. All the pieces have to be assembled together and fitted into one another, such that each piece represents at least the guaranteed and inviolable core of some particular right. Until such a scheme is established the realization of human rights will be, at worst, illusory, and, at best, temporary. For they will remain vulnerable alike to individualist and collectivist philosophies, to policy preferences and fundamental principles, to *ad hoc* judgements where they are secured and to manipulation where they are systemic. Compelling though the rhetoric of human rights may be, it is deontology that must provide the basis for their translation into reality.

Notes

1 As in the Austinian tradition, see John Austin, *The Province of Jurisprudence Determined*, ed. H.L.A. Hart (London: Weidenfeld & Nicolson, 1954), especially Lecture V. By comparison H. Kelsen, though according the status of law to norms established at the international level, treats rights themselves (other than those in a technical sense) as mere 'epiphenomena' of duties, irrespective of derivation. See, e.g., his *Pure Theory of Law* (Los Angeles, California: University of California Press, 1970) Part IV, especially section 29.

2 That is, individual to a state or group of states, as opposed to part of the *ius gentium*.

3 Convention No. 11 (Right of Association – Agriculture Convention, 1921); Convention No. 87 (Freedom of Association and Protection of the Right to Organise Convention, 1948); Convention No. 98 (Right to Organise and Collective Bargaining Convention, 1949); Convention No. 135 (Protection and Facilities to be afforded to Workers' Representatives in the Undertaking Convention, 1971); Convention No. 151 (Labour Relations (Public Service) Convention, 1978).

4 As exemplified by the approach of John Locke: see his 'Second Treatise on Civil Government', in *Two Treatises on Civil Government*, ed. P. Laslett (Cambridge: Cambridge University Press, 1960), esp. ch. 9.

5 See the distinction between 'negative' and 'positive' freedom as made by Isaiah Berlin in 'Two Concepts of Liberty', in *Four Essays on Liberty* (Oxford: Oxford University Press, 1969). The common-law approach is reflected by Sir Robert

Megarry in *Malone* v. *Commissioner of Police of the Metropolis* (No. 2) [1979] 2 All E.R., 620 at 638.

6 C.-A. Colliard, *Libertés Publiques* (France: Dalloz, 1972), 20, the notion flowing from Jean-Jacques Rousseau, *The Social Contract*, ch. 8, see e.g. *Social Contract: Essays by Locke, Hume and Rousseau* (Oxford: Oxford University Press, 1966).

7 Liberty-rights – rights to do or be, not to do or not to be – are to be contrasted with receipt-rights, which are rights to be accorded certain benefits. Where a liberty-right is established in such a way as to require cooperation in its exercise, the distinction between the two becomes blurred. If rights of either type simply form part of the positive law, they are unsecured. Should the Constitution preclude their abrogation by the public authorities, however, they may be regarded as secured; should it enjoin the public authorities to sustain them, they may be regarded as systemic.

8 Accordingly, for there to be a substantive liberty-right, both these aspects must be catered for. Thus the establishing of a right at positive international law both inhibits the public authorities from taking certain measures and enjoins them to take other ones to ensure that the right is freely exercised.

9 In December 1983 the UK Government decided that membership of national trade unions and access to industrial tribunals should no longer be open to staff at GCHQ and their conditions of service were revised under Article 4 of the Civil Service Order in Council 1982. The staff were given the alternative of remaining at GCHQ and ceasing to be union members, receiving a payment of £1,000, or of retaining union membership but transferring to a department not concerned with security work.

10 Thus the Combination Act of 1800 was repealed in 1824, but the effect of the repeal was limited by the Combination of Workmen Act, 1825. See also the Combination of Workmen Act, 1859.

11 E.g. the Trade Union Act 1871, Section 23; Trade Union (Amendment) Act 1876; Trade Union Act 1913, Sections 1 and 2.

12 Since 1971 the term 'trade union' has been limited to the first two of these.

13 This alone was not sufficient to constitute the association a trade union.

14 [1901] A.C. 426.

15 [1901] A.C. 495.

16 Trade Disputes Act 1906, Section 3.

17 E.g. *Kelly* v. *NATSOPA* (1915) 84 L.J.K.B. 2236; *Bonsor* v. *Musicians' Union* [1956] A.C. 104. The 1971 Act conferred status as a legal entity on registered unions only; the 1974 Act restored trade unions to the position of unincorporated associations but accorded them certain capacities proper to corporate bodies.

18 Cmnd 3623 (1968).

19 Cmnd 3888 (1969).

20 Roger W. Rideout, *Principles of Labour Law* (3rd edn) (London: Sweet & Maxwell, 1979), 248.

21 ILO Convention No. 87, Article 10.

22 Power shortages brought about by a miners' strike led to short-time working throughout British industry. A General Election was called, the Conservative Government defeated and a Labour Government returned with a very narrow majority.

23 Employment Protection Act 1975, Section 7.

24 Trade Union and Labour Relations Act 1974, Section 30(1).

25 Ibid., Section 14.

26 Ibid., Section 29.

27 Ibid., Section 13.

28 Section 3(2).
29 Employment Act 1980, Section 7, as amended by the Employment Act 1982, Section 3.
30 Employment Act 1982, Section 17.
31 Ibid., Section 18. (For the list, see the 1974 Act, Section 29(1).)
32 Employment Act 1980, Section 17.
33 Ibid., Section 18.
34 Employment Act 1982, Section 14.
35 Ibid., Section 15.
36 Trade Union Act 1984, Sections 10 and 11, Sections 1–9, Sections 12–19 respectively.
37 [1959] I.R. 254.
38 [1966] 2 Q.B. 633. Strictly, it seems, the cause of action arose out of public policy, with reference to the idea of 'a right to work'; the declaration sought being granted in respect of the arbitrariness of the rule.
39 Industrial Relations Act 1971, Section 65(2).
40 Trade Union and Labour Relations Act 1974, Section 5.
41 See, e.g., *Lee* v. *Showman's Guild of Great Britain* [1952] 2 Q.B. 329; *Bonsor* v. *Musicians' Union* [1956] A.C. 104; *Lawlor* v. *Union of Post Office Workers* [1956] Ch. 712; *Radford* v. NATSOPA [1972] I.C.R. 484; *Stevenson* v. *Road Transport Union* [1977] I.C.R. 893; also Trade Union and Labour Relations Act 1974, Section 6(13).
42 Industrial Relations Act 1971, Section 5.
43 Trade Union and Labour Relations Act 1974, Schedule I, Part II, Section 24.
44 Employment Protection Act 1975, Section 53; Employment Protection (Consolidation) Act 1978, Sections 23 and 58.
45 Employment Act 1980, Section 15.
46 Employment Act 1982, Section 13.
47 Industrial Relations Act 1971, Sections 6, 8 and 9.
48 Ibid., Sections 17 and 18.
49 Trade Union and Labour Relations Act 1974, Schedule I, Part II, Section 24.
50 Trade Union and Labour Relations (Amendment) Act 1976, Section 2.
51 Employment Protection (Consolidation) Act 1978, Sections 23 and 58.
52 Employment Act 1980, Section 7.
53 European Court of Human Rights, Series A, vol. 44.
54 Judge Evrigenis.
55 Ratified by 97 states.
56 Article 2. The only exceptions, by Article 9, are for the armed forces and police.
57 Ibid.
58 Article 6.
59 Article 3.
60 Article 6.
61 Article 8, para. 2.
62 Article 3, para 2.
63 Article 4.
64 Article 7.
65 Article 11.
66 Article 22 of the ILO Constitution. Statistics for 1982–4 show a return rate for reports from the governments of ratifying states of approximately 80%. Also under Article 19 of the Constitution reports may be called for in relation to progress toward ratification in respect of unratified Conventions.
67 Under special procedures adopted in 1950 by common consent of the Governing

Body of the ILO and the Economic and Social Council of the UN. By the end of 1984 the Committee on Freedom of Association had received in the region of 1,300 complaints.

68 Complaint No. 1,261: 'the Committee considers that the unilateral action taken by the Government to deprive the category of public service workers of their right to belong to a trade union was not in conformity with the Freedom of Association and Protection of the Right to Organise Convention 1948 (No. 87), ratified by the United Kingdom.' ILO Official Bulletin, vol. 67/84, Series B, No. 2. Contrast with this *R. v. Secretary of State for Foreign and Commonwealth Affairs* ex parte *Council of Civil Service Unions* [1984] IRLR 353 C.A. See also *Council of Civil Service Unions and Others* v. *Minister for the Civil Service* [1984] 3 All E.R. 935.

69 See, e.g., the General Survey submitted to the 69th (1983) session of the International Labour Conference, para. 223.

70 See, e.g., Reports of the Committee of Experts on the Application of Conventions and Recommendations: 'The Committee notes with satisfaction . . .'.

71 As of April 1985 the number of member states is 151.

72 Article 3.

73 Article 4.

74 Article 2, para. 2.

75 Recommendation No. 143.

76 Reports of the Committee of Experts on the Application of Conventions and Recommendations, 1982, 1983 and 1984, M. Ivanov. Endorsed by M. Gubinski of Poland.

77 Algeria (Report of the Committee of Experts on the Application of Conventions and Recommendations, 1983).

78 Ibid.

Index